W9-AAY-540

AA

STEAMING ACROSS BRITAIN

Published by AA Publishing, a trading name of AA Media Ltd, whose registered office is Fanum House, Basing View, Basingstoke, Hampshire RG21 4EA.
Registered Number 06112600.

Managing Editor: David Popey
Art Editor: Louise Turpin
Picture Researcher: Julian Holland
Image manipulation and internal repro: Sarah Montgomery
Verifiers: Matthew Thompson and Alexander Medcalf
Proofreader: Alison Moore
Indexer: Julian Holland
Production: Lorraine Taylor

Commissioning Editor: Paul Mitchell

Cartography provided by the Mapping Services Department of AA Publishing

Visit AA Publishing at theAA.com/shop

A CIP catalogue record for this book is available from the British Library.

A04538

ISBNs: 978-0-7495-7077-4 and 978-0-7495-7105-4 (SS)

Printed in China by Toppan Printing

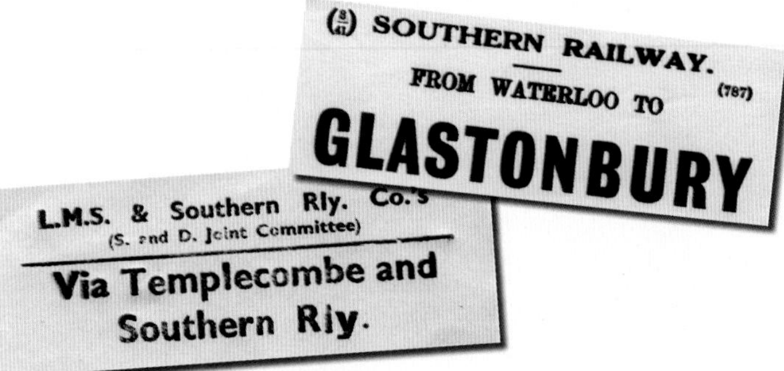

Page 1 **A 'Castle' Class 4-6-0 gets ready to leave Platform 1 at Paddington with a down express in March 1958 (see pages 54–61).**

Opposite **BR Standard Class 2 2-6-0 No. 78049 crosses the Royal Border Bridge over the River Tweed on 25 May 1962 (see pages 200–205).**

STEAMING ACROSS BRITAIN

JULIAN HOLLAND

▲ John Cameron's LNER Class 'K4' 2-6-0 No 61994 'The Great Marquess' near Attadale on the shores of Loch Carron with the Inverness to Kyle of Lochalsh leg of the Railway Touring Company's 'Great Britain III' nine-day railtour on 12 April 2010 (see pages 208–213).

▲ A busy scene at Moat Lane Junction on 7 June 1960. From left to right: Ivatt Class 2 2-6-0 No. 46523 waits in the bay with a Mid-Wales line train to Three Cocks Junction; in the centre the 2.30pm Aberystwyth to Oswestry train departs; and Standard Class 2 2-6-0 No. 78002 heads the 4.20pm Newtown to Machynlleth local train (see pages 32–41).

Contents

◀ Allocated to York shed, Class 'A2/3' 4-6-2 No. 60522 'Straight Deal' heads into Durham with a fast-fitted freight, c.1960 (see pages 176–181).

Introduction

The sights, sounds and smells of working steam railway locomotives still have a very special place in the hearts of many people. As the birthplace of steam railways, Britain has witnessed the amazing evolution of these living, breathing monsters over the past 200 years. Despite the official end of standard gauge steam on British Railways in 1968, there seems no limit to its current renaissance.

Tracing the fascinating history of some of the country's best-loved steam railway routes, this book is an unashamedly nostalgic celebration of the golden years of steam traction on Britain's nationalised railways from 1948 to 1968 – a time capsule journey with not a diesel in sight!

I hope that *Steaming Across Britain* will transport you back to a time when steam railways were still part of everyday life across the length and breadth of Britain. From the romantically named expresses hurtling up and down the East Coast and West Coast main lines and Summer-Saturday trains packed with holidaymakers heading for Devon and Cornwall to long-closed railways such as the Midland & Great Northern Joint Railway in East Anglia, the Somerset & Dorset Joint Railway and the long-lamented Waverley route in the Borders, this book is 100 per cent steam.

The 'Modernisation Plan' of 1955 effectively sounded the death knell for steam on British Railways and the 'Beeching Report' of 1963 simply speeded up the process – by the mid-1960s nearly new steam locomotives were being sent to the scrapyard after less than 10 years' service and replaced by unproven and unreliable diesels. However, the end of standard gauge steam on British Railways in 1968 was not the end of steam.

In fact, quite the opposite happened; the preservation movement surged into top gear, reopening many closed railways as heritage lines and lovingly restoring rusting hulks back to life. To satisfy the current insatiable appetite for steam, this book also includes information on where to see restored steam locomotives hard at work again – from the standard gauge double-track Great Central Railway in Leicestershire and the 18-mile North Yorkshire Moors Railway to Welsh narrow gauge enterprises such as the recently reopened Welsh Highland Railway in Snowdonia.

Long live steam!

Following the Lines
Every line in this book is accompanied by a map to show the featured route and its main stations. Heritage lines in the local area are also shown and many are described in the panel at the end of each section.

Legend

Thick line	Featured route
Thin line	Non-featured existing line
Faint line	Non-featured closed line
Dashed double line	Heritage line
■	Route start/finish point
●	Station
○	Railway museum/centre
▲	Route summit
▬	Route feature

The charm of Isle of Wight steam – ex-L&SWR Class 'O2' 0-4-4T No. 22 'Brading' slips violently on the weed-infested track while leaving Wroxall with the 7.46am Ryde to Ventnor train on 1 September 1965. Less than a year later, this scene had disappeared for ever.

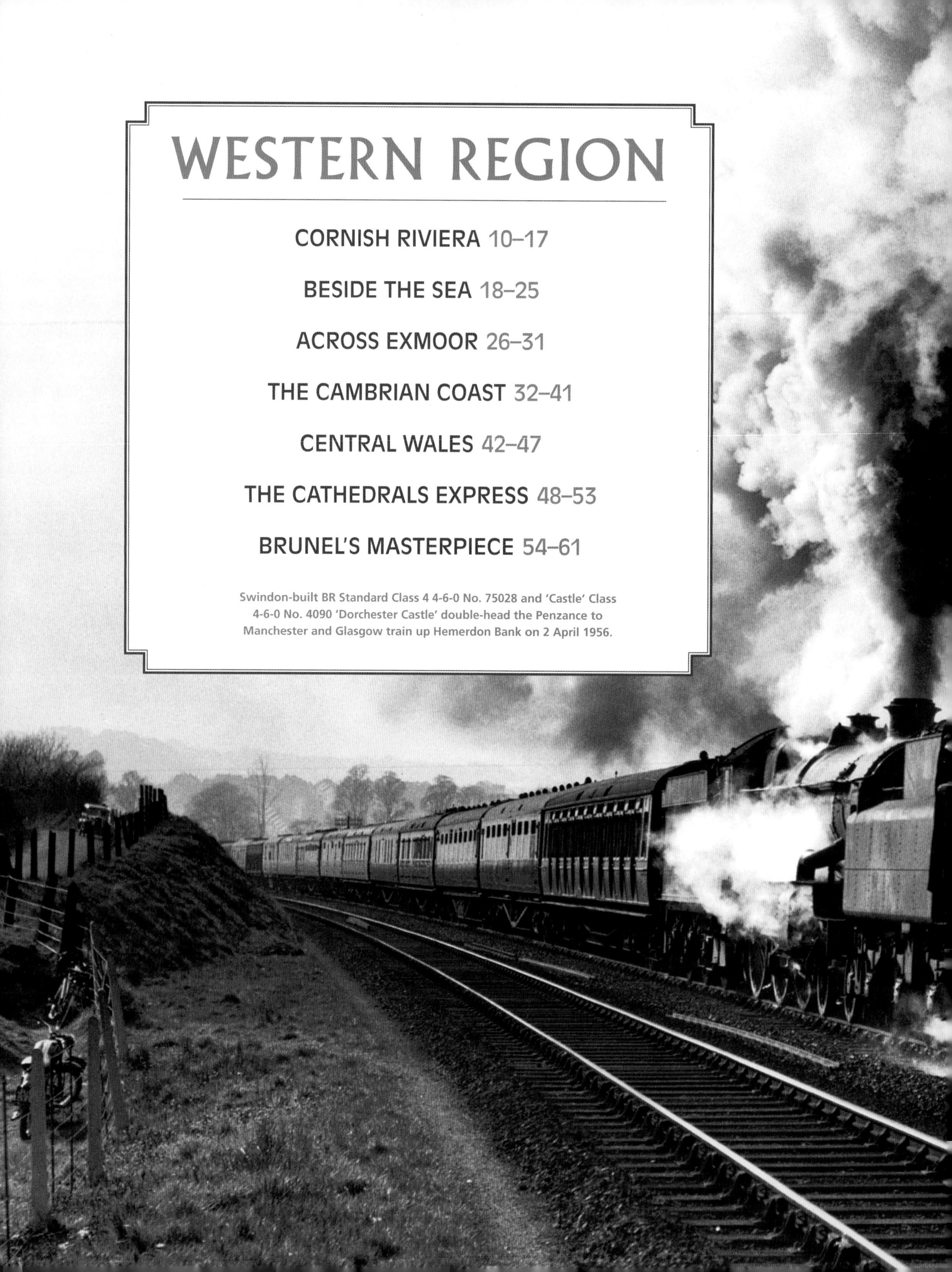

WESTERN REGION

Swindon-built BR Standard Class 4 4-6-0 No. 75028 and 'Castle' Class 4-6-0 No. 4090 'Dorchester Castle' double-head the Penzance to Manchester and Glasgow train up Hemerdon Bank on 2 April 1956.

CORNISH RIVIERA

Plymouth to Penzance

Despite the early construction of a network of horsedrawn tramways and steam-hauled mineral railways that linked mines and harbours throughout Cornwall, the county remained isolated from the rest of Britain's rail system until 1859.

▲ Class '6400' 0-6-0PT No. 6420 propels its auto trailer out of Saltash station before crossing Brunel's Royal Albert Bridge in August 1959. The view was spoilt by the parallel road bridge of 1961 with the Plymouth to Saltash auto trains becoming a thing of the past.

Although the South Devon Railway from Exeter had reached Plymouth (Laira) in 1848 (see pages 18–25), the county of Cornwall remained cut off from the rapidly expanding national rail network until 1859. However, this isolation had not stopped the building of a system of tramways and mineral railways that had started in the early 19th century. Most of these had been built to serve the then important copper-mining industry, carrying copper ore from the mines to harbours from where it was exported around the world.

As early as 1801 the Cornish engineer Richard Trevithick had built a steam-powered carriage and ran it on roads around Camborne. His first steam locomotive for railway use operated at Penydarren in South Wales in 1803 but, despite the work of this local inventor, many Cornish lines remained horsedrawn for many more years. Early Cornish lines included the horsedrawn Poldice Tramway from the Gwennap copper mines to Portreath (opened c.1809, closed c.1860); the Redruth & Chacewater Railway (1826–1915), which was horsedrawn until 1854; the Pentewan Railway (1829–1918), built to carry china clay from near St Austell to the port of Pentewan, which remained horsedrawn until 1874; the steam-hauled Bodmin & Wadebridge Railway, which opened in 1834 to carry sea sand from the Camel Estuary to moorland farms; the Hayle & Portreath Railway, which opened in 1837 to carry copper ore from Tresavean and Redruth to the harbours at Portreath and Hayle (this line included inclined planes at Angarrack and Penponds); the Liskeard & Caradon

▲ Heading a down goods train from Plymouth to Cornwall, 'Grange' Class 4-6-0 No. 6845 'Paviland Grange' halts at Saltash for the driver to hand over the single-line tablet after crossing the Royal Albert Bridge on 2 May 1959 – exactly 100 years to the day since Prince Albert had opened the bridge.

Railway, which opened in 1844 to carry copper ore and granite from Caradon down to Looe; the Par Railway, which opened in 1847; the Newquay Railway from East Wheal Rose Mine and St Dennis to Newquay Harbour, which opened in 1849; the West Cornwall Railway, which opened in 1852 and was an extension of the Hayle Railway connecting Penzance, Redruth and Truro.

BRUNEL'S CONTRIBUTION

The West Cornwall Railway, engineered by Isambard Kingdom Brunel, eventually formed the western half of the Plymouth to Penzance main line that we know today. Brunel bypassed the inclined planes at Angarrack and Penponds with timber viaducts; passenger traffic between Penzance and Truro commenced in 1852. This temporary arrangement remained until 1855, when a new terminus was opened at Truro. Strangely, the railway was built to standard gauge, although this had to be relaid to broad gauge after the Cornwall Railway had opened from Plymouth to Truro.

Meanwhile, the missing link from Plymouth to Truro and on to Falmouth had been authorised by an Act of Parliament in 1846. The Cornwall Railway, as it was then known, allowed for

▲ Bathed in glorious sunshine, Class '4300' 2-6-0 No. 7321 restarts the 3.40pm Plymouth to Penzance train from Liskeard on 14 June 1956. Liskeard is also the starting point for the scenic branch line down to Looe, saved from Beeching's axe because of the difficult road access to the popular harbour village.

the building of a broad gauge double-track main line between the up-and-coming port of Falmouth to Saltash via Truro with a single-track bridge across the Tamar to Plymouth. Financial backing for this venture came from various interested parties including the Great Western Railway (GWR), the Bristol & Exeter Railway and the South Devon Railway. However, its construction was delayed for six years due to the severe financial crisis brought on by nationwide 'Railway Mania' – the speculative bubble that saw the eventual expansion of the railway network at the expense of the UK's economy and many individual livelihoods.

Eventually, with Brunel again at the helm, work started on building this heavily engineered line in 1852. The statistics are staggering – the heavily graded line being carried through several tunnels, on numerous embankments and across more than 30 viaducts, The latter were originally built of timber resting on stone piers but the high cost of maintenance led them to be replaced in later years by stone or steel viaducts and occasionally by embankments.

▼ Looking very handsome with its train of chocolate and cream Mk 1 coaches, the down 'Cornishman' express from Wolverhampton (Low Level) to Penzance approaches Bodmin Road station behind 'County' Class 4-6-0 No. 1002 'County of Berks' on Whit Monday, 18 May 1959. The train would have taken a journey that is no longer possible via Stratford-upon-Avon, Cheltenham Spa (Malvern Road) and Gloucester (Eastgate) and would have involved engine changes at Bristol and Plymouth.

▼ 'Grange' Class 4-6-0 No. 6805 'Broughton Grange' leaves Truro station with a down parcels train on 15 May 1959. Immediately behind the locomotive is an empty milk road tanker returning to the creamery at St Erth. Many young lads would have given their right arm to live in one of those fairly new estate houses with their panoramic view of Truro station and engine shed.

'Castle' Class 4-6-0 No. 7031 'Cromwell's Castle' takes on water at Truro before departing with the up 'Cornish Riviera Express' on 16 May 1959. Although the class was introduced by the GWR in 1923, the final members, including No. 7031, were built by BR at Swindon in 1950. A Plymouth Laira regular, the loco ended its days at Worcester before being withdrawn in 1963 – a great waste.

'County' Class 4-6-0 No. 1023 'County of Oxford' passes through Lostwithiel station with the 11.30am Paddington to Penzance train on 11 June 1956. Although the branch line from here to Fowey lost its passenger service in 1965, the line still sees regular china clay traffic to Carne Point.

The crossing of the River Tamar is one of Brunel's masterpieces and the opening of the Royal Albert Bridge, on 2 May 1859, finally gave Cornwall its link with the outside world. Passenger services between Plymouth and Truro commenced on that date but the Falmouth branch had to wait until 1863 before it was granted its own passenger service.

RAPID CHANGE IN CORNWALL

The immediate years following the opening of the Cornwall Railway saw a major rationalisation of railway operating in Cornwall. First, operations on the West Cornwall Railway west of Truro were taken over by the broad gauge consortium of the Great Western, the Bristol & Exeter and the South Devon railways in 1866. The line was then relaid to broad gauge, thus allowing through running between Paddington and Penzance for the first time – the journey in 1867 took nine hours. In 1876, the GWR took over the Bristol & Exeter Railway and two years later the South Devon Railway, but, although the now mighty GWR continued to work the line, the West Cornwall Railway surprisingly remained in existence as a company until it was dissolved on nationalisation in 1948.

To the east, the Cornwall Railway from Plymouth to Truro and Falmouth, plagued by accidents during its early years, remained independent until 1877 when the GWR took over the working of the line. Despite this, the company itself remained as a separate entity until being swallowed up by the GWR in 1889.

Although Cornwall had once been the world's leading exporter of copper ore, the 1870s saw a dramatic decline in mining fortunes as worldwide prices fell. Although this decline soon led to the abandonment of the early tramways, an upsurge in the worldwide demand for china clay from the St Austell area soon led to the generation of new railborne traffic not only to

▼ *Main image* Reallocated to Penzance shed only two months earlier, immaculately turned-out 'County' Class 4-6-0 No. 1002 'County of Berks' nears the summit of the line between Truro and Chacewater with the down 'Cornishman' on 16 May 1959. Sadly, none of F. W. Hawksworth's powerful 'Counties' were preserved, although a replica (No. 1014 'County of Glamorgan') is being built at the Didcot Railway Centre.

▼ *Inset* Looking in immaculate ex-works condition, 'Grange' Class 4-6-0 No. 6875 'Hindford Grange' passes the engine shed at Long Rock, Penzance, with the 1.55pm Penzance to Plymouth train in May 1959. Closing to steam on 10 September 1962, Penzance shed (83G) once boasted a healthy allocation of 'County' and 'Grange' Class 4-6-0s for working trains on the Cornish main line to Plymouth.

the Potteries but also to Fowey Harbour for onward export by ship. The subsequent opening of branch lines to St Ives, Helston (for The Lizard), Fowey, Newquay and Looe also led to an influx of Victorian travellers and the development of these once small fishing villages into thriving seaside towns. Local produce in the form of fish, milk, potatoes, broccoli and cut flowers could also now reach the all-important London markets overnight. By 23 May 1892 all of Brunel's original broad gauge west of Exeter had been relaid to standard gauge and tourism was fast becoming an important factor in Cornwall's economy.

THE CORNISH RIVIERA EXPRESS

The Great Western Railway, its public relations department never slow to extol the virtues of its destinations and capitalise on a new trend, introduced the 'Cornish Riviera Express' from Paddington to Penzance in 1904. Originally travelling via Bristol, its journey was shortened the following year by the opening of a new line between Westbury, Castle Cary and Taunton. The train became so popular with holidaymakers that it ran in two portions before the First World War. The introduction of the 'King' Class 4-6-0s in 1927 saw speeded-up and heavier trains reaching Plymouth in four hours and soon there were through coaches for Falmouth and St Ives. On summer Saturdays, the train ran non-stop to St Erth with passengers for Falmouth and Helston being carried in a relief express – although it was scheduled as 'non-stop' this train actually changed engines at Devonport as the 'King' Class locos were too heavy to work over the Royal Albert Bridge. From the 1930s until the early 1960s the switchback Cornish main line saw a steady procession of Summer Saturday trains, many of them double-headed and packed with holidaymakers from the North, the Midlands and London. During this period, the mainstay of passenger steam-haulage on the line until the onset of diesels in the early 1960s were 'Castle', 'Hall', 'Grange' and 'County' Class 4-6-0s from Plymouth Laira and Penzance sheds. These were gradually replaced by the Western Region's short-lived 'Warship' and 'Western' Class diesel-hydraulics, followed by English Electric Type 4 (Class 50), Brush Type 4 (Class 47) and then by HST diesel sets. Now overdue for replacement, these latter trains have performed sterling service on the Cornish main line for more than 30 years.

For years branch-line traffic in Cornwall was normally handled by the 'Small Prairie' 2-6-2 tanks (4500 and 4575 Classes) but by the early 1960s these had been replaced by the short-lived North British Type 2 diesel-hydraulics, Beyer-Peacock Hymeks and diesel multiple units or single 'Bubble' cars.

▼ Complete with small alloy headboard, the 'Cornish Riviera Express' waits to depart from Penzance in June 1957 behind 'Castle' Class 4-6-0 No. 5069 'Isambard Kingdom Brunel'. The famous train left Penzance at 10am, running non-stop between Plymouth and Paddington, where it arrived at 4.40pm.

THE LINE TODAY

Despite the disappearance of most of its freight traffic (apart from china clay traffic), the scenic Cornish main line is very much alive and kicking today. In recent years, passenger numbers have seen a dramatic increase – those using Penzance station have increased by a staggering 65 per cent since 2000. The line is served by local stopping trains between Plymouth and Penzance and by through express trains to and from Paddington (including the Night Riviera overnight sleeper train) all operated by First Great Western. In addition, CrossCountry operates through services to and from Birmingham, Edinburgh, Glasgow, Aberdeen and Manchester. Despite the complete closures of the Gwinear Road to Helston branch (1962), the Chacewater to Newquay branch (1963), the Lostwithiel to Fowey branch (to passengers only in 1965) and Bodmin Road to Bodmin General (see Bodmin & Wenford Railway, right), the following former GWR branch lines radiating from the Cornish main line are still open for passengers on trains run by First Great Western:

St Erth to St Ives
Truro to Falmouth
Par to Newquay
Liskeard to Looe

HERITAGE RAILWAYS

BODMIN & WENFORD RAILWAY

General Station, Bodmin,
Cornwall PL31 1AQ

Tel: 0845 125 9678 or 01208 73555

Website:
www.bodminandwenfordrailway.co.uk

Route: Bodmin Parkway – Bodmin General – Boscarne Junction

Length: 6½ miles

Nearest main-line station:
Bodmin Parkway

The only standard gauge preserved steam railway in Cornwall, the Bodmin & Wenford Railway was originally the GWR branch from Bodmin Road to Boscame Junction, opened in May 1887, which was closed to passengers in 1967 and to all traffic in November 1983 following the ending of china clay trains from Wenfordbridge. Reopened as a heritage line in 1989, the section from the terminus at Bodmin General to Bodmin Parkway includes an intermediate station at Colesloggett Halt that gives passengers access to Cardinham Woods and its waymarked trails, café, picnic area and cycle-hire facilities. Trains are mainly steam-hauled by former GWR locomotives along this scenic line, which includes gradients as steep as 1 in 37. An extension from Bodmin General to Boscarne Junction (for the Camel Trail) was opened in 1997. Trains connect with First Great Western services between Plymouth and Penzance at Bodmin Parkway station.

HELSTON RAILWAY

Trevarno Manor, Crowntown,
Helston, Cornwall TR13 0RU

Website: www.helstonrailway.co.uk

Tel: 07136 796456

Opened in 1887, the 8¾-mile branch line from Gwinear Road to Helston closed to passengers in 1962 and completely in 1964. Once famous for its GWR connecting bus service to The Lizard, the trackbed, viaduct and bridges of the line disappeared into the undergrowth until 2005 when a group of volunteers started restoring a short length of track in Trevarno Gardens. Now the Helston Railway Preservation Company (a 'not for profit' company) has cleared about a mile of the trackbed and relaid ¼ mile. They currently have a shop and exhibition of railway memorabilia in a converted mail van at their new station in Trevarno Gardens and planning permission has been given for an extension of the line to Truthall.

◀ Although it is normally a passenger-carrying heritage line, the Bodmin & Wenford Railway occasionally runs demonstration goods trains for the benefit of photographers and enthusiasts. Here, preserved '4575' Class 2-6-2T No. 5552 makes a fine sight as it works a goods train from Bodmin Parkway to Bodmin General in September 2006.

BESIDE THE SEA

Exeter St Davids to Kingswear and Plymouth

Originally an expensive and unsuccessful experiment for Brunel's eccentric atmospheric railway system, the former GWR main line between Exeter and Plymouth with its coastal route, sea views and Dartmoor vistas must rate as one of the most scenic railway journeys in Britain.

Engineered by Isambard Kingdom Brunel and leased to the Great Western Railway, the broad gauge Bristol & Exeter Railway opened throughout on 1 May 1844 amid great rejoicing in the city of Exeter. Meanwhile, Brunel had witnessed earlier trials of an innovative railway propulsion system in West London known as an atmospheric railway. Avoiding the need for normal steam locomotives, the system consisted of a steel pipe (with a diameter of 22in on gradients and 15in on level surfaces) located between the rails from which stationary steam engines pumped out the air to create a vacuum. The iron pipe had a slot in the top, sealed by a leather flap, and a 15ft-long piston, secured on a rod beneath the leading carriage, fitted into the pipe. The pressure of the air that was sucked into the vacuum pipe as the flap was opened moved the piston, and hence the

▼ 'Castle' Class 4-6-0 No. 5007 'Rougemont Castle' bursts out of the tunnel at Horse Cove near Dawlish with a down express on 13 August 1957. Even today the crumbling red sandstone and winter storms along this stretch can bring a halt to proceedings!

train, forward. As the piston moved forward, two small wheels in front of and behind it first opened the flap and then sealed it. Stationary pumping houses were to be located at intervals of 3 miles along the line to ensure a permanent vacuum in the pipe.

ATMOSPHERIC PROBLEMS

Brunel was so impressed by what he saw that he advocated for an atmospheric system to be installed on his next broad gauge railway engineering project, the South Devon Railway from Exeter to Plymouth. Financially backed by the Great Western, the Bristol & Exeter and the Bristol & Gloucester railways, the South Devon Railway received Parliamentary approval just two months after the Bristol & Exeter had opened. Progress in building the line was swift but delivery of the atmospheric equipment was behind schedule and the first trains from Exeter to Teignmouth on 16th August 1846 had to be run behind borrowed GWR locomotives. Passenger-carrying atmospheric trains finally started operation between Exeter and Teignmouth on 13 September 1847, to Newton Abbot on 10 January 1848 and to Totnes by July of that year.

▼ **Fitted with a straight-sided Hawksworth tender, 'Castle' Class 4-6-0 No. 5073 'Blenheim' restarts a northbound express from the West Country at Exeter St Davids in 1958. This locomotive was originally built in 1938 as 'Cranbrook Castle' but, was renamed in 1941, its old name being given to No. 7030 when that loco was built in 1950.**

▲ **This time seen with a Collett tender, 'Castle' Class 4-6-0 No. 5073 'Blenheim' heads along the seawall at Dawlish with an up express in spring 1960. This famous stretch of coast-hugging line still sees the steam-hauled 'Torbay Express' from Bristol to Kingswear during the summer.**

Work continued on building the line towards Plymouth, but the atmospheric system was already experiencing serious problems with high maintenance costs due to the failure of the supposedly air-tight leather seals. The South Devon Railway's shareholders pulled the plug on it in August and it ceased to operate on 6 September 1848, being replaced by conventional steam haulage.

Meanwhile the remaining section of line between Totnes and Plymouth had opened on 5 May 1848, although trains were being hauled using borrowed GWR locomotives. A branch line from Newton Abbot to Torre was opened in December that year and later extended to Paignton in 1859, to Churston (for the Brixham branch) in 1861 and finally to Kingswear in 1864. A railway-operated ferry ran from here across the River Dart to a 'railway station' at Dartmouth. In this period the railway's arrival transformed previously small fishing villages and soon excursion trains packed with Londoners were bringing thousands of holidaymakers to the area – by the end of the 19th century, both Torquay and Paignton had grown beyond all recognition.

By 1876 the Bristol & Exeter Railway had been amalgamated with the GWR and, two years later, the South Devon Railway followed suit – with the GWR also by now working the main line through Cornwall it now controlled the entire railway route from Paddington to Penzance. Brunel's dream of the luxurious broad

▼ Superpower at Newton Abbot – the second portion of the down 'Cornish Riviera Express' makes an impressive sight behind 'King' Class 4-6-0s No. 6026 'King John' and No. 6025 'King Henry III' on 27 July 1957. A few miles farther on these two powerful locos would have made easy going of the notorious South Devon Banks around the southern slopes of Dartmoor.

▼ A jolly seaside holiday scene at Dawlish in the late 1950s as Plymouth Laira's 'Castle' Class 4-6-0 No. 5023 'Brecon Castle' passes through at the head of the 8am Saturdays-only Sheffield to Paignton train. Built at Swindon in 1934, this loco was allocated to Laira for most of the 1950s and withdrawn in 1963.

'Hall' Class 4-6-0 No. 5943 'Elmdon Hall' heads out of Teignmouth with an up fitted freight on 8 August 1956. This locomotive was built at Swindon in 1935 and withdrawn in 1963.

gauge finally ended in a massive operation over a weekend in May 1892 when the GWR relaid the entire system west of Exeter to standard gauge – a feat almost unimaginable today.

A LINE FOR BEAUTY

Featuring the famous seawall at Dawlish, the main line between Exeter and Plymouth is still one of the most scenic railway journeys in Britain. In addition to the seawall, where the track is often lashed by winter storms, the section of fairly level coast-hugging line between Dawlish and Teignmouth includes five tunnels. After Newton Abbot, where the South Devon Railway had its headquarters, the main line climbs at 1 in 37 to Dainton Tunnel before dropping down to Totnes from where the branch line to Ashburton opened in 1872. Beyond Totnes the main line climbs around the southern edges of Dartmoor up Rattery incline to the summit near Wrangaton before descending across graceful stone viaducts, through Ivybridge and down the 1 in 42 Hemerdon incline to journey's end at Plymouth.

Apart from the Ashburton branch line already mentioned (closed 1962), which is now a heritage line as far as Buckfastleigh, the opening of the South Devon Railway spawned three other branch lines including Newton Abbot to Moretonhampstead (opened 1866, closed to passengers 1959), the Churston to Brixham line (opened 1868, closed 1963) and Brent to Kingsbridge (opened 1893, closed 1963). The line between Paignton and Kingswear was closed in 1972 and is now a steam-hauled heritage railway.

END OF AN ERA

Until the introduction of the 'King' Class 4-6-0s in 1927, heavy trains had to be double-headed over the South Devon banks west of Newton Abbot. This practice continued until the end of steam in the early 1960s and made Newton Abbot a mecca for railway enthusiasts. Here, on summer Saturdays in the 1950s a long procession of trains packed with holidaymakers from the North, the Midlands and London bound for Cornwall,

▶ The end of the line alongside the River Dart at Kingswear. 'Castle' Class 4-6-0 No. 5028 'Llantilio Castle' takes on water before hauling the 'Torbay Express' back to Paddington in September 1953.

▼ Pounding up Dainton Bank, 'Grange' Class 4-6-0 No. 6813 'Eastbury Grange' of Exeter shed (83C) pilots 'Modified Hall' Class 4-6-0 No. 6991 'Acton Burnell Hall' with a Bristol to Plymouth relief holiday train on 3 August 1960 while the driver of the 'Grange' gives a cheerful 'V' for Victory sign to the photographer, Hugh Ballantyne. This dramatic scene soon disappeared with the introduction of 'Warship' Class diesel-hydraulics.

having just steamed along the coastal route through Dawlish and Teignmouth, would stop at the station to take on a pilot locomotive for the onward journey to Plymouth. All types of former GWR main-line 4-6-0 locomotives could be seen from 'King' and 'Castle' to 'Hall', 'Modified Hall', 'Grange' and 'County'. Even the newer BR Standard Class 9F 2-10-0s and occasionally Western Region 'Britannia' 4-6-2s were often pressed into service during peak holiday times. Alongside these comings and goings, an equally busy service of trains, including the 'Torbay Express', could be seen heading for Torquay, Paignton and Kingswear. Other famous named trains that processed through the station were the 'Cornish Riviera Express' (in several portions), 'The Royal Duchy' and 'The Mayflower'. Sadly, by the early 1960s and the introduction of diesel-hydraulics, later followed by the HST, this wondrous scene was swept away for ever.

▼ Even the new diesels required assistance over the South Devon Banks – here Newton Abbot-based 'Castle' Class 4-6-0 No. 4098 'Kidwelly Castle' pilots NBL 'Warship' Class diesel-hydraulic D602 'Bulldog' into Brent station with the 6.25am Penzance to Paddington train on 5 August 1960. Brent was also the station for the 12½-mile Kingsbridge branch, which closed in 1963.

▲ All steamed up and ready to tackle the South Devon Banks, 'Hall' Class 4-6-0 No. 4976 'Warfield Hall' and 'Castle' Class 4-6-0 No. 4087 'Cardigan Castle' head out of Plymouth with the 9.30am Falmouth to Paddington train on 18 August 1960.

THE LINE TODAY

Fortunately, the dramatic rail journey from Exeter to Plymouth, with its far-reaching views of the Exe Estuary and the sea and of Dartmoor, can still be enjoyed today. Passenger numbers are rising – in fact, they have nearly doubled in the past ten years and, apart from the occasional seasonal difficulties caused by inclement weather along the seawall at Dawlish, the line has a bright future. The line is served by First Great Western trains from Paddington including the overnight Night Riviera sleeping car train and CrossCountry trains from Scotland and the North of England via Bristol. Local stopping trains are also operated by First Great Western.

As an alternative to the clogged rounds surrounding Torquay, the branch from Newton Abbot to Torquay and Paignton is also served by First Great Western stopping services from Exeter and by through trains from Paddington. CrossCountry also operates through services from Manchester Piccadilly via Bristol.

Not all is lost for the steam enthusiast either because on certain Sundays during the summer months the steam-hauled 'Torbay Express' provides a memorable return trip from Bristol to Paignton and Kingwear. The sight of No. 6024 'King Edward I' hauling its packed train of brown and cream coaches along the seawall at Dawlish cannot fail to evoke those halcyon days of GWR main-line steam along this scenic stretch of line.

HERITAGE RAILWAYS

DARTMOUTH STEAM RAILWAY & RIVER BOAT COMPANY

Queens Park Station, Torbay Road, Paignton, Devon TQ4 6AF

Website: www.dartmouthrailriver.co.uk

Tel: 01803 555872

Route: Paignton to Kingswear

Length: 7 miles

Nearest main-line station: Paignton

A broad gauge line from Torquay was built by the Dartmouth & Torbay Railway Company, reaching Paignton in 1859 and Churston in 1861. A branch to Brixham was opened in 1867. Originally intending to bridge the Dart to Dartmouth, it was finally terminated at Kingswear in 1864, being converted to standard gauge by the GWR in 1892. Scheduled for closure by BR in 1972 (the Brixham branch having succumbed in 1963), the line was taken over by the Dart Valley Light Railway Ltd that year. Services began in 1973 and were worked by this company until 1991, when the Paignton & Dartmouth Steam Railway operated it until 2010. This company has recently joined forces with Riverlink to provide combined rail and river trips along the River Dart with the advantage of a link to the national rail system at Paignton. At the other end, in Kingswear, passengers from the trains can take a ferry across the River Dart to Dartmouth. A journey along the line offers three viaducts and a tunnel, sandy beaches and a river estuary. Ex-GWR steam locomotives run regular services with an ex-'Devon Belle' observation car attached to certain trains.

▲ Preserved ex-GWR 2-6-2T No. 4555 arrives at Kingswear with a train from Paignton on 8 June 2006. With its main-line connection at Paignton and the scenic delights of the River Dart, the Dartmouth Steam Railway is ideally placed for holidaymakers to the English Riviera.

SOUTH DEVON RAILWAY

The Station, Dart Bridge Road,
Buckfastleigh, Devon TQ11 0DZ

Website: www.southdevonrailway.co.uk

Tel: 0845 3451420 or 01364 642338

Route: Buckfastleigh to Totnes (Littlehempston)

Length: 7 miles

Originally opened as a broad gauge branch line to Ashburton in 1872, converted to standard gauge by the GWR in 1892, and closed by BR in 1962, the South Devon Railway evokes all the atmosphere of a sleepy GWR West Country branch line as it follows the winding valley of the River Dart. One of the earliest preserved lines, it was reopened in 1969 (by Lord Beeching!) and was eventually jointly operated with its seaside cousin, the Paignton & Dartmouth, by the Dart Valley Light Railway Ltd. One of the main drawbacks to the success of the preserved railway was the lack of access for passengers at the Totnes end of the line. For a short period between 1985 and 1988, Dart Valley trains were able to run into the BR station at Totnes, but the practice was abandoned, due partly to the high charges made by the state operator for this privilege. In 1990 the South Devon Railway Trust took over the running of the railway and has been a great success. One of the highlights of recent years this has been the opening of the South Devon Railway station at Totnes (Littlehempston), which is connected via a footbridge over the River Dart to the car park of the nearby BR station. Trains are currently mainly steam-hauled and rolling stock includes superbly restored vintage GWR carriages. A railway museum, adjoining Buckfastleigh station, contains many fascinating railway artefacts and relics, including the only surviving broad gauge locomotive, 'Tiny'.

▲ Beautifully preserved ex-GWR 0-6-0PT No. 5786 runs round its auto coach at the northern terminus of the South Devon Railway at Buckfastleigh in September 2010. Like many other heritage lines, the SDR offers driver training courses to members of the public.

ACROSS EXMOOR

Taunton to Barnstaple

Despite a rather dismal start to life, the old Devon & Somerset Railway eventually came into its own as an important route for GWR holiday trains to North Devon in the 1930s. Competition from road transport in the 1950s eventually sounded the death knell for this delightfully rural line.

Originally known as the Devon & Somerset Railway, the broad gauge railway line between Taunton and Barnstaple was authorised in 1864 but its construction was painfully slow due to the widespread repercussions of the financial crisis in 1866 when a London wholesale discount bank, Overend, Gurney & Co., collapsed (owing nearly a billion pounds at today's rate). The subsequent rapid collapse in stock and bond prices hit railway stocks particularly hard.

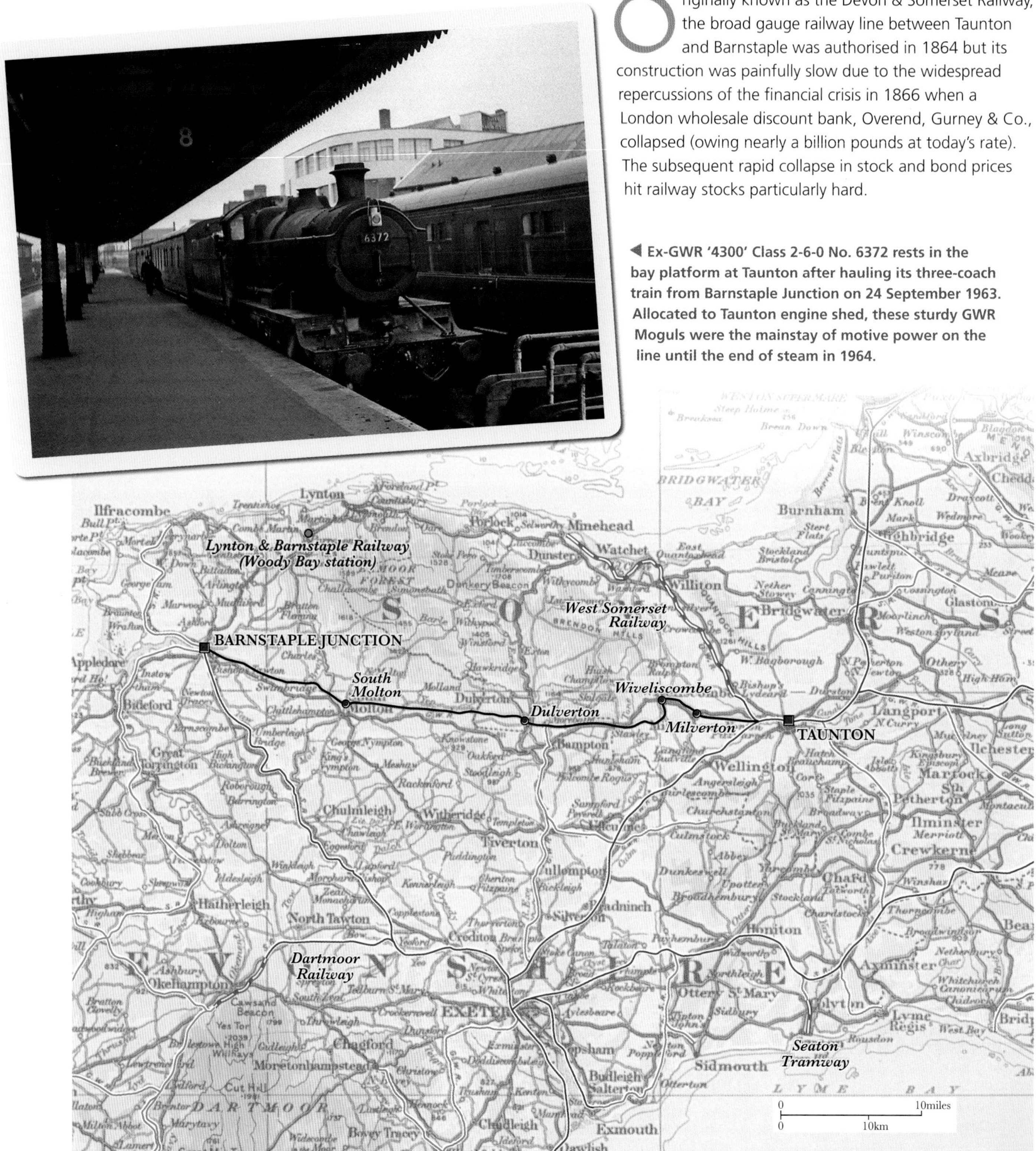

◀ **Ex-GWR '4300' Class 2-6-0 No. 6372 rests in the bay platform at Taunton after hauling its three-coach train from Barnstaple Junction on 24 September 1963. Allocated to Taunton engine shed, these sturdy GWR Moguls were the mainstay of motive power on the line until the end of steam in 1964.**

'4300' Class 2-6-0 No. 7333 leaves Milverton station with a Taunton to Barnstaple train on a sunny 14 September 1963. By this date the line was living on borrowed time having been listed for closure in that year's Beeching report.

BUDGET RAILWAY

Worked from the outset by the Bristol & Exeter Railway, the 43-mile single-track line finally opened between Norton Fitzwarren Junction and Wiveliscombe in 1871 and to Barnstaple (renamed Victoria Road in 1949) in 1873. Although involving the construction of three tunnels and two substantial viaducts, this was a budget-priced line with low-cost stations and only three passing loops. Services were initially appalling with neither mail nor coal being carried for some years because of disputes. The line continued its torpid existence until 1881, when it was converted to standard gauge along with the inclusion of more crossing loops. Further improvements to services occurred in 1887, when a connecting line to Barnstaple Junction station was opened, thus allowing through trains from Taunton and beyond to run over the London & South Western Railway's line to Ilfracombe. Even so, direct running to Junction station still required the train to reverse at Victoria Road until 1905, when a new spur was opened.

HOLIDAY TRAFFIC

The Devon & Somerset Railway was taken over by the GWR in 1901 and soon the introduction of holiday trains on summer Saturdays from other parts of the network to the up-and-coming resort of Ilfracombe were choking the line's capacity during the summer months. To cope with this increased traffic, the Great Western Railway doubled the section between Norton Fitzwarren and Milverton in the 1930s and lengthened passing loops. Except during the Second World War, these holiday trains continued to run until the early 1960s, when the line was listed for closure in Dr Beeching's report. Barnstaple (Victoria Road) station had already been closed in 1960 (although it was still used for freight until 1970) and all passenger trains from Taunton were diverted along the 1905 spur to Junction station. By then freight traffic, including the all-important cattle and milk trains, had been reduced to a trickle, and steam operations were to end in October 1964 when Taunton shed was closed. Any freight traffic left was

▲ A Barnstaple-bound train heads out of Dulverton behind '4300' Class 2-6-0 No. 6372 on 25 August 1962. Even after receiving the death sentence from Dr Beeching in 1963, the station flower beds were still being cared for by the staff.

▼ *Main image* No. 7333 restarts from Venn Cross station with a Taunton-bound train on 14 September 1963. Curiously, the Devon–Somerset border cut through the station, with the goods shed being in Devon and the station buildings in Somerset. All of these buildings have survived since closure and are now private residences.

sent via Exeter, and passenger services were reduced to single-car diesel multiple units, which continued in service until total closure came on 3 October 1966.

For most of the last 30 years of its life, motive power on the line was provided by the sturdy GWR 'Mogul' 2-6-0s, often working in tandem on heavy holiday trains, based at Taunton shed. They were also often to be seen working on the Barnstaple Junction to Ilfracombe line with through trains to and from other parts of the GWR system via Taunton. The only branch line to feed into the Devon & Somerset route was the Exe Valley line, which ran from Exeter to Dulverton via Stoke Canon, Tiverton and Morebath Junction. The line opened in two stages: Tiverton to Morebath Junction in 1884 and Stoke Canon to Tiverton in 1885. Traffic was never heavy and was usually handled by a GWR auto train. The line closed to passengers on 7 October 1963.

▼ A regular performer on the Taunton to Barnstaple line No. 7337 is seen here taking on water at South Molton at the head of a Barnstaple-bound train on 8 May 1961. Sadly, the station building has been demolished and the trackbed of the railway has been swallowed up by the A361 North Devon Link Road.

▲ Barnstaple Junction, today a former shadow of itself, was once a busy rail hub with lines radiating out to Torrington, Ilfracombe (seen curving away under the road bridge), Exeter and Taunton. Here, '4300' Class 2-6-0 No. 6327 is performing a shunting operation after arriving from Taunton in April 1963.

THE LINE TODAY

Much of the trackbed of this line is fairly intact, while many former station buildings are now private residences. West of Taunton, the B3227 Milverton bypass now follows the route of the railway and, farther west at Exebridge, there are tantilising glimpses of a high railway embankment and the remaining arch of the bridge over the River Exe. At Brushford the station building, plaform and goods shed of Dulverton station (more than a mile away from the town it once served) are in a well-preserved state, while the trackbed to the west is now a footpath and cycleway to East Anstey. From South Molton to Barnstaple several sections of the old railway trackbed have been swallowed up by the A361 North Devon Link Road. The former goods shed at Victoria Road station can be seen alongside the A361 on the approach to Barnstaple.

HERITAGE RAILWAYS

WEST SOMERSET RAILWAY

The Railway Station, Minehead,
Somerset TA24 5BG

Website: www.west-somerset-railway.co.uk

Tel: 01643 704996

Route: Minehead to Bishop's Lydeard

Length: 20 miles

Nearest main-line station: Taunton

Britain's longest heritage railway, running past the rolling Quantock Hills to the sea, was originally opened as a broad gauge line from Norton Fitzwarren, on the main Taunton to Exeter line, to Watchet in 1862 and extended to Minehead in 1874. The line was initially operated by the Bristol & Exeter Railway and then by its successor, the Great Western Railway, who converted it to standard gauge in 1882. Although the opening of Butlin's holiday camp at Minehead in 1962 brought an increase in traffic, the line was eventually closed by British Rail (BR) in 1971, much to the consternation of local people and businesses. Prior to closure Minehead station had been one of the locations used in the filming of The Beatles' film *A Hard Days Night*. The line was partly reopened, from Minehead to Williton, in 1976 by the newly formed West Somerset Railway Company (WSR), who leased it from Somerset County Council. By 1979, it had been extended to its present terminus at Bishop's Lydeard. The section from here to Norton Fitzwarren is not currently used on a regular basis but there is a turning triangle and a physical connection with the national network, with a limited number of through trains being run from the national system on to the WSR. Plans to run a regular service to Taunton have been obstructed for many years, originally by opposition from the National Union of Railwaymen and then by official BR bureaucracy. A bus service links Bishop's Lydeard with Taunton. The present West Somerset Railway is home to a variety of steam and diesel locomotives (the diesel preservation group being based at Williton) as well as the Somerset & Dorset Trust's museum at Washford. Steam locomotives include S&DJR Class 7F 2-8-0 No. 88 and a wide variety of former GWR types. Visiting locomotives can regularly be seen at work on the line, making use of the turntable (originally from Pwllheli) that has recently been installed at Minehead. All ten of the picturesque

▲ The driver and fireman of preserved '4575' Class 2-6-2T No. 5553 pass the time of day at Minehead, the seaside terminus of the West Somerset Railway, after preparing their steed to haul the 'Quantock Belle' dining train.

stations on the line have been painstakingly preserved and the journey evokes all the atmosphere of a GWR country railway.

LYNTON & BARNSTAPLE RAILWAY

Woody Bay Station, Martinhoe Cross,
Parracombe, Devon EX31 4RA

Website: www.lynton-rail.co.uk

Tel: 01598 763487

Route: Woody Bay station to Killington Lane

Length: 1 mile

Nearest main-line station: Barnstaple

Opened in 1898, the 1ft 11½in-narrow gauge Lynton & Barnstaple Railway was closed by the Southern Railway in 1935. After many years trying to reopen part of the line, the Lynton & Barnstaple Railway Association purchased the former Woody Bay station in 1995. Since then about a mile of track has been laid to a temporary terminus at Killington Lane. With far-reaching views towards the North Devon coast, most trains are steam-hauled during the period from April to October. Extensions to Lynton in the north and Wistpoundland Reservoir in the south are a long-term plan as the Lynton & Barnstaple Trust now owns much of the former trackbed.

▲ Built by Kerr, Stuart & Co. in 1915, the Lynton & Barnstaple Railway's 0-6-0T 'Axe' is seen here at picturesque Woody Bay station after working a First World War demonstration goods train on 20 April 2009.

THE CAMBRIAN COAST

Shrewsbury to Aberystwyth and Pwllheli

Narrowly escaping closure under the 'Beeching Axe' and one of the last outposts of steam on British Railways, the long and tortuous route from Shrewsbury to the Cambrian Coast remains one of the most scenic railway journeys in Britain.

The history of the present-day railway route from Shrewsbury to the Cambrian Coast is a long and convoluted tale. Ever since the 1830s, various schemes had been proposed for railways to be built linking the Midlands with the ports and harbours of the Welsh west coast. Following the failure of other schemes to get off the ground, the small market town of Llanidloes promoted its own railway, the Llanidloes & Newton Railway, which was authorised in 1853 and opened in 1859. This 14-mile line remained totally isolated from the rest of the growing national railway network until 1864 when the Oswestry & Newtown Railway

▼ Then allocated to Machynlleth shed, 'Manor' Class 4-6-0 No. 7818 'Granville Manor' waits to leave Shrewsbury station with a Cambrian line stopping train on 5 August 1961. Built at Swindon in 1939, this locomotive was finally withdrawn from Tyseley shed in January 1965.

▲ **The end of an era – BR Standard Class 4 4-6-0 No. 75006 leaves Shrewsbury with the last regular steam-hauled 'Cambrian Coast Express' to Aberystwyth and Pwllheli on 11 February 1967.**

▼ **Sporting its new LMR Shrewsbury shed code of 6D, 'Manor' Class 4-6-0 No. 7819 'Hinton Manor' heads out of Shrewsbury with the down 'Cambrian Coast Express' on 12 September 1964. Replaced by BR Standard Class 4 4-6-0s, this loco was withdrawn less than four months later but escaped the cutter's torch at Woodham's scrapyard in Barry and has since been preserved.**

opened for business. In 1863, the Newtown & Machynlleth Railway opened westwards from Moat Lane Junction and a year later these three railway companies and the Oswestry, Ellesmere & Whitchurch Railway joined forces to become the Cambrian Railways with its headquarters in Oswestry.

ABERYSTWYTH & WELCH

The westward tentacles of this network were soon extended by the opening of the Aberystwyth & Welch [sic] Coast Railway, first from Machynlleth to the growing tourist resort of Aberystwyth in 1864. Two years later, the company was absorbed by the Cambrian Railways. The northward coastal line from Dovey Junction to Pwllheli was built in fits and starts and involved seawalls, tunnels and the daunting crossing of the Mawddach Estuary at Barmouth. Held up by the building of the 121-span Barmouth Bridge at 990yd, the line was not completed until 1867. The timber bridge was subsequently fitted with a pivoting steel swing bridge to allow shipping to pass through in 1899 and rebuilt in the early 20th century.

The all-important connection from the Cambrian main line at Buttington, north of Welshpool, to Shrewsbury was opened by the Shrewsbury & Welshpool Railway in 1861 and was jointly operated by the London & North Western Railway (in 1923 becoming part of the LMS) and Great Western Railway until nationalisation in 1948.

With its slow journey times and elderly locomotives and rolling stock, the straggling and mainly single-track network of the Cambrian Railways struggled to make ends meet and was taken over by the Great Western Railway in 1922. A year earlier, a head-on collision between two trains near Abermule had caused the deaths of 17 people, with the blame being put on the unauthorised passing of a single-line tablet by careless station staff to the driver of one of the trains involved.

THE CAMBRIAN COAST EXPRESS

Under GWR management, the Cambrian main-line saw many improvements carried out to stations and the opening of numerous halts along the coastal route north of Dovey Junction. By far the biggest improvement, though, was the introduction of a new weekday restaurant car service from Paddington to Aberystwyth and Pwllheli. The train was officially named the 'Cambrian Coast Express' in 1927 and, except during the Second World War, ran continuously until the end of steam on the line in 1967. The train was normally hauled from Paddington to Shrewsbury by an Old Oak Common or Wolverhampton Stafford Road 'Castle'. At Shrewsbury, the train reversed and headed out for its journey to the mountains and the coast behind a beautifully turned-out 'Manor' Class 4-6-0 complete with headboard. The train split at Machynlleth with the main portion continuing on to Aberystwyth and the second portion heading north along the coast to Barmouth, Porthmadog, the Butlin's camp at Penychain and Pwllheli. In the last couple of years of its life the 'CCE' was usually headed by BR Standard Class 4 4-6-0s, often double-heading for the difficult climb up to Talerddig Summit. Apart from this train and a mail train, all other services were effectively dieselised late in 1964.

Dr Beeching's 1963 'Report' spelt the end for many loss-making railways in Wales and it was close-run as to whether the Cambrian line or the Ruabon to Barmouth line would be closed. In the end the Cambrian was reprieved and the Ruabon to Barmouth line effectively closed at the end of 1964. A second

▲ Working through from Crewe on the West Coast Main Line, 'Manor' Class 4-6-0 No. 7819 'Hinton Manor', soon to be withdrawn, arrives at Welshpool with a train for Aberystwyth in October 1964. On the right, a grubby No. 7821 'Ditcheat Manor' waits for its next duty. Fortunately, both of these locomotives have since been preserved.

▼ *Main image* Following a heavy snowfall in December 1964, 'Manor' Class 4-6-0 No. 7827 'Lydham Manor' makes a fine sight as it slogs up the 1 in 52 Talerddig Bank with the up 'Cambrian Coast Express'. This locomotive was one of the first departures from Woodham's scrapyard in Barry when it was saved for preservation in 1970.

7827

death knell was later sounded for the coastal route to Pwllheli but this too was reprieved despite a major insect infestation being found in the timbers of Barmouth Bridge in the mid-1980s. With the added attraction of special steam trains operating during the summer months, the journey along this scenic route today is one of the highlights of Britain's rail network.

While the Cambrian main line north of Buttington to Oswestry and Whitchurch closed early in 1965, followed by the closure of many smaller stations on the remaining section westwards, the fate of the many branch and connecting lines and feeder narrow gauge lines along the route had already been sealed.

HISTORY OF THE BRANCH LINES

At Welshpool, the 2ft 6in-gauge Welshpool & Llanfair Railway (see page 40) had opened in 1903, taken over by the GWR in 1923 and closed by British Railways in 1956. Farther south, the short Abermule to Kerry branch line was opened in 1863 and closed in 1956. Moat Lane Junction also served trains on the Cambrian's rambling line through mid-Wales to Builth Wells and Three Cocks Junction. The section to Llanidloes had opened in 1859 with the rest of the route southward completed by 1864. It was closed at the end of 1962. A short distance west of Moat Lane Junction is Caersws from where a 6½-mile branch line was opened to lead mines at Van in 1871. The line had a chequered history, closing temporarily in the 1890s, until complete closure in 1940.

Farther west the 6¾-mile privately owned Mawddwy Railway from Cemmes Road to Dinas Mawddwy was opened in 1867 to serve slate quarries at the head of the Dovey Valley. It closed in 1908 but was rebuilt and reopened by the Cambrian Railways in 1911. This scenic standard gauge line finally closed in 1951.

▼ The 120ft-deep cutting dug through gritstone at Talerddig Summit was, for a while, the deepest railway cutting in the world. Here, on 4 March 1967, immaculately turned-out BR Standard Class 4 4-6-0 No.75033 surefootedly breasts the summit with the up 'Cambrian Coast Express' enthusiasts' special.

▼ Watched keenly by a young trainspotter, a rather grimy '4300' Class 2-6-0 No. 6371 departs from Aberystwyth with the 5.15pm train for Machynlleth on August Bank Holiday Monday, 1 August 1960. In the background, the recently arrived carriages of the 'Cambrian Coast Express'.

In glorious sunshine and complete with headboard, 'Manor' Class 4-6-0 No. 7823 'Hook Norton Manor' leaves Machynlleth with the down 'Cambrian Coast Express' in May 1962.

'Manor' Class 4-6-0 No. 7803 'Barcote Manor' of Machynlleth shed is cleaned by staff at Aberystwyth shed before hauling the up 'Cambrian Coast Express' on a cold 18 February 1961. Poor old 'Barcote Manor' was withdrawn in April 1965 before being unceremoniously disposed of at Bird's scrapyard in Bridgend.

At Machynlleth the 2ft 3in gauge Corris Railway (see Heritage Lines, page 40) opened to slate quarries near Aberllefeni in 1859. It was closed by BR following floods in 1948.

At Aberystwyth, the Cambrian line met the former grandly titled Manchester & Milford Railway from Carmarthen, which had opened throughout in 1867. Following floods it was closed by BR in 1964. Aberystwyth is also the terminus of the 1ft 11¾ in-gauge Vale of Rheidol Railway (see Heritage Lines, page 40) to Devil's Bridge which opened at the end of 1902. Once British Railway's last steam-operated line, it is still open for passenger traffic.

Northwards from Dovey Junction, the Cambrian coast line once met the previously mentioned GWR route from Ruabon and Llangollen at Barmouth Junction (now Morfa Mawddach). At Tywyn, the 2ft 3in-gauge of the Talyllyn Railway meets the Cambrian coastal line. Opened in 1866 to carry slate down from Nant Gwernol, it was saved from closure in 1951 by a group of enthusiasts (see Heritage Lines, page 41). At Minffordd the 1ft 11¾ in-gauge Ffestiniog Railway (see Heritage Lines, page 41) has an interchange station with the Cambrian line and at Porthmadog the newly opened 1ft 11½ in-gauge Welsh Highland Railway (see page 140) from Caernarfon crosses the line on a level diamond crossing. Finally, the London & North Western Railway's line from Caernarfon, opened in 1864, once connected with the Cambrian line at Afonwen station until it was finally closed at the end of 1964.

▲ Once the mainstay of motive power on the Cambrian line, the ex-GWR 'Dukedog' 4-4-0s were the last outside-frame locomotives to work on British Railways. Here, No. 9012 arrives at busy Towyn station with a Barmouth-bound train in 1956. One member of this class, No. 9017, has been preserved.

▼ The main engineering feature on the Cambrian Coast line is Barmouth Bridge across the Mawddach Estuary. Here, double-headed 'Dukedog' 4-4-0s Nos 9017 (since preserved) and 9021 look in fine fettle as they approach Barmouth with an enthusiasts special' on 20 April 1958.

THE LINE TODAY

Fortunately, the Cambrian line from Shrewsbury to Aberystwyth and Pwllheli is still open today with trains being operated by Arriva Trains Wales. Some trains from Aberystwyth and Pwllheli combine at Machynlleth and continue beyond Shrewsbury to Birmingham International. In recent years, a steam train service has been operated by West Coast Railways along the coastal route between Pwllheli and Machylleth from the end of July to the end of August. This area of mid and north Wales is also lucky to possess so many restored steam-operated narrow gauge lines that connect with the Cambrian coast line.

▲ Complete with GWR copper-capped chimney and one of the original locomotives used on the line, Beyer-Peacock 0-6-0T No. 823 'Countess' heads a mixed bag of foreign carriages along the pretty Banwy Valley on the Welshpool & Llanfair Light Railway.

HERITAGE RAILWAYS

WELSHPOOL & LLANFAIR LIGHT RAILWAY

The Station, Llanfair Caereinion, Powys SY21 0SF

Website: www.wllr.org.uk

Tel: 01938 810441

Route: Welshpool (Raven Square) to Llanfair Caereinion

Length: 8 miles

Nearest main-line station: Welshpool

The Welshpool & Llanfair, opened in 1903, was one of the first railways built under the Light Railways Act of 1896. It has some of the steepest gradients (maximum 1 in 24) on any adhesion railway in Britain, and was built to carry general merchandise, coal, timber and livestock between farms in the Banwy valley and the local market town of Welshpool. Until closure, W&L trains ran through the back streets of the town to an interchange at the Cambrian Railways standard gauge station. From the beginning, the railway was run by the Cambrian until it was absorbed into the GWR in 1922. The last passenger train ran in 1931 but goods traffic continued, and in 1948 the line became part of the nationalised British Railways. BR closed the line in 1956 but a preservation group stepped in and reopened the first section to passengers in 1963. The line, following the delightful Banwy valley from Llanfair Caereinion, now ends at the new Raven Square station on the west side of Welshpool, using buildings from the 1863 Eardisley station. The two original Beyer-Peacock locomotives, 'The Earl' and 'Countess', still work on the line alongside steam engines from Austria, Finland, Sierra Leone and Antigua, continental-style balcony carriages from Austria and bogie coaches from Sierra Leone.

CORRIS RAILWAY AND MUSEUM

Station Yard, Corris, Machynlleth, Mid Wales SY20 9SH

Website: www.corris.co.uk

Tel: 01654 761303

Route: Corris to Maespoeth

Length: 2 miles

Nearest main-line station: Machynlleth

Housed in former 2ft 3in-gauge Corris Railway buildings, the Corris Railway Museum is devoted to many exhibits and photographs from that railway. Opened in 1859 to transport slate from the quarries around Corris to the main line at Machynlleth, this narrow gauge line was originally worked as a horse-tramway. Steam locomotives and passenger trains were later introduced and in 1930 the railway was taken over and worked by the Great Western Railway. Passenger traffic ceased at the end of 1930 and goods traffic in 1948. A preservation group has reopened the line south to Maespoeth and planning permission has been obtained for a farther 2 miles southwards through the beautiful Esgairgeiliog Gorge. The original engine shed at Maespoeth, built in 1878, has been restored and adapted to meet the current-day needs of the railway. Steam-operated trains run on most weekends between May and September.

VALE OF RHEIDOL RAILWAY

Park Avenue, Aberystwyth, Cardiganshire SY23 1PG

Website: www.rheidolrailway.co.uk

Tel: 01970 625819

Route: Aberystwyth to Devil's Bridge

Length: 11¾ miles

Nearest main-line station: Aberystwyth

The Vale of Rheidol Light Railway was opened in 1902 as a narrow gauge line to serve lead mines, the timber industry and tourism. In 1913, the railway was amalgamated with its larger neighbour, Cambrian Railways, which in turn was taken into the GWR empire in 1922. The GWR then virtually rebuilt the line, scrapped two of the original locomotives, rebuilt one and built two new ones. These three 2-6-2T locomotives, No. 7 'Owain Glyndwr', No. 8 'Llywelyn' and No. 9 'Prince of Wales' still work the line, although they have now all been converted to oil-burning. Goods traffic ceased in 1920, winter passenger services in 1931, and thereafter the railway had to earn its living purely from tourism. Following temporary closure during the Second World War, the railway was nationalised in 1948, unlike its near neighbour the Talyllyn Railway, eventually becoming the only BR-operated steam line in 1968. In 1989, in a controversial move, BR sold the whole operation and it is now privatised.

TALYLLYN RAILWAY COMPANY

Wharf Station, Tywyn, Gwynedd, LL36 9EY

Website: www.talyllyn.co.uk

Tel: 01654 710472

Route: Tywyn Wharf to Nant Gwernol

Length: 7½ miles

Nearest main line station: Tywyn

Opened in 1866 to carry slate from the quarries above Nant Gwernol to Tywyn, this scenic narrow gauge railway has never actually closed. When the slate quarry closed in 1946 the owner, Sir Henry Haydn Jones, managed to keep the railway running, but with little or no maintenance the line was in a very run-down state by the time of his death in 1950. However, a group of volunteers saved it from imminent closure by taking over the running of the line to Abergynolwyn, thus making it the world's first successful railway preservation scheme. In 1976, the Preservation Society reopened the ¼-mile section of mineral line from Abergynolwyn to Nant Gwernol at the foot of the first incline that led to the quarry. Trains are still hauled by some of the original and beautifully preserved Talyllyn Railway locomotives, over 130 years old, and four-wheeled coaches are used as well as more recent additions with one from the Corris Railway. Locomotives, including three diesels, are numbered 1 to 9 and are named 'Talyllyn' (0-4-2 saddle tank built 1865), 'Dolgoch' (0-4-0 well tank built 1866), 'Sir Haydn' (0-4-2 saddle tank built 1878), 'Edward Thomas' (0-4-2 saddle tank built 1921), 'Midlander' (diesel mechanical built 1940), 'Douglas' (0-4-0 well tank built 1918), 'Tom Rolt' (0-4-2 tank built 1949), 'Merseysider' (diesel-hydraulic built 1964) and 'Alf' (diesel-mechanical built 1950). The railway's workshop at Pendre has constructed bogie coaches and a new steam engine. A journey on the line today evokes all the atmosphere of a Victorian narrow gauge railway as the train slowly climbs along the wooded side of the valley of the Afon Fathew, affording panoramic views of Dolgoch Falls and the Welsh mountains.

FFESTINIOG RAILWAY

Harbour Station, Porthmadog, Gwynedd LL49 9NF

Website: www.ffestiniograilway.co.uk

Tel: 01766 516000

Route: Porthmadog Harbour to Blaenau Ffestiniog

Length: 13½ miles

Nearest main-line station: Minffordd or Porthmadog

Opened in 1836 as a horsedrawn and gravity tramway to take slate from the quarries at Blaenau Ffestiniog down to the harbour at Porthmadog, the Ffestiniog Railway was converted to steam power in 1865. Always independent, the Ffestiniog managed to keep operating through to 1946, although passenger services ceased in 1939. In 1951, an early railway preservation group was formed and the first length of line across The Cob to Boston Lodge was reopened in 1955. In stages the line was reopened to Tan-y-Bwlch, Dduallt – where a spiral was built to take the railway at a higher level past the new hydro-electric reservoir – and finally to Blaenau Ffestiniog in May 1982. Here FR trains run into a newly built station adjacent to the standard gauge Conwy Valley terminus, while at Minffordd passengers can make a connection with the Cambrian Coast line. Original Victorian rolling stock and locomotives (dating from 1863), including the unique double Fairlies (introduced in 1872), have been beautifully restored at the company's Boston Lodge works. Carriages Nos 15 and 16, introduced in 1873, were the first true bogie coaches in Great Britain and were among the earliest iron-framed coaches in the world. A trip on the line affords the traveller wonderful views of Snowdonia as the train steadily climbs high above Porthmadog hugging the contours, round sharp curves, through tunnels and along ledges cut into the mountainside. The Ffestiniog Railway Museum at Porthmadog Harbour Station depicts the history of the line and includes the 1863-built 0-4-0 saddle and tender tank locomotive 'Princess' and the famous hearse wagon as well as many other historic wagons.

▼ One of the Ffestiniog Railway's 'Double-Fairlie' 0-4-0+0-4-0 locomotives heads an impressive 10-coach train for Blaenau Ffestiniog across the one-mile-long Cob at Porthmadog.

CENTRAL WALES

Craven Arms to Swansea Victoria

By taking control of the long and heavily graded Central Wales line, the London & North Western Railway entered GWR territory through the back door and gained lucrative traffic from Swansea Docks and the surrounding coalfield.

What was to become known as the Central Wales line was originally built by several different railway companies until they were swallowed up by the mighty London & North Western Railway to form an important route between London Euston, the Midlands and Swansea.

At the southern end of the line, the Llanelly Railway & Dock Company took 18 years to complete its railway from Llanelly to Llandilo via Pontardulais. Llandilo was reached in 1857 and from here to Llandovery the company leased the Vale of Towy Railway, which opened a year later. A branch line from Llandilo to Carmarthen was opened by the Llanelly Railway in 1865 and the final link in the southern chain from Pontardulais to Swansea via the Gower Peninsula was opened in 1867.

At the northern end of what was to become the Central Wales line, the Knighton Railway had opened from Craven Arms, on the Hereford to Shrewsbury line through the Welsh Marches, westwards to the town of Knighton in 1861. This 12¼-mile line was seen by the London & North Western Railway (LNWR), as a first stepping stone to reaching its final goal of creaming off lucrative freight and mineral traffic from the GWR at Swansea. In 1863, the Knighton Railway merged with the uncompleted Central Wales Railway, which eventually opened from Knighton to the up-and-coming spa resort of Llandrindod Wells in 1865. This was followed by the Central Wales Extension Railway, which

▼ **Watched intently by a group of young trainspotters, ex-LNWR Class 'G2a' 7F 0-8-0 No. 48895 of Springs Branch (Wigan) backs onto a Central Wales line freight train at Craven Arms on 16 August 1962. Behind is the former LNWR/LMS engine shed, by then a sub-shed of Shrewsbury (89A) which closed in May 1964.**

▼ **Stanier 'Black Five' 4-6-0 No. 45283 slows for the driver to hand over the single token at Llandrindod Wells while hauling the 4.30pm Swansea to York mail train on 2 July 1962. The passing loop here was to the north of the station.**

▲ The powerful Stanier '8F' 2-8-0s were the mainstay of motive power for Central Wales freight trains. Here, No. 48369 is seen taking the Central Wales line at Craven Arms with a fitted freight in the early morning of 27 July 1963.

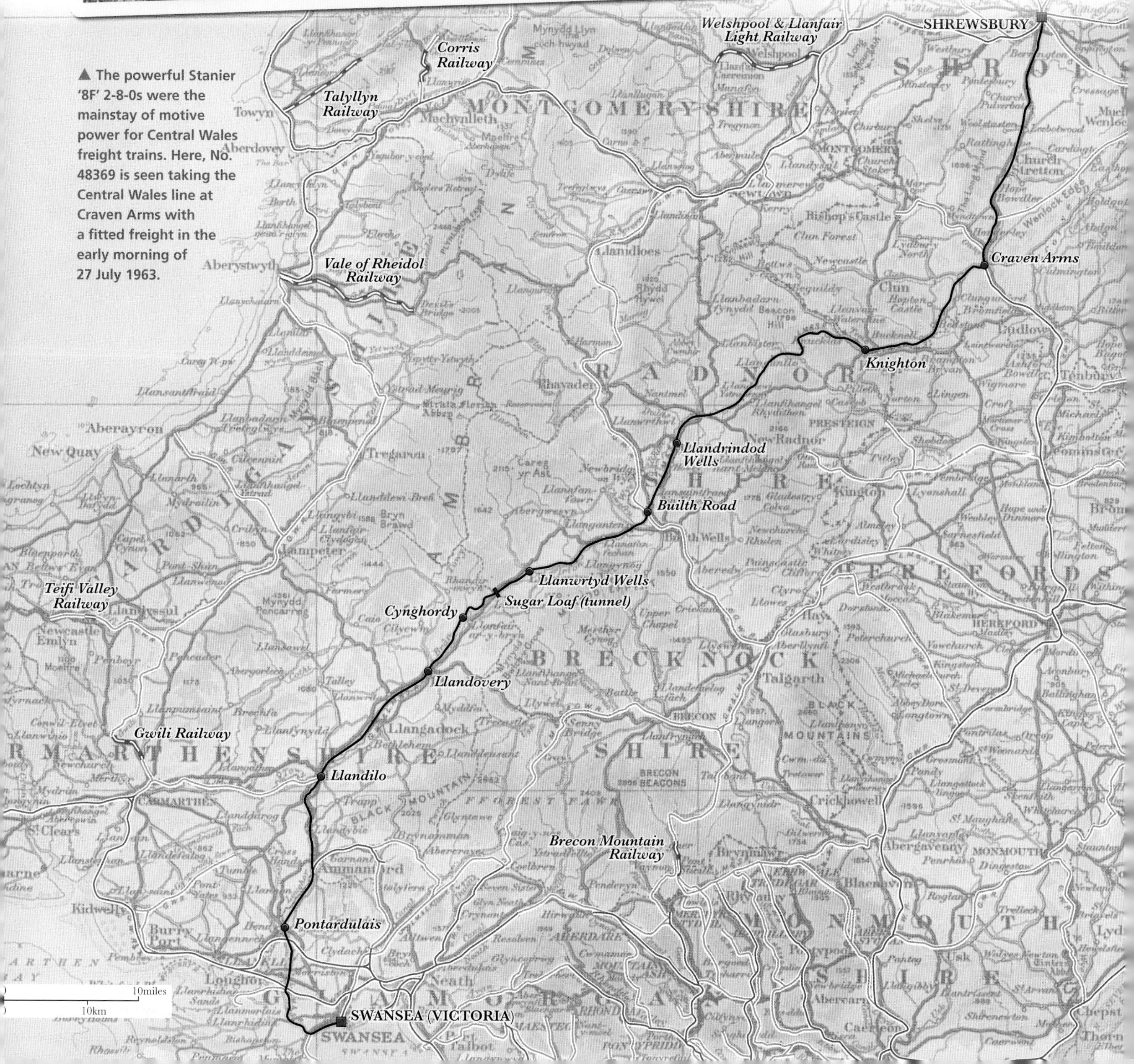

opened from Llandrindod to Llandovery, where it met the Vale of Towy Railway in 1868. Both the Central Wales and the Central Wales Extension railways were taken over by the LNWR in the same year. In 1873, the LNWR was granted running powers from Llandovery to Swansea and also on the branch to Carmarthen. The route of Central Wales line was complete but not yet totally in the hands of the LNWR.

The LNWR did eventually get its own way in 1891 when it finally absorbed the Swansea and Carmarthen lines, although the section between Llandilo and Pontardulais was operated jointly with the GWR. The direct route from Euston to the unprepossessing terminus at Swansea Victoria, albeit rather circuitous, was now complete. With the opening of the railway and the introduction of through carriages from many parts of the LNWR system, the tiny spa resorts of Llandrindod, Builth, Llangammarch and Llanwrtyd soon proved popular destinations for Victorians seeking to reap the health benefits of the resorts' mineral waters.

ENGINEERED FOR STEAM

Built as a heavily graded, mainly single-track line with passing loops, the 95¼-mile Central Wales line features many dramatic engineering features including the spectacular castellated 13-arch Knucklas Viaduct across the Heyop Valley close to the English/Welsh border and the 1,000yd-long Sugar Loaf Tunnel between Llanwrtyd Wells and Cynghordy. Approached from either side by fairly strenuous gradients, the single-bore curved tunnel must have been a hell hole during the days of steam when heavily laden freight trains, banked in the rear, laboured up the gradient to the line's summit. South of the tunnel the graceful, curving 18-arch Cynghordy Viaduct, built in sandstone and lined with brick, towers rises to a height of 102ft above the valley below.

During its heyday, the Central Wales line was not only heavily used as a freight route carrying minerals (in particular vast amounts of anthracite northwards), cattle and even beer from Burton-upon-Trent but also provided a regular passenger service from Swansea to Shrewsbury with through carriages to the Midlands, the North and Euston. Through carriages bound for resorts on the Pembrokeshire coast were also carried along the LNWR's heavily engineered branch line from Llandilo to Carmarthen. The all-important Swansea to York mail train continued to use the Central Wales line until the end of steam in 1964. Heavy freight trains also laboured along the line behind powerful LNWR Class 'G2a' 0-8-0 freight locos, later superseded by Stanier 8F 2-8-0s and 'Black Five' 4-6-0s while 'Jubilee' and BR Standard Class 5 4-6-0s along with Fowler 2-6-4 tanks provided the mainstay of passenger motive power until the end of steam. Due to its single-track construction with passing loops, journey times along the line were pretty slow. In 1922, the 2.40pm departure from Shrewsbury conveying through carriages from Euston, Birmingham, Liverpool and Manchester arrived at Swansea at 6.58pm; in British Railways' days, by which

▼ The passing loop at Llandrindod Wells station was lifted in the early 1960s as an economy measure. Here, ex-LMS Fowler 2-6-4T No. 42388 enters the single-line station with the 6.15am Swansea to Shrewsbury train on 3 July 1962.

Not long after a works overhaul, Shrewsbury-based Stanier '8F' 2-8-0 pauses at Builth Road High-Level station with a southbound freight train on 25 July 1959. The station sign, one of the biggest in the UK, refers to the Low-Level station, which served the Mid-Wales line between Moat Lane and Three Cocks Junction and closed at the end of 1962.

time the Central Wales line had come under Western Region management, the overnight mail train from York left Shrewsbury at 3.45am, arriving at Swansea Victoria at 8.06am.

REPRIEVED FROM CLOSURE

With high operating and maintenance costs, loss of passengers and freight to road and serving only small towns and villages along its long route, it is hardly surprising that the Central Wales line was listed for closure by Dr Beeching in 1963. Fortunately, most of it was reprieved at the last moment, although the Llandilo to Carmarthen branch closed in 1963 and the section southward from Pontardulais to Swansea Victoria closed on 13 June 1964. From that date all steam-hauled passenger trains were replaced by diesel multiple units shuttling between Shrewsbury and Swansea via Pontardulais and Llanelly where they reversed. All through freight trains along the line ceased in August 1964 and were rerouted via Cardiff and Newport. A second closure threat in 1967 was also seen off because of the impact it would have had on isolated rural communities along the route. Since 1986, the entire line has been controlled from the one remaining signalbox at Pantyffynnon, using a system known as 'No Signalman Token Remote'.

Over much of its long route the Central Wales line met very few other railway lines. The exception was at Builth Road where it crossed over the Cambrian Railways' Mid-Wales line from Moat Lane Junction to Three Cocks Junction. Builth Road Low-Level station closed along with the rest of the Mid-Wales line at the end of 1962. As previously mentioned the Llandilo to Carmarthen line closed in 1963. A branch from Pantyffynnon to anthracite mines around Brynamman opened throughout in 1842 and although passenger services ceased in 1926 part of the line is still in use for coal trains. On the now closed section between Pontardulais and Swansea, a branch from Gowerton to Panclawdd was opened by the Llanelly Railway in 1867 and extended to Llanmorlais by the LNWR in 1884. Known locally as 'the Cockle line' it closed to passengers in 1931 and to freight in 1957.

▶ Llandilo was once the junction for the LNWR branch to Carmarthen, which closed in 1963. South of here the Central Wales line as far as Pontardulais was in GWR territory, hence the lower quadrant semaphore signals seen in this August 1961 photo. With the Llandilo branch train on the left, BR Standard Class 5MT 4-6-0 No. 73049 coasts into the station with a Swansea-bound train while the driver waits to hand over the single-line token.

▼ Alan Jarvis's precarious position, 100ft up at the southern end of the curving 18-arch Cynghordy Viaduct, is rewarded with this shot of a Stanier 'Black Five' hauling a Shrewsbury to Swansea train on 16 May 1964. Steam-hauled passenger trains on the Central Wales line ended less than a month later.

THE LINE TODAY

Now marketed as the 'Heart of Wales Line', the scenic Central Wales line, dependent on government subsidies, still clings precariously to life. The 28 intermediate stations and halts between Craven Arms and Llanelli are served by four trains daily each way on weekdays (two on Sundays from mid-July to early September) between Shrewsbury and Swansea via Llanelli. Operated by Arriva Trains Wales, services are normally provided by single-car diesel units, but during the summer months these are increased to two cars. Journey time between Craven Arms and Llanelli is just under three hours.

While none of the intermediate stations is now manned, passenger numbers have seen a marked increase in recent years. However, increasing the frequency of trains is currently not possible as several of the passing loops are out of action due to a lack of spare parts! Occasionally frequented by walkers, the request halt at Sugar Loaf has the dubious distinction of being the least-used station in Wales. Charter trains also occasionally use this route but only on a Sunday when there is excess line capacity. For more details about the line visit www.heart-of-wales.co.uk.

HERITAGE RAILWAYS

GWILI RAILWAY

Bronwydd Arms Station,
Carmarthen SA33 6HT

Website: www.gwili-railway.co.uk

Tel: 01267 238213

Route: Bronwydd Arms to Danycoed

Length: 2½ miles

Nearest mainline station: Carmarthen

The ex-GWR branch from Carmarthen to Aberystwyth, opened in 1860 as a broad gauge (7ft 0¼in) line and, following flooding at the northern end of the line, was closed by British Rail to passengers in 1964 and to goods in 1973. In 1978, a preservation group had starting running services over a short length of track at Bronwydd Arms station three miles north of Carmarthen. By 1987, the line was extended to Llwyfan Cerrig, where there is a picnic site and 7¼in gauge miniature railway. More recently the line has been opened to Danycoed with plans to extend to Llanpumpsaint. Aided by material and equipment from the closed Swansea Vale Railway, the railway is also being extended southwards from Bronwydd Arms to Abergwili Junction on the northern outskirts of Carmarthen. The railway owns a large collection of mainly industrial steam and diesel locomotives and a wide variety of passenger and goods rolling stock, including an award-winning Taff Vale Railway coach, dating from 1891, which was fully restored after being found in a field in Herefordshire. Bronwydd Arms signalbox originally stood at Llandybie on the Central Wales Line and was bought in 1985 for use on the Gwili Railway. Dating from 1885, the 21-lever box is now fully restored and operates signals in the station area. The railway runs regular events and experience days including a 1940s Day and days out for children throughout the year.

▼ Preserved ex-GWR Class 4575 2-6-2T No. 5541 (masquerading as local engine No. 5549) hard at work in the autumn sunshine on the Gwili Railway.

THE CATHEDRALS EXPRESS

Oxford to Worcester and Hereford

Once an important cross-country route through the Cotswold and Malvern Hills, the Oxford to Hereford route fell on hard times in the 1960s and 1970s, when it was relegated to secondary status. Recent improvements to the line have seen a welcome upsurge in passenger numbers.

What became known as the 'Old Worse & Worse', the Oxford, Worcester & Wolverhampton Railway was incorporated in 1845 to connect these places with 89 miles of broad gauge track. Financially supported by the GWR and with Isambard Kingdom Brunel as engineer, the line had a troubled construction period with the original costs ending up 250 per cent over the estimated price and the line being completed to standard gauge. The GWR had seen the railway as an alternative to the London & Birmingham Railway but pulled the rug out from under OW&WR's shareholders by purchasing the Birmingham & Oxford and Birmingham, Wolverhampton & Dudley railways in 1848. In doing so, the GWR availed itself of a shorter, more direct route between London and Birmingham than was offered by the then unfinished OW&WR.

GETTING A BAD NAME

With the newly formed London & North Western Railway (successor to the London & Birmingham) unsuccessfully trying to muscle in on the act and lease it, the OW&WR had opened northwards from Worcester to Stourbridge and eastwards to Evesham by 1852. To the east of Evesham, near the summit of

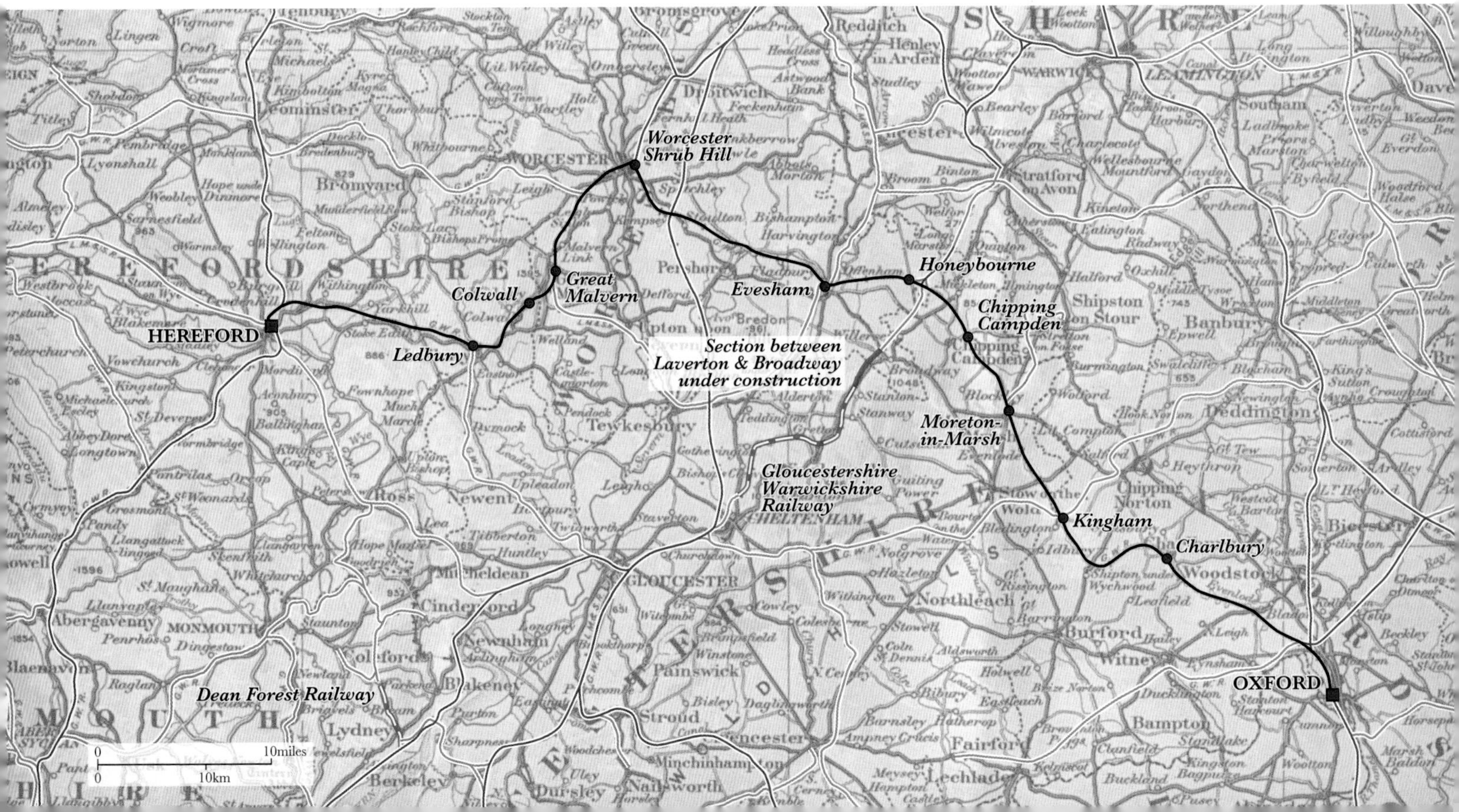

▲ Oxford was once an unrivalled railway crossroads with trains from the Southern, Western, Eastern and London Midland regions all converging at the station. Here, watched by two young trainspotters, ex-GWR 'Hall' Class 4-6-0 No. 5931 'Hatherley Hall' waits for its fireman to board before departing on a southbound train in the 1950s.

▲ **Ex-GWR '5101' Class 2-6-2T No. 4101 has arrived at Kingham with the 14.50 from Cheltenham in October 1962. By that date the cross-country line to King's Sutton (once the route of the short-lived 'Ports to Ports Express' between Cardiff and Newcastle) had already closed and passenger services from Cheltenham were about to end.**

the line at Chipping Campden and the 875yd tunnel, Brunel had a spot of trouble when a sacked contractor who had not been paid refused to leave the site. He backed down only after Brunel brought in two thousand navvies and threatened the use of troops from Coventry. The railway finally opened eastwards to Wolvercot Junction, north of Oxford, in 1853 and northwards to Wolverhampton in 1854. For the first few years of its life the OW&WR gained an appalling reputation for its poor passenger services, hence receiving its well-deserved nickname, which unfortunately, it took years to rid itself of.

UNDER THE MALVERNS

To the west of Worcester, the cathedral city of Hereford had already been reached by the Newport, Abergavenny & Hereford Railway in 1854. In between the two cities were the daunting Malvern Hills and, when the 29¾-mile Worcester & Hereford Railway was authorised in 1853, the cost of tunnelling through them was greatly underestimated. An alternative route north of the hills would have left the growing spa resort of Malvern off the railway map, a situation that local townsfolk were not prepared to accept. Seen as part of a scheme to link the West Midlands with South Wales, the W&HR opened between Worcester and Malvern Wells in 1860. To the south of here, the single-bore Colwall Tunnel (1,567yd), with its gradient of 1 in 23, proved the undoing of two sub-contractors and it was not completed, along with the slightly shorter Ledbury Tunnel, until 1861 by the herculean efforts of a large group of Welsh miners.

In the meantime, the W&HR, along with the Newport, Abergavenny & Hereford and OW&W railways, had merged to form the West Midland Railway in 1860. In its short working life, the newly formed company with around 200 miles of line and operating powers over many others, was leased by the GWR a year later until being absorbed by it in 1863.

With its single bore and steep gradient, Colwall Tunnel proved to be the Achilles heel of the Worcester to Hereford section of the line. Following the partial collapse of the tunnel in 1907, the GWR decided to build a new tunnel that was slightly longer but with a less demanding gradient. It opened in 1926 and the old tunnel was put to use during the Second World War to store torpedoes for the Royal Navy. It is now bricked up and home to a colony of bats.

For years, the GWR ran the 'Wolverhampton, Kidderminster, Malvern & Worcester Express'. Both luncheon and tea cars ran in the formation, which ran non-stop between Worcester and Oxford and provided a morning up service to Paddington and a return down journey in the afternoon. To speed up services the GWR introduced water troughs between Charlbury and Ascott-under-Wychwood. The GWR's 'Hereford, Malvern, Kidderminster and Worcester Express' and the 'Malvern Express' had only limited stops between Oxford and Worcester and were the forerunner of the 'Cathedral Express', which was introduced by British Railways in 1957. The latter train was the last steam-hauled named train to run on the Western Region, with its motive power usually being provided until 1965 by one of Worcester shed's allocation of immaculate 'Castle' Class 4-6-0s.

'NO ONE LEFT AND NO ONE CAME...'

Until 1965 both the Oxford to Worcester and Worcester to Hereford routes carried significant amounts of freight traffic. The Oxford to Worcester section lost its cross-country traffic in that year when the Yarnton Loop north of Oxford closed – the loop had enabled trains to run from the former LNWR main line at Bletchley via Verney Juncton and Bicester and to bypass the Oxford bottleneck. In the same year, the Worcester to Hereford section lost its through heavy freight services from South Wales to the West Midlands, which were then diverted via the Gloucester to Birmingham route. Gone were the days

▲ Built by BR at Swindon in 1949, double-chimney 'Castle' Class 4-6-0 No. 7023 'Penrice Castle' approaches Chipping Campden Tunnel with the 10.05am Hereford to Paddington train on 15 June 1963.

◀ Built by BR at Swindon in 1950, 'Castle' Class 4-6-0 No. 7031 'Cromwell's Castle' leaves Chipping Campden Tunnel with the 1.15pm Paddington to Hereford train on Whit Monday, 3 June 1963. Brunel's 875yd tunnel is currently having its second track reinstated following singling of much of the line in the 1970s.

▼ Ex-GWR 'Castle' Class 4-6-0 No. 7006 'Lydford Castle' crosses the Worcester & Birmingham Canal north of Foregate Street station with the 10.35am train from Hereford on 27 August 1961. It was practice to change engines and add carriages to the train at Shrub Hill station before proceeding to Oxford and Paddington.

when a procession of heavy coal trains headed by GWR 2-8-0s and banked in the rear would struggle through the steeply graded single-bore Malvern Tunnel.

The 1960s and the implications of the 'Beeching Report' also saw a major run-down of passenger services between Oxford and Hereford. Branch and connecting lines were closed and many intermediate stations between Oxford and Worcester, including Adlestrop made famous in Edward Thomas's poem, were also shut down. Freight services were diverted away from the route and in the 1970s much of it was singled. This once-important cross-country route had finally been relegated to secondary status.

In addition to the Yarnton Loop already mentioned, the Oxford to Hereford line had many branch lines and important cross-country connections along its 86¼-mile route. West of Oxford the long Fairford branch opened throughout in 1873, closed to passengers in 1962 and completely in 1970. At Kingham, there was a connection with the Cheltenham to King's Sutton line, which was opened throughout in 1887 and formed part of the route of the short-lived 'Ports to Ports Express' between Cardiff and Newcastle-upon-Tyne. This cross-country route closed in stages between 1951 and 1964. Next along the route was the Shipston-on-Stour branch from Moreton-in-the-Marsh, which opened in 1889 and closed in 1960. At Honeybourne, the Cheltenham to Stratford-upon-Avon line crossed the Oxford to Worcester route. This once-important GWR

⯭ *Top* 'Castle' Class 4-6-0 No. 7033 'Hartlebury Castle' receives attention inside the small engine shed at Worcester motive power depot on 28 August 1962. Behind is 'Black Five' 4-6-0 No. 44776 and to the right '5700' Class 0-6-0PT No. 4664. Worcester shed was once home to nine 'Castle' Class locos, including No. 7005, which was named after the local resident and composer, Sir Edward Elgar.

▲ *Bottom* Ex-GWR '5101' Class 2-6-2T No. 4147 leaves Colwall Tunnel with the 4.34pm Worcester (Foregate Street) to Ledbury train on 16 May 1964. This single-bore tunnel was opened in 1926 to replace an older tunnel that had a steep gradient and was difficult to work. The old tunnel was put to use during the Second World War to store torpedoes for the Royal Navy.

north–south route had opened throughout in 1908 and closed completely in 1976. Farther west, the line meets the Bristol to Birmingham line at Norton Junction and at Worcester the city is still served by two stations: Shrub Hill and Foregate Street. West of Worcester, the Worcester, Bromyard & Leominster Railway was opened in stages between 1874 and 1897. The Bromyard to Leominster section closed in 1952 and the rest in 1964. At Malvern Wells the Midland Railway's branch to Ashchurch opened throughout in 1860 and was closed in stages between 1952 and 1964. At Ledbury, the GWR's branch to Gloucester opened in 1885 and closed completely in 1964.

▲ Hereford is also the junction for the north–south route from Shrewsbury to Newport. Here, BR Swindon-built 'Modified Hall' Class 4-6-0 No. 6992 'Arborfield Hall' enters the station with a train from the south in the 1950s.

▼ Ex-GWR '2800' Class 2-8-0 No. 2859 approaches Ledbury Tunnel with a down freight on 16 May 1964. This long-lived engine was built at Swindon in 1918 and withdrawn at the end of 1964.

THE LINE TODAY

After languishing for around 40 years as a poorly served secondary route, the Oxford to Hereford line is set for a long-overdue renaissance. With increasing passenger numbers and marketed as 'The Cotswold Line', work is in hand to reinstate around 20 miles of double track between Oxford and Worcester, including through Chipping Campden Tunnel, to allow a more frequent service of trains. The work is scheduled to be completed in 2011 and also involves opening new stations at Rushwick, Withington and Chipping Campden. Train services from Paddington to Oxford, Worcester, Malvern and Hereford are provided by First Great Western. The Worcester to Hereford section is also served by London Midland trains between Birmingham and Hereford.

▲ Ex-GWR 'Manor' Class 4-6-0 No. 7802 'Bradley Manor' appears in fine fettle with the rolling stock of the 'Cardigan Bay Express' on the Severn Valley Railway. Withdrawn in 1965, this loco was saved from Barry scrapyard in 1979 and restored.

HERITAGE RAILWAYS

GLOUCESTERSHIRE WARWICKSHIRE RAILWAY

The Railway Station, Toddington, Gloucestershire GL54 5DT

Website: www.gwsr.com

Tel: 01242 621405

Route: Toddington to Cheltenham Racecourse

Length: 10 miles

Nearest main-line station: Cheltenham

A heritage railway linking Toddington and Cheltenham along the former GWR main line from the Midlands to the Southwest that was closed to passengers by BR in 1969 and to freight in 1976. Trains currently run from Toddington to Cheltenham Racecourse with intermediate stations at Winchcombe (originally the station building at Monmouth Troy) and Gotherington via the 693yd Greet Tunnel. The railway is currently extending its route northwards to Broadway. Motive power is drawn from a fleet of GWR steam and BR diesel locomotives. Visiting main-line locomotives are a common sight on the railway. A journey along the line takes passengers through the picturesque North Gloucestershire countryside with fine views of the Cotswold escarpment, past Hailes Abbey to the beautifully restored station at Winchcombe (for Winchcombe Railway Museum, see below right), and then through the 693yd Greet tunnel to the terminus at Cheltenham Racecourse.

SEVERN VALLEY RAILWAY

The Railway Station, Bewdley, Worcestershire DY12 1BG

Website: www.svr.co.uk

Tel: 01299 403816

Route: Bridgnorth to Kidderminster

Length: 16 miles

Nearest main-line station: Kidderminster

One of Britain's premier preserved lines, the Severn Valley Railway is situated on the former GWR branch from Hartlebury to Shrewsbury, opened in 1862 and closed to passengers by BR in 1963. The initial preservation group started fund-raising in 1965, and the first public train ran in 1970 from Bridgnorth to Hampton Loade. The service was extended to Bewdley in 1974 and to Kidderminster in 1984. Since then it has become a huge success with its large collection of steam and diesel locomotives and rolling stock. Much restoration work is carried out by the railway's workshops, which are famed for their high standards. The country stations on the line have all been carefully restored to their former GWR glory and a journey along the scenic route, which mostly follows the River Severn, evokes all the heyday of steam travel. The major engineering structure on the line is the graceful cast-iron Victoria Bridge, built in 1861, which carries trains on its 200ft span, high above the River Severn. Several enthusiasts' weekends are held every year, when visiting locomotives from other preserved railways can be seen in action. Good connections with the main line network at Kidderminster and a frequent steam-operated service, have ensured the railway's continuing success. It featured in the 1978 version of *The Thirty Nine Steps*.

MUSEUM

WINCHCOMBE RAILWAY MUSEUM

23 Gloucester Street, Winchcombe, Gloucestershire GL54 5LX

Website: www.winchcomberailwaymuseum.co.uk

Tel. 01242 609305

Features thousands of artefacts including signalling equipment and a large collection of line-side notices.

BRUNEL'S MASTERPIECE

Paddington to Bristol

Built by navvies with only basic tools and designed for speed and comfort, Isambard Kingdom Brunel's broad gauge railway between London and Bristol was a masterpiece of engineering unsurpassed anywhere in the world.

▲ An early-evening line-up at Paddington in April 1958 with, left to right: 'Castle' Class 4-6-0 No. 5015 'Kingswear Castle' has just arrived on Platform 9 with the up 'The Bristolian'; another 'Castle' has arrived 15 minutes before on Platform 10 with the up 'Cambrian Coast Express.

By the early 19th century the port of Bristol was a busy place, with ships plying their international trade across the Atlantic and beyond. Apart from slow and dangerous seagoing coastal traffic, communications between the city and other parts of Britain, in particular London, were poor. A scheme to link the two cities by railway had been proposed as early as 1824 but this came to nothing, as did another in 1830. The turning point came in March 1833 when a group of Bristol businessmen appointed a young engineer (only 27), Isambard Kingdom Brunel, to survey the route of yet another proposed railway to London. By August the survey of a near-level route via Bath, the little village of Swindon and the Thames Valley to Paddington had been completed, two boards of directors established (one at Bristol and one at Paddington) and the Great Western Railway (affectionately known by its supporters as God's Wonderful Railway) was born.

▶ Sonning Cutting, east of Reading, is over a mile long and up to 60ft deep. Here, 'Hall' Class 4-6-0 No. 5989 'Cransley Hall' speeds through on the fast line with an up express on 20 June 1959.

THE GENESIS OF A RAILWAY

After an initial rejection of the scheme, Parliament finally authorised the building of the London to Bristol line along Brunel's surveyed route on 31 August 1835. Two months later, the GWR directors opted to build their line for speed and comfort to the broad gauge of 7ft 0¼in – unfortunately, apart from in the southwest, most other railways around Britain went ahead with what became the standard gauge of 4ft 8½in, but more about this later. In 1837 Brunel appointed Daniel Gooch as the GWR's first chief mechanical engineer, a position to be held later by exalted men such as William Dean, George Jackson Churchward, Charles Collett and Frederick Hawksworth.

The railway was built in nine sections over 118¼ miles, with the first section from Paddington to Maidenhead opening on 4 June 1838, to Twyford on 1 July 1839, to Reading on 30 March 1840, to Steventon on 1 June, to Faringdon Road on 20 July, to Hay Lane (near Swindon) on 17 December and to Chippenham on 31 May 1841. From the Bristol end, the section to Bath from Temple Meads opened on 31 August 1840 but the construction of Box Tunnel delayed the full opening of the line until 30 June 1841. The northern section of the Bristol & Exeter Railway also opened on the same day. In addition to the 3,212yd-long Box Tunnel (the longest railway tunnel at that time in the world), which was built with extreme accuracy, the other major engineering feat on the line was Sonning Cutting, east of Reading. Taking two years to complete, the cutting is over a mile long and up to 60ft deep and was excavated by hundreds of navvies using picks and spades.

At each end of the line Brunel designed imposing termini fit for his modern railway. His train shed at Bristol Temple Meads still stands today, albeit without any train tracks. Much of the Paddington station that we know today was also designed by Brunel along with his associate Matthew Wyatt but was not completed until 1854. It is interesting to note that when the line opened there were no stations at Swindon or Didcot but this was all soon to change when the former became the junction for what was to be the GWR's route to South Wales via Gloucester and the location of the company's main works. Didcot soon developed as an important junction for the Oxford, Worcester and Birmingham lines. From a small village Swindon grew to become the largest railway town in Britain, with the railway works employing around 14,000 people in its heyday.

By the 1860s, it was obvious that Brunel's unique broad gauge was now out of step with the rest of the nation's expanding standard gauge system. The problem was eventually addressed after Brunel's death by gradually converting GWR track to standard gauge between 1864 and 1892. The GWR prospered and within a few years had spread its tentacles across southwest England, the West Midlands and South Wales. By 1921, prior to the Big Four Grouping, it had a route mileage of 3,797 miles.

The opening of the Severn Tunnel in 1886 saw the flow of traffic through Bristol increase dramatically. Heavy coal trains from South Wales heading for London now competed for line occupancy with the increasingly popular through services from Paddington to the West of England – the double-track line between Bristol and Swindon via Bath was full to bursting. The GWR tackled this problem by building a new line from Wootton Bassett, west of Swindon, to Patchway where it joined the line from Bristol to the Severn Tunnel.

▲ **Built at Swindon in 1927, 'King' Class 4-6-0 No. 6000 'King George V' was exhibited at the Baltimore & Ohio Railway's Centenary Exhibition later that year when it was fitted with a commemorative brass bell above its buffer beam. Here, in all its glory, the 'King' thunders through Sonning Cutting with the down 'The Merchant Venturer', c.1960.**

4

◀ **Shrouded in steam – getting ready to leave Platform 1 at Paddington with a down express in March 1958, a 'Castle' Class 4-6-0 is fitted with its train reporting number.**

Known as the Badminton cut-off, this 29½-mile line opened throughout in 1903 and greatly relieved the Bristol bottleneck. The GWR was also known as the Great Way Round for its circuitous route from London to the West Country via Bristol, so the opening of the more direct route for West Country trains via Westbury and Castle Cary, which opened in 1906, further reduced pressure on the Reading to Bristol section.

Swindon's prolific output of classic ground-breaking steam locomotive types probably reached its zenith in 1923 with the introduction of Collett's 'Castle' Class 4-6-0s, which saw 35 years of sterling service on the Paddington to Bristol line. From the world-beating 'Cheltenham Flyer' of the early 1930s to their unforgettable performances on 'The Bristolian' in the 1950s, their feats have passed into railway folklore. This was, and still is, a railway line laid out for speed and the steady steam-hauled procession of named Western Region expresses thundering through Swindon in the late 1950s was a sight for sore eyes for any railway enthusiast – 'The South Wales Pullman', the 'Capitals United Express', 'The Red Dragon', 'The Bristolian', 'The Pembroke Coast Express', the 'Cheltenham Spa Express', and 'The Merchant Venturer' are all now fading memories. Sadly this glorious era of GWR steam ended with the introduction of Swindon's diesel-

▲ *Top* **Fitted with a double chimney, green-liveried BR Standard Class 4 4-6-0 No. 75029 receives the attention of a gaggle of young trainspotters at Reading General station on 28 July 1962. On withdrawal from revenue-earning service, this loco was purchased directly from British Railways by the artist David Shepherd and given the name 'The Green Knight'. It can be seen at work on the North Yorkshire Moors Railway.**

▲ *Bottom* **Much admired by their crews, Cardiff Canton's well-groomed BR 'Britannia' Class 4-6-2 No. 70029 'Shooting Star' thunders into Reading with the up 'Capitals United Express' in the late 1950s. Delivered new from Crewe Works, Cardiff's allocation of 12 Britannias was reallocated to Crewe and Carlisle in 1961 and ended their life pounding up and down the West Coast Main Line north of Crewe.**

hydraulic locomotives in the early 1960s – like Brunel's broad gauge, their non-standard design soon led to their early demise with the introduction of the HST sets that we know today. Recent plans to electrify the former GWR main line to Bristol and also to Cardiff and Swansea have recently been announced, but, apart from the Heathrow Shuttle, Paddington is still the only major London terminus not electrified.

▲ 'County' Class 4-6-0 No. 1028 'County of Warwick' pollutes the early-evening skies near Chippenham with the 5.05pm Paddington to Bristol express. Sadly, none of these fine locos was ever preserved, although a replica is currently being built at the Didcot Railway Centre.

LONDON TO BRISTOL BRANCH LINES

In addition to several important connections with other lines along its route, the opening of the London to Bristol line soon spawned a number of branch lines. From east to west these included the following:

WEST DRAYTON TO UXBRIDGE
(opened 1856, closed completely 1964)

WEST DRAYTON TO STAINES
(opened throughout in 1885, closed to passengers 1965 and completely 1991)

SLOUGH TO WINDSOR & ETON CENTRAL
(opened 1849, still open)

MAIDENHEAD TO BOURNE END AND MARLOW
(opened 1873, still open)

TWYFORD TO HENLEY-ON-THAMES
(opened 1857, still open)

CHOLSEY & MOULSFORD TO WALLINGFORD
(opened 1866, closed to passengers 1959. Now a heritage line.)

WANTAGE ROAD TO WANTAGE
(opened 1875, closed completely 1945)

UFFINGTON TO FARINGDON
(opened 1864, closed completely 1963)

SWINDON TO HIGHWORTH
(opened 1883, closed completely 1962)

DAUNTSEY TO MALMESBURY
(opened 1877, closed completely 1962)

CHIPPENHAM TO CALNE
(opened 1863, closed completely 1965)

▶ A classic GWR location – fitted with a Hawksworth tender 'Castle' Class 4-6-0 No. 7019 'Fowey Castle' emerges from Brunel's Box Tunnel with a down express of 'blood and custard' coaches in 1956. When it opened in 1841, the 3,212yd-long tunnel was the longest railway tunnel in the world.

▶ The down 'Merchant Venturer' express changed engines at Bristol Temple Meads before resuming its journey from Paddington to Weston-super-Mare. Here, c.1960 and sporting different styles of headboards, Old Oak Common's 'Castle' Class 4-6-0 No. 5044 'Earl of Dunraven' prepares to come off the train in favour of Taunton-allocated 'Hall' Class 4-6-0 No. 5992 'Horton Hall'.

▼ With a backdrop of giant cumulo-nimbus clouds and headed by a 'Castle' class 4-6-0, the up 'Merchant Venturer' express streaks across the Wiltshire landscape near Thingley Junction, Chippenham, in April 1954.

THE LINE TODAY

Trains between Paddington and Bristol are operated by First Great Western. The company also operates trains on the Windsor & Eton Central branch, the Marlow branch and the Henley-on-Thames branch. In 2010, a steam-hauled 'The Bristolian' once again ran between Paddington and Bristol on four Saturdays between June and December.

▲ Visiting preserved ex-LBSCR 'Terrier' Class 'A1X' 0-6-0T No. 662 hauls a short train on the Cholsey & Wallingford Railway in 2008. Built in 1875 and originally named 'Martello', the loco was withdrawn from the Hayling Island branch as BR No. 32662 in late 1963 after which it was displayed for some years at Butlin's Holiday camp in Ayr.

HERITAGE RAILWAYS

CHOLSEY & WALLINGFORD RAILWAY

5 Hithercroft Road, Wallingford, Oxfordshire, OX10 9GQ

Website: www.cholsey-wallingford-railway.com

Tel: 01491 835067

Route: Cholsey to Wallingford

Length: 2¼ miles

Nearest main-line station: Cholsey

Opened in 1866, the ex-GWR branch line to Wallingford was closed to passengers in 1959 and to goods in 1965. Part of the line was left open to serve a mill until 1981. Since then a preservation society has reopened the line, and limited services with a borrowed locomotive ran until 1990, when the line bought its first engine. A Light Railway Order was granted in 1995 and trains now connect with the national network at Cholsey on the main line to Paddington. Although the railway does not own a resident steam loco, visiting locomotives are a regular feature.

DIDCOT RAILWAY CENTRE

Didcot, Oxfordshire OX11 7NJ

Website: www.didcotrailwaycentre.org.uk

Tel: 01235 817200

Route: Within site

Nearest main-line station: Didcot

The Great Western Society, founded in 1961, moved its base to the former BR engine shed at Didcot in 1967 and now evokes all the atmosphere of a working 1930s GWR running shed with turntable and coaling stage. Now housing the largest collection of GWR locomotives and rolling stock in Britain, it is also frequently visited by other locomotives employed on main-line steam specials. Locomotives on display include a wide range of GWR types including 'Castle' class 4-6-0s No. 4079 'Pendennis Castle' and No. 5051 'Drysllwyn Castle', 'Hall' class 4-6-0 No. 5900 'Hinderton Hall', 'King' Class 4-6-0 No. 6023 'King Edward II', 'Modified Hall' Class 4-6-0 No. 6998 'Burton Agnes Hall' and 'Manor' Class 4-6-0 No. 7808 'Cookham Manor' along with former Wantage Tramway 0-4-0 well tank 'Shannon', built in 1857. Short rides are given on two demonstration lines within the site, which also boasts a rebuilt small country station (Didcot Halt) complete with working signalbox, originally used at Frome Mineral Junction. A short section of Brunel's broad gauge (7ft 0¼in), with a section of mixed gauge trackwork, has also been built. On Steam Days, demonstrations are given using the restored Travelling Post Office. A library houses the Society's collection of books and papers relating to the history of the Great Western Railway.

SWINDON & CRICKLADE RAILWAY

Blunsdon Station, Tadpole Lane, Blunsdon, Swindon, Wilts SN25 2DA

Website: www.swindon-cricklade-railway.org

Tel: 01793 771615 (weekends only)

Route: Northwards from Blunsdon to South Meadow Lane (Southward extension from Hayes Knoll to Mouldon Hill Country Park under construction)

Length: 1 mile

Nearest main-line station: Swindon

Situated on the former Midland & South Western Junction Railway between Cheltenham Spa and Swindon Town, Blunsdon station was itself closed in 1937 and the line closed by BR in the early 1960s. A preservation group took over the station area in 1979 and now provide mainly steam-hauled trains along a short section of reinstated track northwards towards Cricklade.

▲ A night-time line-up of preserved ex-GWR locos at Didcot Railway Centre, from left to right: 'City' Class 4-4-0 No. 3717 (previously numbered 3440) 'City of Truro', 'Hall' Class 4-6-0 No. 5900 'Hinderton Hall' and 'Castle' Class 4-6-0 No. 5029 'Nunney Castle'. The last two locos spent 7 years and 12 years respectively at Woodham's scrapyard at Barry before they were saved for preservation.

▲ Preserved ex-GWR '5700' Class 0-6-0PT No. 4612 at work on the Swindon & Cricklade Railway in June 2010. It is hard to imagine that this lovely loco spent over 15 years as a rusting hulk at Woodham's scrapyard at Barry before being saved for preservation in January 1981.

BRISTOL HARBOUR RAILWAY

Bristol Industrial Museum, Princes Wharf, City Docks, Bristol BS1 4RN

Tel: 0117 922 3571

Route: Along dockside between Bristol Industrial Museum, SS *Great Britain* and the 'B' Bond Warehouse

Length: 1 mile

The railway is part of the newly opened Bristol Industrial Museum, which houses a large transport collection with excellent ship and railway models. The Bristol Harbour Railway originally opened to the quayside in 1866 and the present operation started in 1978. Steam trains operate on some weekends between April and October. The two restored steam locomotives, which originally worked at Avonmouth Docks, are 0-6-0 saddle tanks No. 1764 'Portbury', built by Avonside in 1917, and No. 1940 'Henbury', built by Peckett in 1937. Passengers are carried in an open wagon and a Great Western Railway 'Toad' brakevan. The industrial museum also operates the restored steam tug 'Mayflower' and a 35-ton steam crane, and Brunel's restored iron ship, SS *Great Britain*, is open for viewing by the public at the nearby Great Western Dry Dock.

MUSEUM

STEAM – MUSEUM OF THE GREAT WESTERN RAILWAY

Kemble Drive, Swindon SN2 2TA

Website: www.swindon.gov.uk/steam

Tel: 01793 466646

Nearest main-line station: Swindon

Housed in part of the former GWR's Works, the museum opened in 2000 and contains many interesting exhibits including locomotives, rolling stock, a series of reconstructed work areas, a steam-engine simulator and an enormous collection of GWR archive material. Locomotives on display include replica broad gauge loco 2-2-2 'North Star', a Dean Goods 0-6-0, 'King' Class 4-6-0 No. 6000 'King George V', 'Castle' Class 4-6-0 No. 4073 'Caerphilly Castle' and the last steam locomotive to be built at Swindon, BR Standard Class 9F 2-10-0 No. 92220 'Evening Star'.

SOUTHERN REGION

One week before being unceremoniously despatched to a scrapyard in Newport, 'Merchant Navy' Class 4-6-2 No. 35008 'Orient Line' rests at Weymouth's terminus after hauling a special on 2 July 1967.

SPL
1

THE ATLANTIC COAST

Exeter to Ilfracombe, Bude, Padstow and Plymouth

Formed from a myriad of early railway companies, what became known as 'The Withered Arm' gave the mighty London & South Western Railway the most westerly and far-flung outposts of its extensive empire at the end of the 19th century.

The broad gauge Bristol & Exeter Railway had reached Exeter as early as 1844, but it took another 16 years before the rival London & South Western Railway reached the city when its line from Waterloo via Salisbury and Yeovil Junction opened throughout (see pages 94–99). In between these two dates the Exeter & Crediton Railway, funded mainly by the LSWR, had opened as a double-track broad gauge line between those two places in 1851. It was initially leased to the Bristol & Exeter but finally became part of the LSWR in 1879, by which time the line had already been converted to standard gauge.

In North Devon, the Taw Vale Railway & Dock Company had already opened its short route between Fremington Quay and Barnstaple some years earlier. The railway became known as the North Devon Railway & Dock Company in 1851 and in 1854 it opened a broad gauge line between Barnstaple and Crediton, thus completing the link with Exeter. Again, the LSWR had a hand in all this and absorbed the company in 1865, converting the line to standard gauge in 1876. Meanwhile the Bideford Extension Railway had already opened from Fremington to Bideford in 1855 and was also taken over by the LSWR in 1862.

▲ *Top* 'West Country' 4-6-2 No. 34003 'Plymouth' stands at Exeter Central with the short-lived Plymouth portion of the 'Devon Belle' Pullman train shortly after nationalisation in 1948. The Ilfracombe portion of the train continued to operate during summer months until 1954. The loco featured was rebuilt in 1957 and withdrawn in 1964.

▲ *Bottom* Unrebuilt 'West Country' 4-6-2 No. 34033 'Chard' departs from Barnstaple Junction with a short stopping train for Exeter Central on 7 September 1953. All that remains today is the station building and a single-line platform.

▲ ***Top*** **Unrebuilt 'Battle of Britain' Class 4-6-2s No. 34075 '264 Squadron' and No. 34069 'Hawkinge' double-head the 2.55pm Ilfracombe to Waterloo train a mile up the bank out of Ilfracombe station, in July 1963.**

▲ ***Bottom*** **A sight that was soon to disappear from the West Country, unrebuilt 'Battle of Britain' Class 4-6-2 No. 34054 'Lord Beaverbrook' stands at Exeter St David's station with the 10.15am (Sundays) train to Ilfracombe on 3 May 1964. The two milk tankers behind the loco are returning empty to the creamery at Torrington.**

A further extension from Bideford to Torrington opened in 1872. North of Barnstaple, the LSWR opened the steeply graded line to Ilfracombe in 1874.

EXPANDING FROM EXETER

Meanwhile what was to eventually become part of the LSWR's growing empire west of Exeter, the Okehampton Railway, opened throughout from Coleford (on the North Devon Railway) to Okehampton in 1871. Three years later, with the completion of the 120ft-high Meldon Viaduct, it was extended to Lydford where it met the broad gauge Launceston & South Devon Railway (an extension of the South Devon & Tavistock

◀ The ex-LSWR Class 'T9' 4-4-0s, nicknamed Greyhounds because of their excellent steaming abilities, were once a common sight on the main line west of Exeter until their withdrawal in 1961. Here, No. 30719 waits at Okehampton with a stopping train for Padstow on 1 September 1960. Only one member of this class, No. 30120, has been preserved.

◀ 'N' Class 2-6-0 No. 31842 at the head of a cattle train waits for the level crossing gates to open at Halwill Junction in 1960. Halwill was once a busy rural crossroads with lines converging from Torrington, Bude, Padstow and Plymouth.

▼ Designed by Richard Maunsell for the South Eastern & Chatham Railway in 1917, the 'N' Class 2-6-0s were another common sight on the LSWR main line west of Exeter. Here, No. 31871 crosses Meldon Viaduct west of Okehampton with a short stopping train on 25 August 1963. Another member of this class, No. 31874, was saved for preservation after spending nearly 10 years at Woodham's scrapyard in Barry.

▲ **A steam scene at Bude terminus in 1964 with 'N' Class 2-6-0 No. 31835 waiting in the siding and BR Standard Class 4 2-6-4T No. 80064 waiting to depart with a two-coach train for Halwill Junction. This was the last year of steam on the Bude branch, with diesel multlple units taking over until complete closure in October 1966.**

Railway). Financially backed by the LSWR, the Okehampton Railway had already changed its name to the Devon & Cornwall Railway in 1865. In 1872 the LSWR acquired the company and in 1879 opened a branch from Okehampton to Holsworthy, later extending it over Holsworthy Viaduct to the small seaside resort of Bude in 1898.

Initially LSWR trains ran through to Plymouth via Lydford and then along mixed gauge track of the South Devon & Tavistock Railway's line through to Marsh Mills Junction. The first trains along this route arrived in Plymouth in 1876 with the LSWR terminus at Devonport being reached over GWR metals through the city. This arrangement was unsatisfactory for the LSWR so the authorisation, in 1883, of the independent standard gauge Plymouth, Devonport & South Western Junction Railway between Lydford and the LSWR terminus at Devonport was manna from heaven. Involving the construction of many bridges and tunnels, the 22½-mile line was expensive to build but opened in 1890 with operations from the outset being in the hands of the LSWR. The PD&SWJR remained fairly prosperous and independent until being absorbed by the LSWR in 1922.

To the north, the LSWR's trek westwards to north Cornwall had been painfully slow. The next link in the chain was a subsidiary company, the North Cornwall Railway, which opened from Halwill Junction, on the LSWR's Holsworthy branch, to Launceston in 1886, to Tremeer in 1892, to Camelford and Delabole in 1893 and to Wadebridge in 1895. The final section of what became known as 'The Withered Arm' reached Padstow, 259¾ miles from Waterloo, in 1899.

The completion of this long and tortuous route and its various tentacles soon brought great benefits to the widely dispersed rural and coastal communities of North Devon and North Cornwall. What were originally small fishing villages, Ilfracombe, Bude and Padstow all developed rapidly as popular holiday destinations after the arrival of the railway. Fresh fish could be sent by special train from Padstow to the London markets, vast quantities of milk were collected from country stations along the route and sent to a new milk-bottling plant at Vauxhall in south London, farm produce and cattle could reach more lucrative and distant markets than ever before as did vast quantities of slate from the enormous quarry at Delabole. The LSWR's 'Ocean Liner' specials also competed for traffic between Plymouth and London until the GWR opened its shorter and quicker route via Castle Cary and Westbury.

THE ATLANTIC COAST EXPRESS

By far the most well-known train serving 'The Withered Arm' was the LSWR's weekday 11am departure from Waterloo to Plymouth, which was the forerunner of what became known as the 'Atlantic Coast Express'. The introduction of powerful 'Lord Nelson' 4-6-0s between Waterloo and Exeter in 1927 greatly speeded up the train, which by the Second World War included through coaches for Ilfracombe, Torrington, Bude, Plymouth and Padstow. The 'ACE' resumed after the war in the charge of Bulleid's new air-smoothed 'Merchant Navy' Pacifics to Exeter and then beyond behind his also new lightweight 'Battle of Britain' and 'West Country' Pacifics. Until the early 1960s, other trains beyond Exeter were usually in the capable hands of ex-LSWR Class T9 4-4-0s (known as 'Greyhounds') or Maunsell's 'Moguls'. A quirk of the GWR and LSWR interchange stations at Exeter St Davids and Plymouth North Road was seeing London-bound trains leaving in opposite directions – a sight that can still be viewed today at Exeter.

Sadly, increasing competition from road transport, foreign holidays, the 'Beeching Report' of 1963 and BR regional boundary changes when Southern Region routes west of Salisbury came under the control of the Western Region, all conspired to kill off most of 'The Withered Arm'. The last 'ACE' ran on 4 September 1964 and soon Western Region diesel-hydraulics were taking over the remaining steam duties. First to go were passenger services between Barnstaple Junction and Torrington, which ceased on 4 October 1965 with total closure for clay traffic from Meeth coming in 1983. Next to close were all of the lines west of Okehampton to Halwill, Bude and Wadebridge on 3 October 1966. Padstow lost its truncated service from Bodmin Road and

▶ Time stands still at Wadebridge – the guard and crew of ex-LSWR Class 'T9' 4-4-0 No. 30709 wait patiently for one of the veteran Beattie well tanks to complete a shunting operation before departing with a train for Padstow on 28 April 1959.

▼ *Main image* Crossing the River Tavy south of Bere Ferrers, the 9am train from Waterloo to Plymouth nears the end of its journey behind appropriately named unrebuilt 'West Country' Class 4-6-2 No. 34104 'Bere Alston' on 4 August 1960. Although now singled, this section of the LSWR main line is still open between St Budeaux and Bere Alston for trains from Plymouth to the Gunnislake branch.

Wadebridge on 30 January 1967. The downgraded Okehampton to Bere Alston section closed completely on 6 May 1968, although the line (now singled) from Bere Alston to Plymouth was retained as part of the surviving Gunnislake branch. Barnstaple Junction to Ilfracombe closed completely on 5 October 1970. While the Coleford Junction to Okehampton section closed to passengers on 5 June 1972, granite track ballast traffic from Meldon Quarry has continued to keep the line open. Apart from that, all that is left of the LSWR network west of Exeter is the 38-mile mainly single-track line from Cowley Bridge Junction at Exeter to Barnstaple. Here the remaining single platform is but a ghost of its former glorious past when trains would arrive or depart from four different directions. Apart from this rather long siding from Exeter, the rest of North Devon and North Cornwall are now totally devoid of rail transport.

NOTABLE BRANCHES

Apart from the major rail connections at Exeter and Plymouth and the various tentacles of 'The Withered Arm', there were four other associated lines worthy of note. At Barnstaple Junction the GWR line to Taunton (see pages 26–31) opened throughout in 1887 and closed in 1966. At Barnstaple Town station the 1ft 11½in Lynton & Barnstaple Railway opened to Lynton in 1898 and closed in 1935 while at Bideford the quirky standard gauge Bideford, Westward Ho! & Appledore Railway opened in stages between 1901 and 1908 and closed in 1917. The latter line was not physically connected with the LSWR station at Bideford, being separated by the River Torridge. Much of the course of this fascinating but short-lived line can still be followed today. At Torrington the standard gauge North Devon & Cornwall Junction Light Railway opened to Halwill Junction in 1925 and was closed to passengers in 1965 and completely (from Meeth to Torrington) in 1983. Much of its route now forms part of the Tarka Trail footpath and cycleway. Finally, the former narrow gauge East Cornwall Railway was rebuilt as a standard gauge light railway between Bere Alston and Calstock by the Plymouth, Devonport & South Western Junction Railway in 1908. From 1966, the branch, which includes the magnificent stone viaduct across the Tamar at Calstock, was cut back to Gunnislake where trains from Plymouth still terminate.

▼ The end of the line at Padstow – 259¾ miles from Waterloo, unrebuilt 'Battle of Britain' Class 4-6-2 No. 34078 '222 Squadron' waits in the sidings with a rake of SR malachite green coaches in July 1964. There was less than two months to go before the withdrawal of the 'Atlantic Coast Express' and the end of steam on this line. Much-loved by John Betjeman, Padstow struggled on with a truncated DMU service to Wadebridge and Bodmin Road until January 1967 when the line finally closed.

THE LINE TODAY

Passenger services between Exeter and Barnstaple, marketed as the 'Tarka Line', are operated by First Great Western. Most trains continue through Exeter to Exmouth. Passenger services between Plymouth and Bere Alston, from where they continue to Gunnislake, are also operated by First Great Western. The line is marketed as the 'Tamar Valley Line'.

In North Devon, the trackbed of the northern part of the Ilfracombe branch is now a footpath while from Braunton to beyond Torrington (via Barnstaple) the trackbed is now the Tarka Trail footpath and cycleway.

Okehampton station is currently served by the Dartmoor Railway (see Heritage Lines, right), which operates a diesel service northward to Sampford Courtenay and southward to Meldon. A summer Sunday service from Exeter St Davids to Okehampton operates as part of the Dartmoor Sunday Rover network. The Devon Coast to Coast Cycleway (National Cycle Network Route 27) parallels the line from Okehampton as far as Meldon from where it uses part of the old trackbed as far as Lydford. The 11-mile section from Okehampton to Lydford is known as the Granite Way and includes a crossing of the famous Meldon Viaduct. Farther west the trackbed of the line from Wadebridge to Padstow now forms part of the popular Camel Trail footpath and cycleway from Wenfordbridge and Bodmin.

HERITAGE LINES

DARTMOOR RAILWAY

Okehampton Station, Okehampton, Devon EX20 1EJ

Website: www.dartmoor-railway.co.uk

Tel: 01837 55164

Route: Sampford Courtenay to Meldon via Okehampton

Length: 5½ miles

Nearest main-line station: Yeoford; also Okehampton on summer Sunday service operated by First Great Western from Exeter St Davids between late May and mid-September.

Originally part of the LSWR main line between Exeter and Plymouth, the Dartmoor Railway is a mainly diesel-hauled heritage line that currently operates on the freight-only line between Meldon Quarry and Sampford Courtenay via Okehampton. Work is currently in hand to extend services to an interchange station at Yeoford on the Exeter to Barnstaple Tarka Line. In 2008, the railway was bought by Iowa Pacific Holdings who aim to increase freight and passenger traffic on the line.

▼ Diminutive 0-4-0ST 'Covertcoat' stands in Launceston station with a train for Newmills on the 2ft-gauge Launceston Steam Railway. The loco was built by Hunslet in 1898 and worked at the Dinorwic Slate Quarry until 1959.

LAUNCESTON STEAM RAILWAY

St Thomas Road, Launceston, Cornwall PL15 8DA

Website: www.launcestonsr.co.uk

Tel: 01566 775665

Route: Launceston to Newmills

Length: 2½ miles

This 2ft-gauge line, opened in 1985, runs along part of the trackbed of the old London & South Western Railway's line from Halwill Junction to Padstow, which closed in 1966. Locomotives, including 'Lilian' and 'Covertcoat', built by Hunslet in 1883 and 1898 respectively, are beautifully restored steam engines that formerly worked in the North Wales slate quarries of Penrhyn and Dinorwic. Passengers are taken through the scenic Kensey Valley in replicas of Victorian narrow gauge carriages. The turn of the century workshop at Launceston, once used by the Launceston Gas Company, is an example of a belt-driven machine shop in daily use, and the British Engineering Exhibition gives an opportunity to view those locomotives not in service. The station's café and booking office were originally built in 1919 for the first Ideal Home Exhibition and then erected as a three-bedroom bungalow in Surrey. A westward extension along the old railway trackbed to the village of Egloskerry is a scheme currently under serious consideration.

THE BOURNEMOUTH BELLE

Waterloo to Bournemouth and Weymouth

After a faltering start, the London & South Western Railway's main line from Waterloo grew to become one of the most intensively used railway systems in the world, finally witnessing the swan song of Bulleid's innovative 'Pacific' locomotives that lasted until the end of steam in 1967.

Originally conceived as a canal, the London & Southampton Railway was born in 1831 as the Southampton, London & Branch Railway & Dock Company. In addition to its main line, a branch to Bristol (not yet connected with a railway) was also proposed. Three years later this had all changed and, as the London & Southampton Railway, the main line between these two cities was authorised by Parliament. The branch to Bristol was later dropped when Brunel's broad gauge route from Paddington found favour instead.

Construction of the line between Nine Elms and Southampton started in 1834, but progress was slow under the direction of the company's first engineer, Francis Giles. With rising costs and

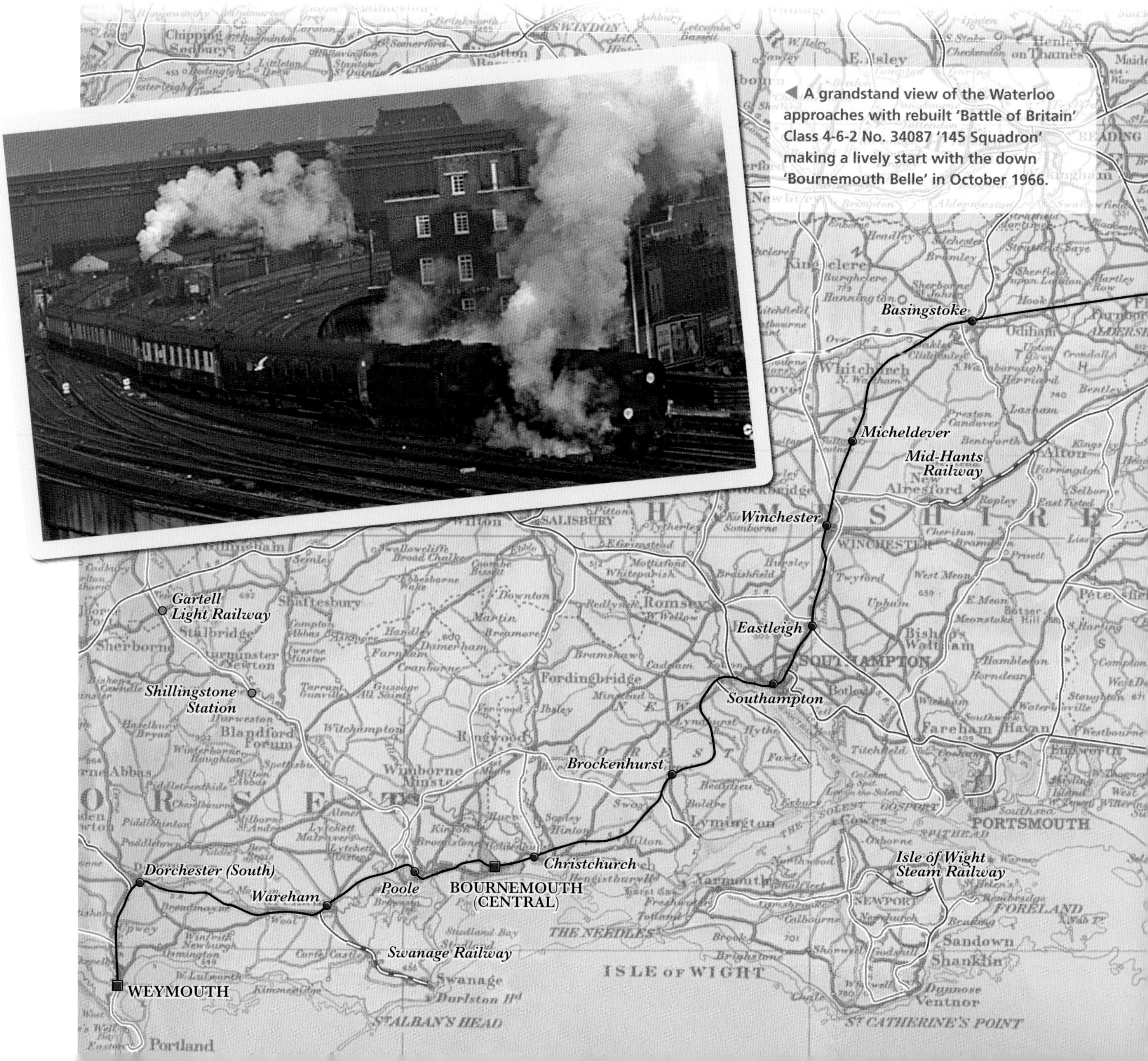

◀ **A grandstand view of the Waterloo approaches with rebuilt 'Battle of Britain' Class 4-6-2 No. 34087 '145 Squadron' making a lively start with the down 'Bournemouth Belle' in October 1966.**

◀ **Watched by a local cool dude, unrebuilt 'West Country' Class 4-6-2 No. 34091 'Weymouth' restarts a down train from Woking on 28 September 1963. The loco had a short working life – built by BR at Brighton in 1949, it was withdrawn in September 1964.**

painfully slow progress, the company became a laughing stock and, in 1837, Giles resigned and was replaced by Joseph Locke who was already renowned for his work on the Stockton & Darlington and Liverpool & Manchester railways.

The line sprang to life in stages with the first section from Nine Elms to Woking opening on 21 May 1838. It was extended to Winchfield on 24 September and to Basingstoke on 10 June 1839, the same day that the Southampton to Winchester section also opened. Amid great rejoicing along the entire line, the intervening gap between Winchester and Basingstoke opened on 11 May 1840.

▼ **Unrebuilt 'West Country' Class 4-6-2 No. 34002 'Salisbury' makes a fine sight as it streaks through New Malden station with the down 'Bournemouth Belle' (normally 'Merchant Navy'-hauled) on a Sunday in 1962.**

Passengers wait to board a Bournemouth to Waterloo express at Winchester station on 27 May 1966. The train engine, 'Merchant Navy' Class 4-6-2 No. 35003 'Royal Mail', was built with an air-smoothed casing at Eastleigh in 1941, subsequently rebuilt in 1958 and withdrawn in July 1967.

▲ **High noon at Southampton Central – BR Standard Class 4MT 2-6-0 No. 76067 prepares to leave the station with an up van train on 12 September 1964. No. 76067 had a short working life of only 11 years after being built at Doncaster in 1956.**

▲ **Unrebuilt 'West Country' Class 4-6-2 No. 34038 'Lynton' makes a dramatic start from Brockenhurst station with the 8.35am Waterloo to Bournemouth train on the cold and crisp morning of 11 December 1965. The loco was withdrawn from service only six months later.**

Meanwhile the London & Southampton Railway had changed its name to the London & South Western Railway in 1839 when it was authorised to build a railway from Bishopstoke (later to become Eastleigh) to Portsmouth. The original London terminus at Nine Elms, designed by Sir William Tite (who also designed the Southampton terminus), soon proved to be insufficient for the rapidly expanding railway and, in 1845, the LSWR received authority to extend the line to a new terminus at Waterloo. This opened in 1848 and the Nine Elms site was expanded to include a goods depot and the company's locomotive works, which remained here until 1910 when they were transferred to Eastleigh.

▼ **Rebuilt 'Battle of Britain' Class 4-6-2 No. 34071 '601 Squadron' streaks through Shawford, in the Itchen Valley south of Winchester, with a down express to Southampton and Bournemouth in the winter of 1963.**

▶ Some railway photographers will go to any lengths to bag a unique photo – shot from an extremely dangerous location inside the tunnel, a decrepit BR Standard Class 5MT 4-6-0 storms up the 1 in 50 gradient through Wishing Well Tunnel north of Upwey with an up express from Weymouth in the spring of 1967.

◀ An evocative 1960s period photo with pedestrians, a cyclist, a Ford Anglia, a Morris Minor and, in the background, a bus all held up by the passage of 'Merchant Navy' Class Pacific No. 35023 'Holland-Afrika Line' heading a Weymouth-bound express over Poole level crossing on 3 June 1967. Bereft of its valuable nameplate, the loco only survived just over a month until the end of steam on the Southern Region in July.

CASTLEMAN'S DOMAIN

To the west of Southampton, a Wimborne solicitor by the name of Castleman had promoted the Southampton & Dorchester Railway, which was part of an early scheme to build a main line from London Waterloo to Exeter and the West. By 1847, the single-track line to Dorchester was opened across the New Forest via Brockenhurst, Ringwood, Wimborne and Broadstone. The terminus at Dorchester faced east ready for the extension to Exeter that never came. Trains between Bournemouth and Weymouth had to reverse out of the station until a new platform was opened for westbound trains in 1877. Eastbound stopping trains had to reverse into the station until 1970 when a new through platform was opened.

In 1848, the railway, known as Castleman's Corkscrew because of its circuitous route, designed to serve as many centres of population along the way as possible, was taken over by the London & South Western Railway. At this time Christchurch and Bournemouth, to the south, were only small hamlets but their rapid growth soon led to calls for a more direct coastal route.

In the early days of the railway, passengers for Christchurch were conveyed by horsedrawn bus from Christchurch Road (later renamed Holmsley) station and for Bournemouth by a similar means from Hamworthy. The demand for a railway to serve these two, by now growing, towns eventually led to the Ringwood, Christchurch & Bournemouth Railway being opened, first to Christchurch in 1862 and then to Bournemouth in 1870. However, this circuitous route was slow and a new direct double-track main line from Lymington Junction, near Brockenhurst, via Sway and New Milton, to Christchurch, together with the doubling of the existing line thence to Bournemouth (what was later to become known as Central station) was opened in 1888. At the western end of Castleman's Corkscrew, a line had already opened from Broadstone to Bournemouth West in 1874.

The opening of the new direct line from Waterloo to Bournemouth had an immediate effect on Castleman's Corkscrew west of Brockenhurst. The Ringwood to Christchurch line lost its importance and, although Weymouth-bound trains continued to use the old route, the opening of new cut-offs at Branksome and Holes Bay in 1893 soon led to its downgrading as a secondary route. The Ringwood to Christchurch line had succumbed in 1935 and, apart from local stopping services, the Castleman's Corkscrew between Brockenhurst and Broadstone came to life only on summer Saturdays when Waterloo to Weymouth trains were diverted along the route. It closed completely in 1964.

WEYMOUTH AND SOUTHAMPTON

The final link in the chain from Dorchester to Weymouth was provided by the broad gauge GWR-backed Wiltshire, Somerset & Weymouth Railway. Facing mounting financial problems and delays, the unfinished railway was taken over by the GWR in 1850 and not completed to Weymouth until 1857. On 20 January that year both broad gauge GWR trains and standard gauge LSWR trains first entered the town along mixed gauge track.

The LSWR were quick to capitalise on their rapidly growing business through Hampshire and Dorset. In 1891, the company transferred its carriage and wagon works from Nine Elms to a green field site at Eastleigh and within a few years the village had grown into a busy railway town. Under the watchful eye of chief mechanical engineer Dugald Drummond, the locomotive works followed in 1909 and Eastleigh remained the main railway works for the Southern Railway (from 1923) and for the Southern Region of British Railways (from 1948) until 1967.

The moribund docks at Southampton were modernised by the LSWR in 1892. Featuring 25 miles of railway, new hydraulic cranes, warehouses, graving docks, sheltered deep-water quays and cold-storage facilities, the docks became one of the finest

▶ 'Merchant Navy' Class 4-6-2 No. 35019 'French Line CGT' makes a cautious exit from Bournemouth Central station with the 11am express to Waterloo on 9 September 1962. The loco was the only member of its class to have script lettering on its nameplate. It was withdrawn in September 1965.

35019

in the world. Vast amounts of freight were carried to and from them by the LSWR and their important rail connections were a vital ingredient to victory in both world wars. Ocean liner expresses between the terminal in the docks and Waterloo also became regular features well into the BR era, while at Weymouth, Channel Island boat trains from Waterloo would process slowly through the streets of the town to Harbour station.

As soon as the direct railway from Southampton had reached Bournemouth in 1888, this once small village quickly developed into a major seaside resort served by expresses from Waterloo and other parts of England. The most famous of these was the 'Bournemouth Belle', which was introduced by the Southern Railway in 1931 and, apart from the period during the Second World War, continued to run until electrification of the line in July 1967. Composed of brown and cream Pullman coaches, the train was usually hauled by a 'Lord Nelson' Class 4-6-0 until the introduction of Bulleid's 'Merchant Navy' Class Pacifics after 1945. The latter remained in charge of the train until the final year of steam on the Southern Region in 1967.

MAIN-LINE ELECTRICIFCATION

Among the major pre-Grouping railway companies, the LSWR was the first to grasp the cost-savings of electrified railways on busy commuter routes. Their third rail 660V DC suburban system out of Waterloo was introduced in 1915 on services to Wimbledon via East Putney; by the 1930s, by which time the Southern Railway had taken over, it had grown to become the largest electrified suburban railway in the world. Main-line electrification, operating on 750V DC, followed and on 10 July 1967 the important route from Waterloo to Southampton and Bournemouth was 'switched on'. The era of steam haulage on the Southern Region was over. The electrification of the rest of the line to Weymouth had to wait until 1988, with services in the intervening years being provided by push-pull-fitted Class 33/1 'Crompton' diesels with unpowered 4TC sets.

▲ **Ex-GWR 0-6-0PT No. 1368 departs from Weymouth Quay station with an up Channel Islands Boat Train for Waterloo on 30 September 1961. The train's slow progress along Weymouth's streets was frequently halted by illegally parked cars that were 'bounced' out of the way. A sign in the foreground offers 'boat trips around Portland Harbour to view 'HM ships & submarines'.**

THE LINE TODAY

Passenger services between Waterloo, Southampton, Bournemouth, Dorchester (South) and Weymouth are operated by South West Trains. The section from Dorchester (West) to Weymouth is also operated by First Great Western as part of their Heart of Wessex Line from Bristol, Bath and Castle Cary.

Much of the trackbed of the closed 'Castleman's Corkscrew' line between Brockenhurst and Hamworthy is now a footpath and cycleway.

HERITAGE RAILWAYS

THE MID HANTS RAILWAY WATERCRESS LINE

The Railway Station, Alresford, Hampshire SO24 9JG

Website: www.watercressline.co.uk

Tel: 01962 733810

Route: Alton to Alresford

Length: 10 miles

Nearest main-line station: Alton

Opened in 1865, the railway between Alton and Winchester, known as the Mid Hants (Alton) Railway, was an important link for the armed services between Aldershot and Portsmouth. Heavily used in both world wars, it was also an important diversionary route for main-line trains between Woking and Winchester. Vital local traffic included the transport of locally-grown watercress, which is now used by the present company as its marketing title. Finally closed by BR in 1973, the current section of the line was soon taken over by a preservation group who started services, initially from Alresford to Ropley, in 1977. Services to Alton, where there is an important link with the national network, started in 1985. Steam-hauled trains operate over this steeply graded line, locally known as 'The Alps', necessitating the use of large and impressive locomotives, including ex-SR Bulleid 'West Country' Class 4-6-2 No. 34007 'Wadebridge' and BR Standard Class 5 4-6-0 No. 73096. Visiting locomotives can also be regularly seen hard at work on special event days through the year. The stations along the line are all restored to different periods in the history of the railway, and of special note is the carefully pruned 60-year-old topiary at Ropley station, where the Mid Hants also has its extensive workshops and engine shed.

SWANAGE RAILWAY

Station House, Swanage, Dorset BH19 1HB

Website: www.swanagerailway.co.uk

Tel: 01929 425800

Route: Swanage to Norden

Length: 6 miles

Nearest main-line station: Wareham

The former London & South Western Railway branch line on the Isle of Purbeck was opened from Worgret Junction, a mile west of Wareham, to Swanage in 1885. The opening of the line changed Swanage from a small harbour town

to a thriving seaside resort. Goods traffic was also important with large amounts of clay being carried from the Furzebrook area. Passenger traffic was heavy, especially during the summer months, and included through carriages from Waterloo. The line was controversially closed by BR in 1972, although the section from Worgret Junction to the Wytch Farm oil terminal was retained. A preservation group started to reopen the line from Swanage and the first trains ran along a short section from the station in 1979. By August 1995 the line had been extended to Corfe Castle and Norden, and on its first week of extended operation packed trains carried over 20,000 passengers. A park-and-ride scheme is in operation from Norden, which should help to ease road traffic congestion in the Corfe Castle and Swanage areas. Although the railway has now extended to Worgret Junction, no regular trains run through to Wareham at the moment. Trains are mainly steam-hauled by a variety of locomotives, and the 'Wessex Belle' Pullman dining train service is operated on certain Saturday evenings. Locomotives operating on the line include Southern Railway 'Battle of Britain' class 4-6-2 No. 34070 'Manston', 'West Country' Class 4-6-2 No. 34028 'Eddystone', Class M7 0-4-4 tank No. 30053 and BR Standard Class 4 2-6-4T No. 80104.

▲ *Top* Preserved unrebuilt 'Battle of Britain' Class 4-6-2 No. 34081 '92 Squadron' heads out of Corfe Castle station on the Swanage Railway with a train of happy holidaymakers.

▲ *Bottom* Resident preserved unrebuilt 'West Country' Class 4-6-2 No. 34007 'Wadebridge' hard at work reliving 'The Cunarder' boat train on the switchback Mid Hants Railway near Ropley.

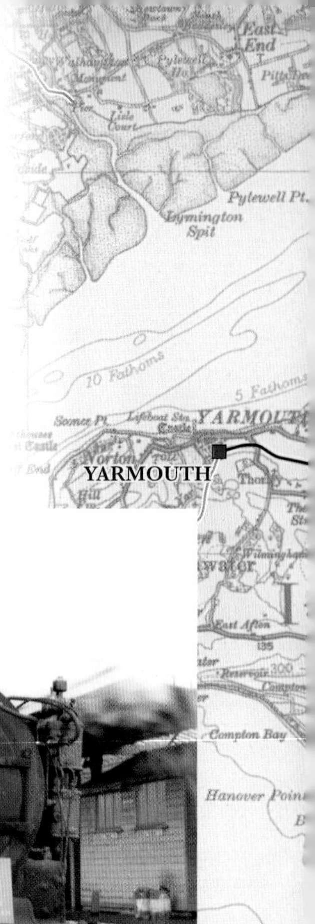

ISLAND LINES

The railways of the Isle of Wight

Isolated from Britain's mainland railway network, the railways of the Isle of Wight became a working Victorian museum until modernised by the Southern Railway. Their demise under British Railways management can only be regretted.

Although measuring only 22½ miles from east to west and 13½ miles from north to south, the Isle of Wight contained 45¼ route miles of railways during its steam heyday. In the early part of the 19th century the main port of entry for ferry passengers from Southampton was at Cowes so it is not surprising that the first railway to be built on the island started from there. The short Cowes & Newport Railway opened for passengers in 1862 and remained isolated from the island's other railways for some years.

The second line to open on the island was the Isle of Wight (Eastern Section) Railway, which opened from Ryde (St John's Road) to Shanklin in 1864 and to Ventnor through a ¾-mile tunnel under Boniface Down in 1866. Renamed the Isle of Wight Railway, the company went on to operate a short branch line from Brading to Bembridge in 1882. At Bembridge a short-lived ferry service out to Hayling Island also came into operation. Originally built by the Brading Harbour Improvement & Railway, the branch

▲ **The last day of steam operations on the Isle of Wight's railways – complete with commemorative wreath, Class '02' 0-4-4T No. 17 (formerly named 'Seaview') heads the 10.12am train from Ryde Pierhead to Shanklin at Ryde Esplanade station on 31 December 1966. The line to Shanklin was then closed while third-rail electrification was installed, reopening with ancient ex-London Underground stock in March 1967.**

▼ Gateway to the Isle of Wight – since its inception in 1880, the railway-operated integrated transport system at Ryde Pier has stood the test of time. Here, on 2 August 1962, the former Southern Railway paddle steamer 'Sandown' has arrived from Portsmouth with a boatload of happy holidaymakers. The two trains, headed by ex-LSWR Class '02' 0-4-4Ts No. 22 'Brading' and No. 27 'Merstone', are about to set off to their final island destinations of Sandown, Shanklin, Ventnor and Cowes.

▲ The end is nigh – Class '02' 0-4-4T No. 30 'Sherwell' trundles along the weed-infested approach to the ¾-mile tunnel under Boniface Down with the 9.25am Ryde Pierhead to Ventnor train on 30 August 1965.

▼ Class '02' 0-4-4T No. 14 'Fishbourne' waits for the road ahead at Shanklin in 1962, while No. 16 'Ventnor' approaches with a train from Ventnor. Shanklin is now the end of the third-rail electrified line from Ryde Pierhead.

line and ferry service proved unprofitable. The former was taken over by the Isle of Wight Railway in 1898 and the latter ceased running altogether.

A TICKET TO RYDE

At Ryde, the 744yd-long pier had been completed by 1833 but a tramway was not built alongside it for another 31 years. Both steam-hauled and horsedrawn at various times, it was extended to St John's Road station in 1871 and electrified with a third rail in 1886. Electricity was replaced by petrol-powered locos in 1927 until the tramway's complete closure early in 1969. A third pier was added alongside the existing structure in 1880 and carried a standard gauge line that linked the Pier Head with St John's Road station. Just to complicate matters, this short stretch of line was owned jointly by the London & South Western and the London, Brighton & South Coast Railways, who by then had serious vested interests across the water in Portsmouth. The new line was worked jointly by the Isle of Wight Railway and the Isle of Wight Central Railway.

In the meantime the Isle of Wight (Newport Junction) Railway had partially opened in 1875 between Newport and Sandown. The viaduct at Newport connecting this line with the Cowes & Newport Railway opened four years later, by which time the company had gone bust. To the east of Newport, the Ryde & Newport Railway opened its line from Smallbrook Junction (south of Ryde) in 1875. The company amalgamated with the bankrupt Isle of Wight (Newport Junction) Railway and the Cowes & Newport to form the Isle of Wight Central Railway in 1887. A short freight-only branch to Medina Wharf from Cowes had been opened in 1875.

Yet another independent concern came into being in 1880, when the Freshwater, Yarmouth & Newport Railway (FY&NR) was authorised to build a 12-mile line to the west of the island. It opened to passengers in 1889 and was initially worked by the newly formed Isle of Wight Central (IWCR). The two companies fell out in 1913 and working the line reverted back to the FY&NR, which stayed independent until the Big Four Grouping in 1923.

The last railway to be built on the Isle of Wight was the Newport, Godshill & St Lawrence Railway's 6¾-mile branch line from Merstone to Ventnor West, which opened throughout in 1900. The line was worked by the IWCR from the outset and amalgamated with that company in 1913. From 1900, the island's railway system remained intact for the next 52 years.

THE TOURIST TRADE

With the island's railway system now complete, the Isle of Wight enjoyed many years of growth as a holiday destination. In 1923 the newly formed Southern Railway took over all of the island's railway-operating companies and found that it had inherited what was essentially a working Victorian museum and set about modernising the system. With the exception of the ex-LB&SCR 'Terrier' tanks, all of the ancient steam locomotives and decrepit

▲ Looking more like a model railway layout, this panoramic view of Ventnor station on 28 August 1965 was taken from above the mouth of the tunnel under Boniface Down. In the foreground Class '02' 0-4-4T No. 20 'Shanklin' waits to depart with a train for Ryde.

▼ Class '02' 0-4-4T No. 26 'Whitwell' crosses over the River Medina at Newport with a Cowes to Ryde Pier Head train in 1962. Closed in 1966, the trackbed of the line between Newport and Cowes now forms part of the Round the Island cycleway.

coaching stock were replaced by modern coaches and newly built Class '02' 0-4-4 tanks. Under SR management, passenger traffic increased year on year until the early 1950s, but competition from road transport was already taking its toll. By now, with cost-cutting British Railways in the driving seat, the future of the island's quaint but out-dated railways looked grim.

First to go was the Merstone to Ventnor West line, which closed in September 1952. A year later the Brading to Bembridge branch and Newport to Freshwater also bit the dust. The 'cross-country' Newport to Sandown line struggled on until early 1956 when it, too, was closed. The future of the remaining two routes from Ryde to Cowes and Ryde to Ventnor remained in doubt and the 'Beeching Report' of 1963 more or less sealed their fate. The end came in 1966 by which time steam was already on its last legs on the mainland – first to go were passenger services between Ryde and Cowes in February followed by Shanklin to Ventnor in April. Freight services on both lines ended in May. Steam services continued between Ryde Pierhead and Shanklin until the end of the year. But all was not lost as the Ryde Pier Head to Shanklin section was then electrified and reopened in March 1967 using clapped-out London Underground trains. A somewhat inglorious end to the island's charming railway system.

▼ *Top* Merstone station was once the junction for the 'cross-country' line to Shanklin and the Newport, Godshill & St Lawrence Railway's 6¾-mile branch line to Ventnor West. The latter became the first island casualty when it closed in 1952. The Brading line remained open until 1956. Seen here on 3 September 1952, less than two weeks before closure, Class '02' No. 35 'Freshwater' waits at Merstone with a train for Ventnor West while on the left No. 27 'Merstone' heads a Sandown train.

▼ *Bottom* The last day of passenger services on the Ryde to Cowes line saw trains packed with enthusiasts wishing to pay their last respects. Here, Class '02' 0-4-4T No. 27 (formerly named 'Merstone') arrives at Cowes on 20 February 1966. Goods traffic lingered on until May when the line closed completely. The station site has long since disappeared beneath a supermarket, while the footbridge can now be seen on the Mid Hants Railway at Medstead & Four Marks station.

THE LINE TODAY

Passenger services between Ryde Pier Head and Shanklin are operated by Island Line Trains. Ferries to Portsmouth are operated by Wightlink. Trains connect with the Isle of Wight Steam Railway (see Heritages Lines, right) at Smallbrook Junction.

The Isle of Wight Steam Railway has restored the Ryde to Cowes line between Smallbrook Junction and Wootton. Other sections of closed railway lines now form part of the 62-mile Round the Island cycleway: between Freshwater and Yarmouth along the east bank of the tidal River Yar; between Newport and Cowes along the west bank of the River Medina; and between Newport and Sandown following the valley of the River Yar (see the Isle of Wight council website for more information).

HERITAGE RAILWAY

ISLE OF WIGHT STEAM RAILWAY

Havenstreet, Isle of Wight
PO33 4DS

Website: www.iwsteamrailway.co.uk

Tel: 01983 882204

Route: Smallbrook Junction to Wootton

Length: 5 miles

Nearest main-line station:
Smallbrook Junction

This line originally opened in 1875 as the Ryde & Newport Railway and eventually became part of the network of rural branch lines run by the Southern Railway on the Isle of Wight. Due to their isolation from the mainland, the railways on the island used a collection of second-hand locomotives and rolling stock. The island rail system, except for the section from Ryde Pier Head to Shanklin, was closed by BR at the end of 1966 and a preservation group moved in to Havenstreet in 1971. Services to Wootton restarted in 1977 and to Ashey and the new station at Smallbrook Junction in 1991, where connection can be made with the electrified Island Line. The ancient and beautifully preserved locomotives and rolling stock, some dating back to the 19th century, all contribute to the Victorian atmosphere that pervades the railway. Included in the line-up are former London Brighton & South Coast Railway Class A1X 0-6-0 tanks, No. W8 'Freshwater' and No. W11 'Newport', built in 1876 and 1878 respectively, and London & South Western Railway Class 02 0-4-4 tank No. W24 'Calbourne' recently restored.

▼ Recently restored in lined BR black livery, Class '02' 0-4-4T No. 24 'Calbourne' heads a short train on the delightful Isle of Wight Steam Railway near Havenstreet.

THE SLOW AND DIRTY

Bath Green Park to Bournemouth West

Known affectionately as the 'Slow and Dirty', the heavily engineered and scenic route over the Mendips to Bournemouth was killed by a thousand cuts following takeover by British Railways. After suffering a slow and painful death, its closure in 1966 can only be described as shameful.

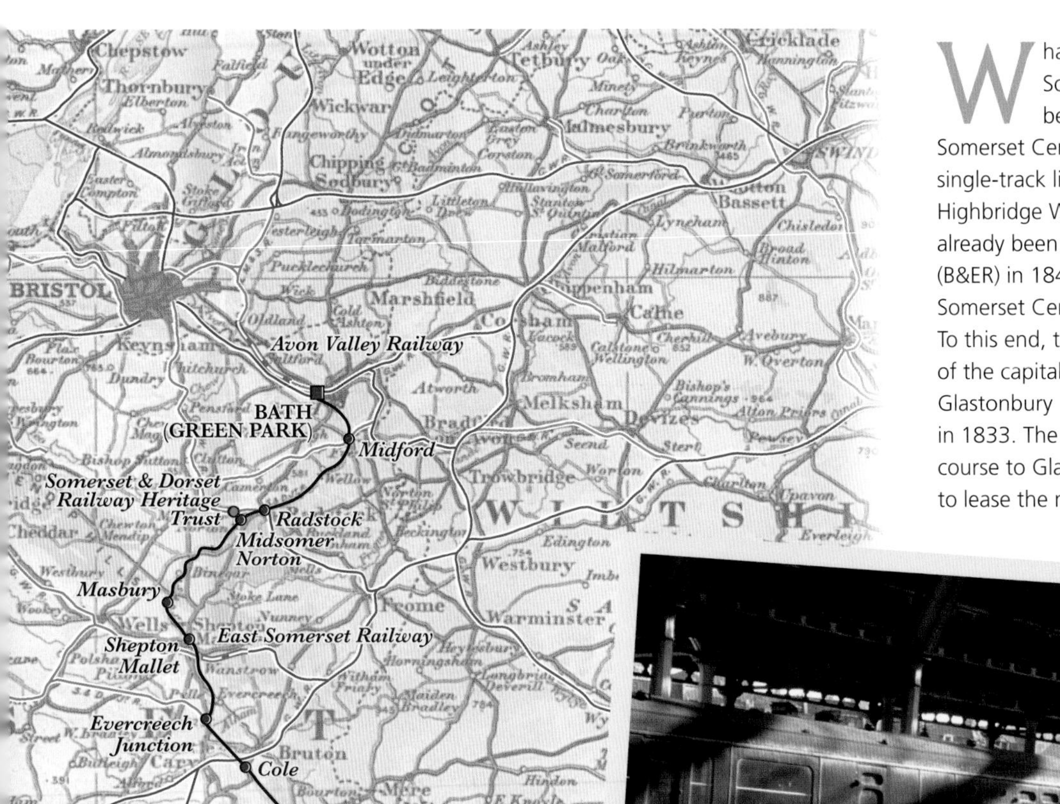

What eventually became the much-loved Somerset & Dorset Joint Railway had its beginnings on 28 August 1854 when the Somerset Central Railway opened its broad gauge single-track line across the Somerset Levels between Highbridge Wharf and Glastonbury. Highbridge had already been reached by the Bristol & Exeter Railway (B&ER) in 1841 and this company was keen to see the Somerset Central Railway (SCR) open for business. To this end, they had subscribed about 15 per cent of the capital having already bought the existing Glastonbury Navigation and Canal, which had opened in 1833. The new railway closely followed the canal's course to Glastonbury closely and the B&ER went on to lease the new railway until 1861.

▲ S&D Class 7F 2-8-0 No. 53806 simmers amid the morning sun beams at Bath Green Park station after hauling the 7am train from Templecombe in August 1962. Within a month all through workings over the S&D between the Midlands, the North and Bournemouth had ceased and this once-important north–south route had been relegated to secondary-line status.

LINKING CHANNELS

From its inception, the Somerset Central was seen as a first step towards building a railway line linking the Bristol Channel and the English Channel, normally a long sea trip around Land's End. To this end, an extension was built from Highbridge to a pier at Burnham-on-Sea, where the company had high hopes of benefiting from seaborne trade and passenger traffic to and from South Wales. The line opened in 1858 and a branch at its eastern end from Glastonbury to Wells opened a year later.

With the English Channel still in its sights, the Somerset Central had already obtained authorisation to extend its main line from Glastonbury to Cole, near Bruton, where it would meet up with the fledgling Dorset Central Railway (DCR). The latter had been authorised in 1856 to build a standard gauge line from a junction with the London & South Western Railway's line at Wimborne (also known as Castleman's Corkscrew; see pages 72–79) to the market town of Blandford. This opened in 1860, by which time the line was already being extended to meet the Somerset Central at Cole. The Somerset Central's dream of reaching the English Channel was about to become a reality but there was one slight problem – the gauges were different. This was overcome when B&ER's lease of the SCR ended in 1861 and the decision was made to convert the broad gauge SCR to standard gauge. (B&ER trains continued to run over mixed gauge track to Cole until 1868.)

▲ In its last year of operation over the S&D, the southbound 'Pines Express' climbs the 1 in 50 gradient out of Bath to the summit at the exit of Combe Down Tunnel on 23 April 1962. The train, double-headed by BR Standard Class 5MT 4-6-0 No 73051 and rebuilt 'West Country' Class 4-6-2 No. 34046 'Braunton' (since preserved), is about to enter the unventilated single-bore 'hell hole' of Devonshire Tunnel.

▼ The ultimate in S&D steam power – in the final summer of through trains over the S&D, BR Standard Class 9F 2-10-0 No. 92245 lifts a southbound express through Midford on 25 August 1962. The 9Fs had recently been drafted in from other WR sheds as they were capable of lifting heavy expresses over the Mendips without assistance. This particular loco spent 25 years at Woodham's scrapyard in Barry before being saved for possible preservation.

TOWARDS A JOINT FUTURE

Meanwhile progress was being made on the intervening gap between Glastonbury and Blandford. The SCR opened to Cole in 1862 and this was extended by the DCR to Templecombe, where it met the Salisbury & Yeovil Railway in the same year. That year also saw the amalgamation of the two companies to form the Somerset & Dorset Railway. The final link from Templecombe to Blandford was opened in 1863 and the important Channel-linking route was open for business, albeit that the railway from Wimborne to the English Channel ports was owned by the amicable London & South Western Railway.

Sadly, the dreams of the original Somerset Central's backers turned into a financial nightmare as the hoped-for traffic from South Wales, Bristol and the Midlands to English Channel ports and over to France failed to materialise – there were very good reasons for this as there was now a change of gauge at Highbridge and a more direct route to the north was blocked by the Mendip Hills. By 1866, also the year of a major financial crash, the company was in dire straits and administrators were appointed. There then followed four years of strict economies until the company managed to get back on its feet.

Now the goal for the S&D was to reach Bath. As well as already being served by the GWR since 1840, the city had also been reached by the Midland Railway in 1869 when that company opened its branch from a junction at Mangotsfield on the Bristol to Birmingham route. Authorised in 1871, the Somerset & Dorset Railway took on its most spectacular and costly extension northwards from Evercreeech Junction (north of Cole) across the Mendips to Bath, where it would join the Midland Railway for the last short section into that company's

▼ The last day of scheduled services on the S&D was 5 March 1966. Here, the penultimate southbound train from Bath Green Park, the 4.25pm to Templecombe, leaves Wellow behind BT Standard Class 4 2-6-4T No. 80043 with driver Cecil Waldron at the controls.

terminus at Queen Square. By taking over the Somersetshire Coal Canal tramway, the new extension also had access to the important coalfields around Radstock. With a summit of 811ft at Masbury, the line was a feat of Victorian engineering involving numerous tunnels and viaducts, but its ever-increasing costs were the final nail in the coffin for the battered finances of the Somerset & Dorset.

The line opened in 1874 and it wasn't long before through trains from the Midlands were using this new north–south route to reach the growing resort of Bournemouth via the newly opened Poole & Bournemouth branch of the LSWR. By 1875 the S&D was looking for a saviour to bail it out of its terrible financial position and approached the GWR with a view to a takeover. On hearing of this potential threat to their territory, the LSWR quickly got together with the Midland Railway and offered to lease the line jointly for 999 years. This offer was manna from heaven to the S&D's directors and they accepted – thus was the Somerset & Dorset Joint Railway born. The GWR was not best pleased as events later told.

▲ Allocated to Bath Green Park shed, BR Standard Class 9F 2-10-0 No. 92212 emerges from the single-bore Winsor Hill Tunnel at the head of a summer Saturdays-only Bristol to Bournemouth train on 26 August 1961. Following withdrawal in 1967, the loco spent more time at Woodham's scrapyard in Barry (11 years) than it did in revenue-earning service (8 years). The loco is currently based at the Mid Hants Railway.

TWENTIETH-CENTURY GROWTH

The opening of the Bath extension eclipsed the original S&D main line from Evercreech Junction to Burnham-on-Sea and, while the S&DJR continued to run steamer services across the Bristol Channel to Cardiff until 1888, the line soon became a rural railway backwater from which it never recovered. Despite

▼ A double-headed express blasts its way northbound near Prestleigh, south of Shepton Mallet, in August 1952. The leading engine is ex-LMS Class 2P 4-4-0 No. 40505, while the second engine is an S&D Class 7F 2-8-0, both fitted with single-line token exchangers on their tenders.

this, the S&D's Works at Highbridge continued to operate until 1930, although locomotive building was carried out by the Midland Railway's works at Derby. The main route, however, soon saw major improvements including the opening of the important Corfe Mullen Junction to Broadstone line in 1885, thus bypassing the awkward connection at Wimborne. With the opening of this cut-off, through trains from the North could run straight through to Bournemouth West.

Apart from the opening of the 7¼-mile Edington Junction to Bridgwater branch in 1890, the S&DJR was now complete. While the original main line slumbered on, the new main line from Bath to Broadstone saw a steady increase of through passenger and freight traffic. Soon the single-line sections couldn't cope with the increased traffic and the line was eventually doubled between Midford and Templecombe and between Blandford and Corfe Mullen Junction. Despite this, working the line over the Mendips with heavy passenger and freight trains became a major operational problem, especially during the First World War. Up until 1914, motive power on the main line was provided by underpowered MR-built 0-6-0s and 4-4-0s but 1914 saw the introduction of six of Fowler's 7F 2-8-0s specifically built to work on the S&DJR. This was such a phenomenal success – they could haul a ten-coach train over the Mendips without assistance – that five more were supplied by Robert Stephenson & Company in 1925.

Following the Big Four Grouping of 1923, the S&DJR was jointly taken over by the newly formed Southern Railway and London, Midland & Scottish Railway. Under the SR and LMS the line was initially still run as a separate entity from Bath Green Park; but this arrangement didn't last long. In a cost-cutting exercise in 1930, the line was divided up with the LMS taking on day-to-day operations and the SR responsible for the structure. Highbridge works was closed and what was left of the old S&D's coastal shipping business in the Bristol Channel was sold off. The Corfe Mullen to Wimborne line had already lost its passenger service in 1920 and this was followed by complete closure in 1933. However, despite the economic turndown of the 1930s and the loss of much local traffic to road transport, the S&DJR

▶ Green-liveried BR Standard Class 5MT 4-6-0 No. 73054 heads the 3.35pm train from Bristol Temple Meads to Bournemouth West a mile north of Templecombe on Whit Monday, 18 May 1964. By then the S&D was living on borrowed time, with less than two years to go before closure.

▼ A southbound train behind S&D 2-8-0 No. 53809 and a BR Standard Class 4 4-6-0 arrives at Evercreech junction on 1 September 1962. Through trains from the north to Bournemouth ceased running at the end of the summer timetable. The 7F was saved after spending 11 years at Woodham's scrapyard in Barry. Restored to working condition, it can be seen at the Midland Railway Centre in Butterley.

continued to see heavy through passenger trains from the Midlands and the North during the summer months. Notable among these was the 'Pines Express', which ran daily, apart from the war years, between Manchester and Bournemouth via the S&DJR from 1927 until September 1962. The final steam-hauled Pines Express over the S&DJR was headed by BR Standard 9F 2-10-0 No. 92220 'Evening Star'. Despite this, nearly all trains had to reverse into or out of Templecombe station before resuming their journey – an archaic working that continued until its closure in 1966.

POST-WAR PROBLEMS

The Second World War saw a massive increase in freight traffic over the line, particularly in the build up to the D-Day landings in 1944. After the war, the through holiday expresses resumed, including one unusual working: the Saturdays-only train between Cleethorpes and Exmouth. The nationalisation of Britain's railways in 1948 soon saw major cutbacks including the complete closure of the Glastonbury to Wells line and also passenger services between Highbridge and Burnham in 1951, followed by complete closure of Edington Junction to Bridgwater in 1954.

The first two years under BR management saw the S&DJR run along similar lines to that of previous years but regional boundary changes in 1950 saw all of the S&DJR north of Cole coming under Western Region and southwards under Southern Region control. However, the entire line was operated throughout by the Southern Region and this period soon saw new SR Bulleid 'West Country' and 'Battle of Britain' Pacifics working through to Bath on through trains to the North. Another boundary change in 1958 saw the S&DJR north of Henstridge come under complete operational control of the Western Region – this was the final straw and all through trains between the Midlands and the North and Bournemouth ceased at the end of the 1962 summer timetable. This act, seen by some as the GWR's revenge for being gazumped in 1875, was the beginning of the end for the S&DJR. Listed for closure in the 'Beeching Report' in 1963, the main line along with the Highbridge branch struggled on for three more years with a pathetic train service deliberately designed by the

WR to be of no social value at all. Closure was fixed for 3 January 1966, by which time the S&DJR, steam-hauled to the end, had become isolated from the rest of the system. Although goods services ceased on that day, a skeleton passenger service had to be introduced as a local bus operator withdrew his application to run an alternative bus service at the last moment. The death of the S&DJR was a slow and painfully sad affair and it was eventually put out of its misery on 7 March 1966.

▼ As there was no train service on a Sunday, the last regular trains had run over the S&D on Saturday 5 March 1966. However, the very last train to run the whole length of the S&D was a Stephenson Locomotive Society special from Bath Green Park to Bournemouth West on Sunday, 6 March. Here, the train is seen approaching Blandford Forum behind ex-LMS Class 8F 2-8-0 No. 48706 and BR Standard Class 4 2-6-4T No. 80043.

▲ Nearing the end of the line – BR Standard Class 4MT 4-6-0 No. 75027 approaches Corfe Mullen with an up express in the Summer of 1960. Although closed to passengers in March 1966, the S&D line northwards from Broadstone to Bailey Gate and Blandford remained open for goods and milk traffic until 1969.

THE LINE TODAY

After 45 years of slumber, the trackbed of the fondly remembered S&DJR is coming back to life, albeit mainly under different guises, at many locations along its route. In the north the graceful overall roof of Bath Green Park station has been preserved and is now a shopping centre, site for market stalls and part of a supermarket car park. The line south from here once climbed steadily through the chokingly smoky, single-bore Devonshire and Combe Down Tunnels, which are now being excavated in readiness for a 4-mile footpath and cycleway to Midford known as 'The Two Tunnels Greenway'.

At Midsomer Norton, National Cycle Network Route 48, which already uses the former GWR line from Radstock, is being extended along part of the old S&D route. It will be known as 'Five Arches Greenway'. Also at Midsomer Norton, the Somerset & Dorset Railway Heritage Trust (see opposite) has restored the former S&D station and is relaying track towards Masbury Summit.

South of Templecombe, the 2ft-gauge Gartell Light Railway runs along the trackbed of the S&D for a short distance while at Shillingstone (see opposite) the S&D station has been preserved and is now open to the public. On the Highbridge branch, a 5-mile section of the original Somerset Central main line west of Glastonbury is now a footpath and cycleway across the Somerset Levels to Shapwick Heath National Nature Reserve.

HERITAGE RAILWAYS

AVON VALLEY RAILWAY

Bitton Station, Bath Road, Bitton, Bristol BS30 6HD

Website: www.avonvalleyrailway.org

Tel: 0117 932 5538

Route: Oldland to Avon Riverside via Bitton

Length: 3 miles

Nearest main-line station: Keynsham

The former Midland Railway route from Mangotsfield to Bath (Green Park) opened in 1869 and closed in 1966. It was used as part of a through route linking the Midlands and the North with Bournemouth via the Somerset & Dorset Joint Railway, route of the famous 'Pines Express'. The first open day was held at Bitton station by the Bristol Suburban Railway Society in 1983. The first trains ran along the mile of line to Oldland in 1987. Oldland station opened in 1991 and in 2004 the section eastwards from Bitton to Avon Riverside was opened. The railway's long-term plan is to reach Bath once again.

◀ One of the last batch of steam locomotives built by BR, Standard Class 9F 2-10-0 No. 92207 was rescued after spending over 21 years languishing in Woodham's scrapyard in Barry. It is now based at Shillingstone station awaiting completion of restoration.

▶ Restored S&D 7F 2-8-0 No. 53809 returned close to home in 2006 when it paid a visit to the Avon Valley Railway near Bath.

GARTELL LIGHT RAILWAY

Common Lane, Yenston, Nr Templecombe, Somerset BA8 ODN

Website: www.glr-online.co.uk

Tel: 01963 370752

Route: Common Lane to Park Lane

Length: 1 mile

Nearest main-line station: Templecombe

This superb 2ft-gauge line partly runs along the trackbed of the old Somerset & Dorset Joint Railway, closed in 1966, a mile south of Templecombe, and is run by three generations of the Gartell family. From small beginnings in 1982 the first public open day was held in 1990. Motive power is provided by both steam and diesel locos and passengers can travel in either open-sided or covered bogie carriages. The line is fully signalled, using ex-BR equipment, and employs two fully operational signalboxes. Open days are on selected Sundays from the end of July to the end of October.

▲ Steam on the S&D again – 0-4-2T No. 6 'Mr G' waits for the road ahead at Pinesway Junction with a train for Common Lane on the Gartell Light Railway.

RAILWAY CENTRES

SOMERSET & DORSET RAILWAY HERITAGE TRUST

Midsomer Norton Station, Silver Street, Midsomer Norton BA3 2EY

Website: www.sdjr.co.uk

Tel: 01761 411221 (Sundays and Mondays only)

Nearest main-line station: none in area

Based at the restored S&D Midsomer Norton station, the Trust has also restored the former stable block and goods shed and reconstructed the signalbox, adjacent greenhouse and vegetable garden. Track has been laid southwards from the station towards Masbury and it is hoped that steam-hauled passenger trains over this short section will start soon. The station site is currently open to the public on Sundays and Mondays when diesel-hauled brakevan rides are operated. Extension of the line to Chilcompton is seen as a long-term goal for the Trust.

NORTH DORSET RAILWAY TRUST

Shillingstone Station, St Patricks Industrial Estate, Station Road, Shillingstone, Dorset DT11 0SA

Website: www.shillingstone.addr.com

Tel: 01258 860696

Nearest main-line station: none in area

Shillingstone station opened in 1863 on the line formed by the 1862 amalgamation of the Somerset Central and Dorset Central railways. The station was occasionally frequented by King Edward VII on his visits to nearby Iwerne Minster House and was closed along with the rest of the S&DJR on 7 March 1966. The signal-box and down platform shelters were demolished in 1967 but the main station building and platform have survived. After several industrial owners the station was leased to the North Dorset Railway Trust in 2003 and has since been restored. It is open to the public every Saturday, Sunday and Wednesday. BR Standard Class 9F 2-10-0 No. 92207 is currently awaiting restoration at Shillingstone.

THE ROLLER COASTER

Basingstoke to Exeter via Salisbury

The London & South Western Railway's switchback route to Exeter was a great success and opened the door to the company's domination of north Devon and north Cornwall. Its relegation to a secondary route in the 1960s can only be regretted.

The way west from Waterloo was fraught with difficulties. One potential route, the Southampton & Dorchester Railway, otherwise known as 'Castleman's Corkscrew' (see pages 72–79), had stopped dead at Dorchester and the proposed western extension along the Dorset and Devon coast to Exeter failed to materialise. Another approach was via the LSWR's long-winded route from Eastleigh, on their main line to Southampton, to Milford, on the outskirts of Salisbury, which opened in 1847. The following year the LSWR put forward a scheme for a railway linking Salisbury and Yeovil but this initially came to nothing.

It became pretty clear that the indirect approach to Salisbury via Eastleigh was clearly not the solution. What was eventually to become the London & South Western's main line to the West

▼ A scene long vanished from the now-sanitised Basingstoke station as rebuilt 'West Country' Class 4-6-2 No. 34025 'Whimple' (minus its valuable nameplates) takes on water while hauling a Waterloo to Salisbury train on 24 May 1966.

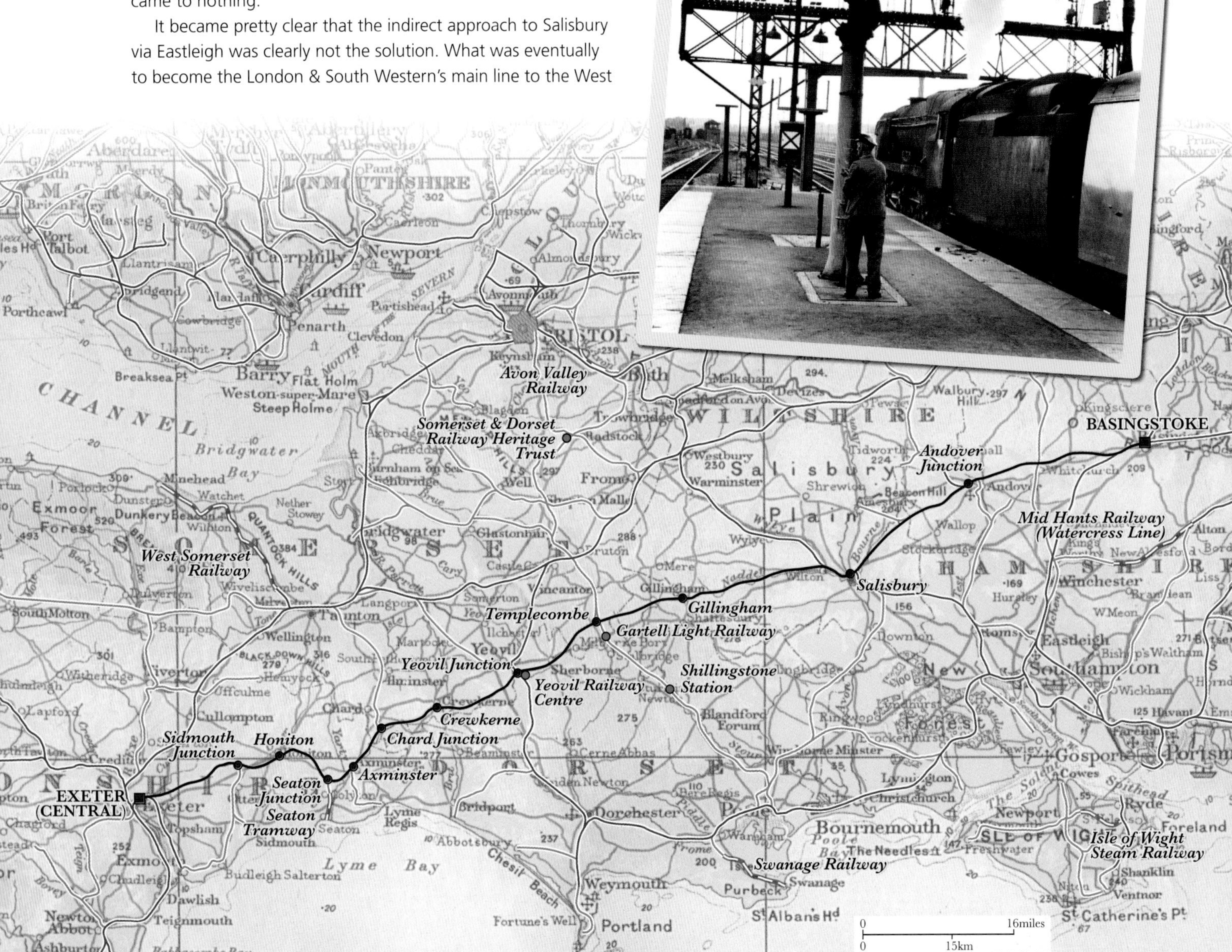

actually had its beginnings in the Basingstoke & Salisbury Railway, which had been authorised in 1846. Although work started on construction, this soon ceased and the abandoned route lay moribund until the LSWR took it over, opening to Andover in 1854 and to Milford station in Salisbury in 1857.

Meanwhile, the LSWR-backed Salisbury & Yeovil Railway had been resuscitated in 1854 with additional powers to extend the line to Exeter being granted in 1856. The first section of this route opened to Gillingham in 1859 and to Yeovil in 1860. Back at Salisbury, the GWR-backed Wiltshire, Somerset & Weymouth Railway had reached the city on broad gauge tracks from Westbury in 1856. Along with the opening of the LSWR line to Gillingham and a new connection with the line from Basingstoke, a new joint station was opened in 1859. Milford station was then closed but continued to be used for goods until the 1960s.

ESTABLISHING THE ROLLER COASTER

Striving to link up with its railway interests already in place west of Exeter (see pages 64–71) the LSWR built its Roller Coaster route in record-breaking time with a single-track line being completed from Yeovil to the city by 19 July 1860. This direct route was built at a cost as it bypassed all of the Dorset and East Devon coastal resorts and most of the important inland centres of population that it purported to serve – Shaftesbury, Yeovil, Crewkerne and Chard were all some distance from their nearest station. Despite this the line prospered financially and was doubled in 1870.

Schemes to link the bypassed resorts and towns with the main line followed in an erratic fashion. Exmouth had been reached from Exeter in 1861, the town of Chard was linked to the main line at Chard Junction in 1863, the branch line from Seaton Junction to Seaton opened in 1868 and that from Sidmouth Junction to Sidmouth in 1874. A proposal for a branch from Axminster to Lyme Regis was put forward as early as 1874 but, despite this early start, the harbour town did not get its railway until 1903. Budleigh Salterton had been reached from Tipton St John on the Sidmouth branch in 1897 and this line was extended to Exmouth by the LSWR in 1903. The situation at Yeovil was complicated as the broad gauge Bristol & Exeter Railway's branch from Durston had already reached the town in 1853 and the Wiltshire, Somerset & Weymouth's broad gauge line had arrived

▼ **The centre of attention, 'Merchant Navy' Class 4-6-2 No. 35015 'Rotterdam Lloyd' halts at Salisbury with the down 'Atlantic Coast Express' in 1964. This famous train made its final journey at the end of that year's summer timetable.**

▲ **Equally at home hauling heavy goods trains or stopping passenger trains, the workhorses of the LSWR main line west of Salisbury were the 'S15' Class 4-6-0s of Salisbury and Exmouth Junction sheds. Here, No. 30843 rumbles into Templecombe with a down goods train on 11 May 1962.**

▼ **A classic Michael Mensing panned shot of unrebuilt 'West Country' Class 4-6-2 No. 34015 'Swanage' as it heads the 7pm Waterloo to Exeter train 3 miles northeast of Salisbury on August Bank Holiday, 3 August 1964. This fine loco has since been preserved.**

at Pen Mill from Frome in 1856. On the completion of its main line to Exeter in 1860, the LSWR opened Yeovil Junction station and ran connecting trains from here via a spur to the new joint Town station.

By the beginning of the 20th century the LSWR empire was complete, stretching for 259¾ miles all the way from Waterloo to Padstow in North Cornwall (see pages 64–71). It not only served the growing coastal resorts of East and North Devon and North Cornwall but also the important ocean-liner terminal at Plymouth. Here passengers could disembark and continue their journey by train to London, a much quicker alternative than waiting to disembark at Southampton. Soon the LSWR and GWR were competing for the fastest service between Plymouth and London and this was to have tragic consequences for the LSWR at Salisbury on 1 July 1906 when a fast-moving boat train from Plymouth became derailed, smashing into a milk train on a sharp curve to the east of Salisbury station. Twenty-eight people lost their lives in this terrible accident and from that date all trains had to call at Salisbury for a water stop and, sometimes, a change of engine.

▼ *Main image* Looking in tip-top ex-works condition, rebuilt 'Battle of Britain' Class 4-6-2 No. 34059 'Sir Archibald Sinclair' heads an up milk train of six-wheeled tank wagons to Clapham Junction west of Milborne Port on Whit Monday, 18 May 1964. Milk traffic on the line from creameries at Chard Junction, Seaton Junction and Sherborne was once an important revenue-earner, ceasing only in 1980.

⯯ *Inset* Superpower at Axminster for the one-coach train to Lyme Regis – ex-LSWR Class '0415' 4-4-2Ts Nos 30582 and 30583 stand in the bay platform with a good head of steam on 17 August 1957. Ideal for travelling round the tight curves of the Lyme Regis branch, these veteran radial-tank locos were introduced in 1882, with three members remaining in service on the Lyme Regis branch until 1962. No. 30583, seen here, was later preserved and can be seen as a static exhibit on the Bluebell Railway.

THE 'ACE'

Without a doubt the most famous of the trains that ran over the LSWR route to Exeter and beyond was the 11am departure from Waterloo. Until the opening of the GWR's shorter route via Westbury and Castle Cary in 1904, this train competed with its GWR rival from Paddington to provide the fastest service to Exeter and Plymouth. Following the introduction of the Southern Railway's powerful 'Lord Nelson' Class 4-6-0s on the route in 1927, the train became known as the 'Atlantic Coast Express' and included through coaches for Sidmouth, Exmouth, Ilfracombe, Bude, Padstow and Plymouth. After the Second World War, the 'ACE', run in several portions, was headed by Bulleid's 'Merchant Navy' Class Pacifics until September 1964 when the train ceased to run. As there were no water troughs on the SR, even this famous train had to make a water stop at Salisbury. While not passing through any industrial areas, the LSWR main line to Exeter also once carried a high volume of agricultural and milk traffic to London – the latter finally ending in 1980.

The year 1963 saw the beginning of the decline of this once-important route. In that year all lines west of Salisbury came under Western Region control. Within a few years all through trains beyond Exeter had ceased, steam had been banished and replaced by worn-out WR diesel-hydraulics, most of the line was singled with passing loops and branch lines closed. Trains services that remained were not only slower but also unreliable – a sad end to this once-mighty holiday highway to the west.

At the eastern end, steam clung on to life between Salisbury and Basingstoke until 9 July 1967 when Salisbury shed closed. Branch-line closures started in 1962 with the closure of the Chard to Chard Junction branch; next was Axminster to Lyme Regis in 1965 followed by Yeovil Junction to Yeovil Town and Seaton Junction to Seaton in 1966 and Sidmouth Junction to Sidmouth and Exmouth in 1967. The north–south Somerset & Dorset Joint Railway (see pages 86–93), which connected with the LSWR main line at Templecombe, also closed in 1966. Only the Exeter to Exmouth line is still open for business.

▼ Rebuilt 'West Country' Class 4-6-2 No. 34100 'Appledore' makes light work of the three-coach 3.05pm train from Salisbury as it leaves Yeovil Junction station on 16 May 1964.

▼ Contrasting light Pacifics at Exeter Central – rebuilt 'West Country' Class 4-6-2 No. 34039 'Boscastle' waits on the centre line with an up ballast train from Meldon Quarry as unrebuilt 'Battle of Britain' 4-6-2 No. 34084 '253 Squadron' leaves with the 3.35pm stopping train to Yeovil Junction on 24 August 1964.

THE LINE TODAY

The Basingstoke to Exeter line is still open for business with trains between Waterloo and Exeter operated by South West Trains. The spur to the Bristol to Weymouth line at Yeovil is occasionally used as a diversionary route by First Great Western trains between Castle Cary and Exeter.

RAILWAY CENTRE

YEOVIL RAILWAY CENTRE

Yeovil Junction Station, Stoford, Nr Yeovil, Somerset BA22 9UU

Website: www.yeovilrailway.freeservers.com

Tel: 01935 410420

Route: within site along Clifton Maybank spur

Length: ¼ mile

Nearest main-line station: Yeovil Junction

The route of this short line, which opened in 1995, is from the former down platform at Yeovil Junction and along part of the former GWR Clifton Maybank spur, which closed over 60 years ago. Motive power currently consists of Peckett 0-4-0 saddle tank 'Pectin', with passengers conveyed in a brakevan. The locomotive turntable at Yeovil Junction, used by steam locomotives on main-line tours, is also leased from Network Rail by the railway's company, South West Main Line Steam Company.

TRAMWAY

SEATON TRAMWAY

Riverside Depot, Harbour Road, Seaton, Devon EX12 2NQ

Website: www.tram.co.uk

Tel: 01297 20375

Route: Seaton to Colyton

Length: 3 miles

Gauge: 2ft 9in

Nearest main-line station: Axminster

Originally opened in 1868 as a standard gauge branch from Seaton Junction, on the main line from Salisbury to Exeter, to Seaton. It was taken over by the London & South Western Railway in 1885 and eventually closed by BR in 1966. In 1969 Modern Electric Tramways of Eastbourne took over the trackbed and stock was moved to Seaton in 1970. The present 2ft 9in-gauge line from Seaton to Colyton was finally completed in 1980 and now miniature replica electric trams, taking their power from overhead wires, take passengers on a delightful trip first alongside the estuary of the River Axe and then, at Colyford station, along the valley of the River Coly to the present terminus (the original 1868 railway station) at Colyton. The fleet consists of five open-top double-deck trams, two enclosed trams, one toast-rack for disabled people and one illuminated tram for evening operating. A new Victorian tram-style terminus at Seaton was opened in 1995.

▲ Miniature replica tramcar No. 8 arrives at Seaton terminus from Colyton on the Seaton Tramway.

60056
4th GREAT YEAR

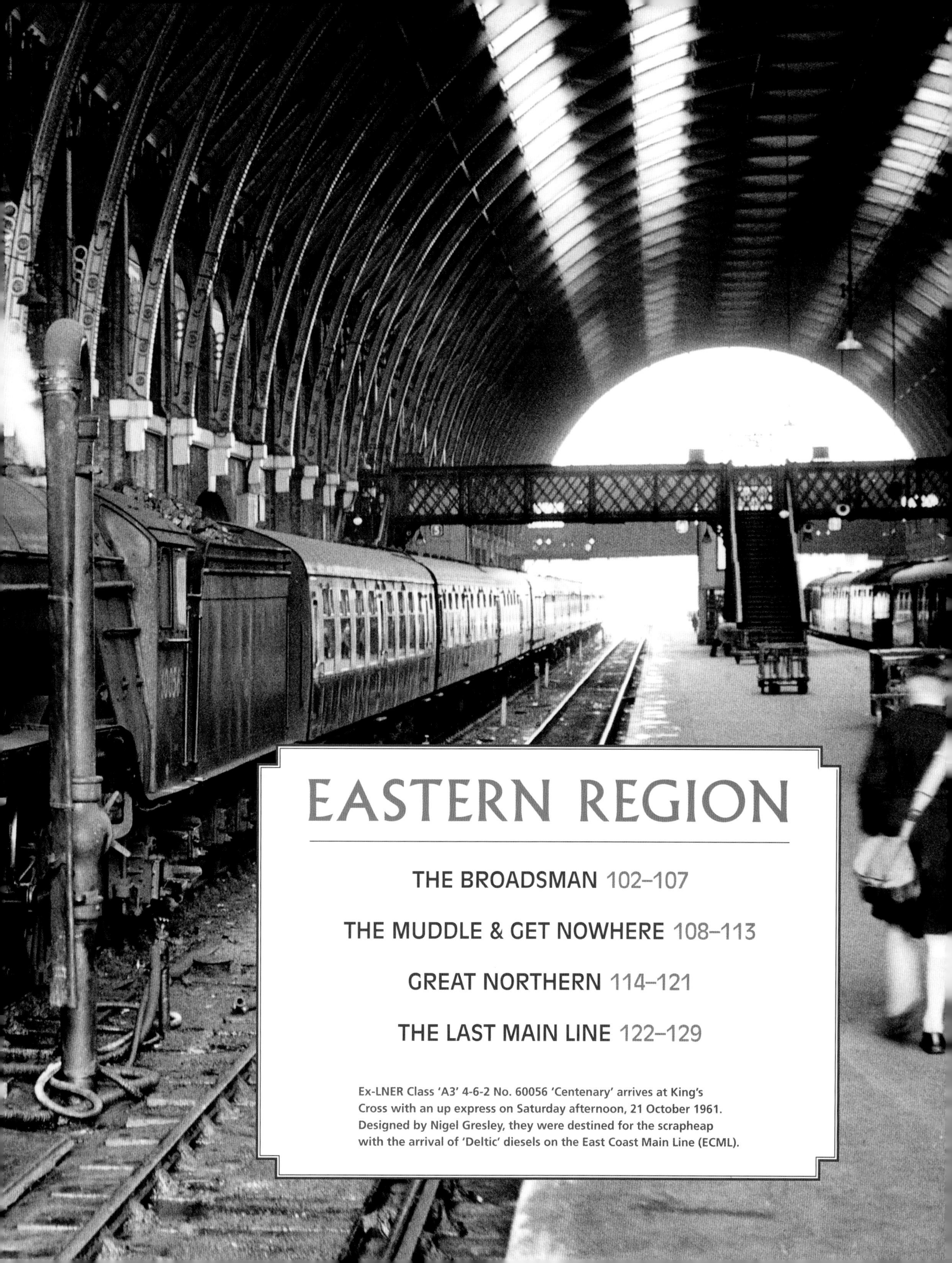

EASTERN REGION

Ex-LNER Class 'A3' 4-6-2 No. 60056 'Centenary' arrives at King's Cross with an up express on Saturday afternoon, 21 October 1961. Designed by Nigel Gresley, they were destined for the scrapheap with the arrival of 'Deltic' diesels on the East Coast Main Line (ECML).

THE BROADSMAN

Liverpool Street to Norwich

First built to a gauge of five feet, the Eastern Counties Railway finally achieved a virtual stranglehold on East Anglian railways by takeovers, leasing and working arrangements. Its lacklustre services were greatly improved by its successor, the Great Eastern Railway.

What was to become the Great Eastern Railway's main line from Liverpool Street to Norwich started life as the Eastern Counties Railway (ECR). Incorporated in 1836, the 126-mile line from London to Great Yarmouth via Norwich was the longest railway in Britain to be authorised at that time. The company's estimate of construction costs was wildly over-optimistic and by the time it had reached Colchester, construction costs had amounted to 50 per cent more than the original budget for the whole route.

Strangely, the railway was built to a gauge of 5ft, although it was converted to standard gauge only a year after opening. The first section from a temporary terminus in Mile End to Romford opened in 1839, from Mile End back to the new terminus at Bishopsgate and from Romford to Brentwood in 1840 and to Colchester in 1843.

▲ **Steam power – ex-LNER Class 'B1' 4-6-0 No. 61004 'Oryx' of Parkeston shed (30F) prepares to leave Liverpool St with the down 'Day Continental' express to Harwich Parkeston Quay on 8 July 1958. Introduced in 1947, this named train replaced the pre-war 'Flushing Continental'.**

▼ **BR Standard 7MT 'Britannia' Class 4-6-2 No. 70007, 'Coeur-de-Lion', a 32A (Norwich) engine, is being turned at Liverpool Street ready for a fast London to Norwich express in the mid 1950s. Introduced in the early 1950s, the 'Britannias' of Stratford and Norwich sheds were replaced in 1961.**

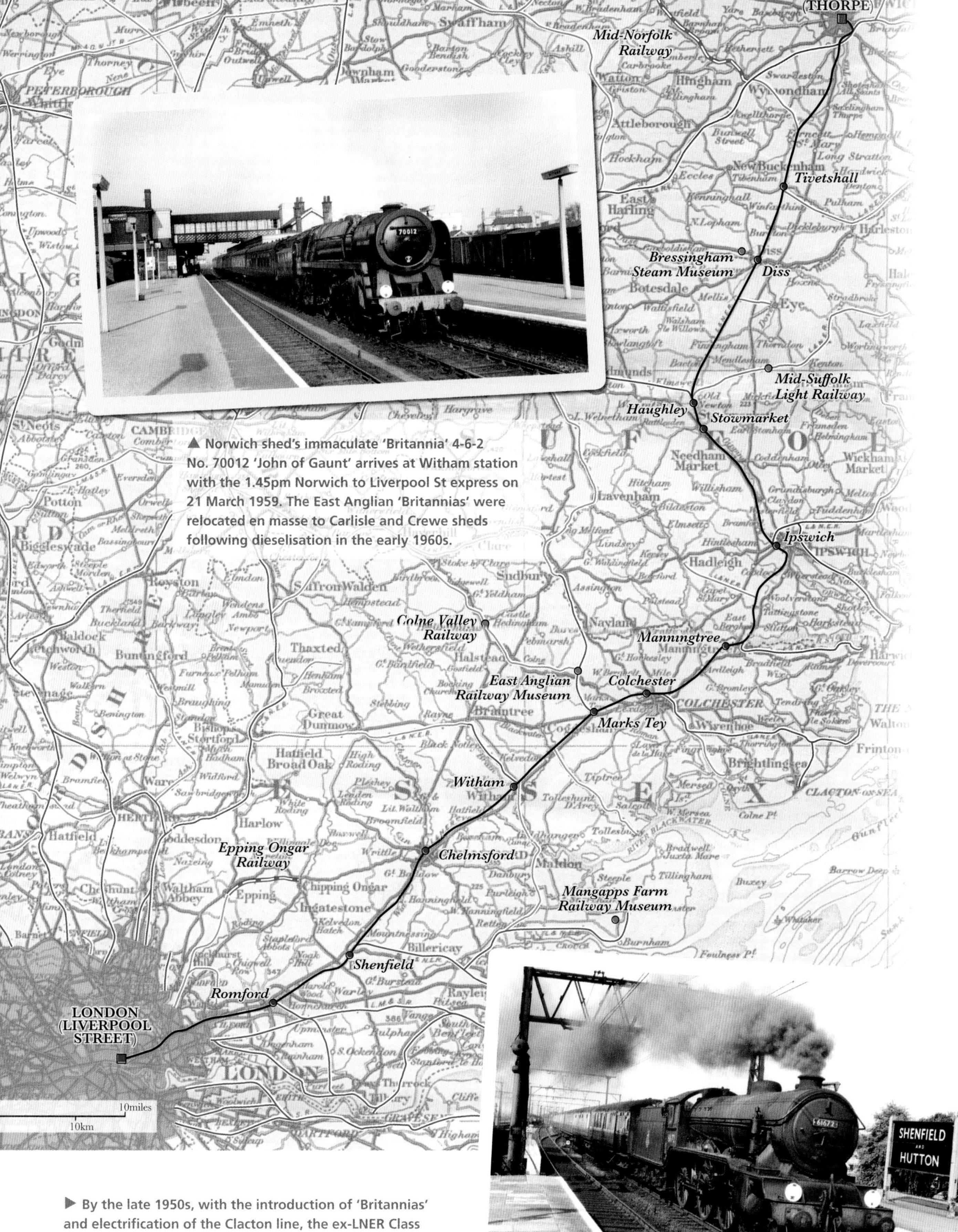

▲ Norwich shed's immaculate 'Britannia' 4-6-2 No. 70012 'John of Gaunt' arrives at Witham station with the 1.45pm Norwich to Liverpool St express on 21 March 1959. The East Anglian 'Britannias' were relocated en masse to Carlisle and Crewe sheds following dieselisation in the early 1960s.

▶ By the late 1950s, with the introduction of 'Britannias' and electrification of the Clacton line, the ex-LNER Class B17 'Sandringham' 4-6-0s' days were numbered. Here, Stratford's No. 61672 'West Ham United' storms through Shenfield with the 2.50pm train from Clacton to Liverpool St on 23 July 1955.

▲Veteran ex-GER locos still clung to life on the East Anglian main line into the 1950s. Here, Class 'E4' 2-4-0 No. 62795 leaves Marks Tey with the 1.15pm train from Cambridge to Colchester on 24 November 1952. One member of this class, No. 62785, has been preserved and can be seen at Bressingham Steam Museum.

AN EAST ANGLIAN RAILWAY

While the Eastern Counties Railway initially failed to reach its goals of Norwich and Great Yarmouth, it did eventually achieve this through various acquisitions, leasing and agreed working arrangements with other lines. First, in 1844, it leased the Northern & Eastern Railway, which had already opened its 5ft-gauge line from Islington to Bishop's Stortford in 1842. This, too, was converted to standard gauge and extended to Cambridge and Brandon in 1845. The ECR then took over the Norfolk Railway in 1848 (this company already owned nearly 100 route miles stretching from Brandon to Yarmouth via Norwich), absorbed the bankrupt East Anglian Railways in 1852 and took over working the Eastern Union Railway in 1854. The latter had already opened its line throughout from Colchester to Norwich (Victoria) and from Ipswich to Bury St Edmunds in 1849. Despite its faltering start only 13 years previously, the Eastern Counties Railway now controlled much of the railway network in East Anglia.

▼ In ex-works condition, ex-GER Class 'B12/3' 4-6-0 No. 61576 looks very smart in lined BR black as it heads the Suffolk Venturer railtour at Colchester in September 1956. Another member of this class, No. 61572, has been preserved and can be seen on the North Norfolk Railway (see page 112).

◀ The photographer's open bag, complete with vital notebooks, seems to be attracting attention from a suspicious bystander at Ipswich station on 20 August 1960. The object of the photographer's desire is Norwich's 'Britannia' Class 7MT 4-6-2 No, 70007 'Coeur-de-Lion' arriving on a down express.

RAPID GROWTH

Despite, or probably as the result of, this extensive railway network, the ECR had a poor reputation for service. In 1862 it became the main constituent company of the newly formed Great Eastern Railway and matters on the ground soon started to improve. The former ECR works at Stratford was expanded and a new London terminus at Liverpool Street completed in 1875. By the end of the century, passenger services between Liverpool Street and Norwich had been transformed. Faster and heavier trains hauled by Stratford-built locomotives designed by Worsdell and the Holdens were providing passengers with services undreamt of only a few years before. The introduction of slip coaches at various stations along the line towards the end of the century also played a major part in accelerating services. The introduction of Stephen Holden's magnificent Class S69 (later classified as LNER Class B12) 4-6-0s in 1911 was also a massive step forward on the GER main line. While the main line went from strength to strength, suburban services out of Liverpool Street also saw a rapid growth with the line to Shenfield experiencing increasing congestion during the rush-hour periods. Norwich (Victoria) station remained open until 1916 by which date all trains from Liverpool Street had been diverted to Norwich (Thorpe).

The Great Eastern Railway became one of the main constituents of the newly formed LNER in 1923. By the 1930s Gresley's Class B17 4-6-0s (known as 'Sandringhams') were putting up electrifying performances on expresses such as the

▼ 'Britannia' Class 7MT 4-6-2 No. 70010 'Owen Glendower' at full throttle as it thunders towards Stowmarket station over Stowupland Road level crossing with an up express on 27 April 1959.

▼ **End of the line at Norwich Thorpe – Stratford's 'Britannia' Class 7MT 4-6-2 No. 70001 'Lord Hurcomb' waits to depart with the up 'East Anglian' express to Liverpool St in the late 1950s.**

'Norfolk Coast Express'. Suburban congestion out of Liverpool Street was improved by adding more tracks, and electrification of what was the most intensive steam-hauled suburban service in the world was on the cards. However, the Second World War intervened and nationalisation of the railways followed in 1948.

THE BRITISH RAIL YEARS

The former GER main line continued to see major improvements under new British Railways management. Liverpool Street to Shenfield was electrified in 1949 and new BR 'Britannia' 4-6-2s, introduced in 1951, were soon putting in sparkling performances on named trains such as 'The Broadsman', 'Hook Continental', 'The Norfolkman', the 'Essex Coast Express' and 'The East Anglian'. Electrification was extended from Shenfield to Chelmsford in 1955 and to Colchester (for the Clacton line) in 1959. In the meantime, the 'Britannias' had been ousted from Liverpool Street to Norwich expresses and been replaced, initially, by English Electric Type 4 diesels and, later, by Brush Type 4 diesels. They in turn were ousted when the Colchester to Norwich section was finally electrified in 1987. The route is currently prospering and passenger numbers have increased more than two-fold in the past five years, while Liverpool Street sees around 56 million passengers each year.

THE LINE TODAY

Passenger services between Liverpool Street and Norwich are provided by National Express East Anglia.

HERITAGE RAILWAYS

MID-SUFFOLK LIGHT RAILWAY

Brockford Station, Wetheringsett, Stowmarket, Suffolk IP14 5PW

Website: www.mslr.org.uk

Tel: 01449 672670

Route: within site at Brockford station

Length: ½ mile

Nearest main-line station: Stowmarket

The Mid-Suffolk Light Railway was an ambitious scheme to build lines from Haughley to Halesworth via Stradbroke and Laxfield, with a branch from Kenton to Westerfield. Work started in 1902, and the line was completed for 21 miles as far as Cratfield by 1904, when goods traffic started. Severe financial difficulties prevented much work on the Kenton to Westerfield line, although it was partly constructed as far as Debenham. The line went into receivership before opening to passengers between Haughley and Laxfield in 1908. There were difficulties crossing the marshes near Halesworth, and before long the line beyond Laxfield, and all of the Westerfield branch were abandoned. The company remained independent of the Great Eastern Railway, and was taken over by the LNER in 1924. It survived the latter's proposal to turn it into a motor road in the 1930s, and closed to all traffic in 1952, being lifted the following year. The present museum was established in 1991, and has brought a number of original MSLR buildings from Mendlesham, Brockford and Wilby on to the site. Steam trains also operate on Sundays. Visitors can use the Trackbed Walk of about 1 mile and also the waymarked Middy Light Railway Long Distance Path between Haughley and Brockford.

▼ **'FD&Co. No3' heads a train of vintage carriages on the Mid-Suffolk Light Railway near Brockford.**

COLNE VALLEY RAILWAY

Castle Hedingham Station, Yeldham Road, Castle Hedingham, Halstead, Essex CO9 3DZ

Website: www.colnevalleyrailway.co.uk

Tel: 01787 461174

Route: either side of Castle Hedingham station

Length: 1 mile

The Colne Valley & Halstead Railway, completely opened in 1863 between Chappel & Wakes Colne and Haverhill, survived as an independent company until 1923 when it was absorbed into the LNER. Following a very busy period during the First World War, the line returned to its normal operation, and after a short experiment with diesel railcars, passenger services ceased in 1961 and the line closed in 1965. In 1973, a preservation group moved in and started to clear the site. The first 'steam up' was held in 1975 and the first of many educational events in 1979. Castle Hedingham station has been re-created on a new site, using the original Colne Valley station building from Castle & Sible Hedingham, and a large quantity of steam and diesel locomotives and rolling stock is preserved here. The railway specialises in educational visits and is well known for its excellent Pullman dining service, operated in three historic carriages creating a luxurious atmosphere. Operating days are usually at weekends and Bank Holidays plus Wednesdays and Thursdays in August.

MUSEUMS

EAST ANGLIAN RAILWAY MUSEUM

Chappel & Wakes Colne Station, Wakes Colne, Essex C06 2DS

Website: www.earm.co.uk

Tel: 01206 242524

Nearest main-line station: Chappel & Wakes Colne

This working museum contains a comprehensive collection of railway architecture, engineering and relics representing over 100 years of railways in the Eastern Counties. It was formed in 1968 as the Stour Valley Railway Preservation Society to preserve a section of the Stour Valley Railway when closure was threatened. When closure did not occur, the museum, a registered charity, was formed in 1986. Chappel & Wakes Colne station is situated on the former GER branch line from Marks Tey to Cambridge via Haverhill. It opened in 1849 and is still open today as far as Sudbury. Built in the 1890s, the station building is a classic example of GER architecture and is restored to its original condition with a heritage centre situated in the storage arches underneath. Two restored signalboxes include the original, no longer in operation, and another from Mistley, near Manningtree, that now controls train movements within the site. The museum is situated near to Chappel Viaduct, which was opened in 1849. It is the longest viaduct in East Anglia and is reputed to be the largest brick structure in Europe, containing more than seven million bricks, with each of the 32 arches being 30ft wide. Running days, vintage train events and a miniature railway day are held on various weekends throughout the year.

BRESSINGHAM STEAM MUSEUM AND GARDENS

Low Road, Bressingham, Diss, Norfolk IP22 2AA

Website: www.bressingham.co.uk

Tel: 01379 686900

Nearest main-line station: Diss

Bressingham is not only known for its extensive steam museum but also for its superb gardens and nurseries, totalling 480 acres. Created by Alan Bloom in 1973, the railway enthusiast is well catered for with 10¼ in, 15in and 2ft steam-operating lines and a standard gauge museum. The 'Garden Line', which opened in 1965, originally 9¼in-gauge but converted to 10¼in during 1995, is the shortest, taking passengers on a 1,350yd ride through the house garden. The 15in-gauge 'Waveney Valley Railway', opened in 1973 and now 2½ miles in length, runs for part of its journey alongside the River Waveney and is powered by two 1937 Krupp-built German 4-6-2s, 'Rosenkavalier' and 'Mannertrau' and a 1976-built 4-6-2 'Flying Scotsman'. The 2ft-gauge 'Nursery Line', at 2½ miles in length, opened in 1966 and takes passengers through the nurseries not normally open to the public. Four steam locos work this line, including two Hunslet 0-4-0 saddle tanks, 'Gwynedd' (built 1883) and 'George Sholto' (built 1909), rescued from the Penrhyn Slate Quarries in North Wales. Passengers are carried in open toast-rack coaches. The standard gauge museum houses royal coaches and main line steam locomotives including London, Tilbury & Southend Railway 4-4-2 tank 'Thundersley', GER Class T26 2-4-0 No. 490 and GNR 4-4-2 No. 990 'Henry Oakley'. A standard gauge demonstration line operates on Sundays and during special events.

▶ **An Austrian (OBB) Class 52 No. 5865 built in 1944 for Norway dwarfs the 2ft-gauge 0-4-0T 'Gwyned' in Bressingham Gardens.**

THE MUDDLE & GET NOWHERE

The Midland & Great Northern Joint Railway

On its formation in 1893, the Midland & Great North Joint Railway, with 182 route miles, was the largest jointly owned railway company in the UK. Once busy with through freight and holiday traffic, mounting losses from road competition brought about its demise in 1959.

The Midland & Great Northern Joint Railway's origins lay not only with the multitude of independent companies that sprouted up around East Anglia in the 19th century, but also with the desires of the mighty Midland Railway and Great Northern Railway to enter Great Eastern Railway territory.

COMPLEX HISTORIES

It all started back in 1866 when the Midland & Eastern Railway had been formed by the amalgamation of the Lynn & Sutton Bridge Railway and the Spalding & Bourn [sic] Railway. The new company also went on to absorb the Norwich & Spalding Railway in 1877. Farther west the Peterborough, Wisbeach & Sutton Bridge Railway had opened in 1866 and was worked from the outset by the Midland Railway.

Thereafter, the story of the railway was far from simple. In 1880 the Lynn & Fakenham Railway opened its 20-mile line from King's Lynn to Fakenham. An extension to Melton Constable, where the company established a railway works, and to Norwich (City) followed in 1882. To the east, the Great Yarmouth & Stalham Light Railway opened between Yarmouth and Hemsby in 1878 and to North Walsham in 1881, by which time the company had changed its name to the Yarmouth & North Norfolk Railway. A much smaller operation, the Yarmouth Union Railway, opened between Yarmouth (Beach) Station and Yarmouth Quay in 1882.

Now it gets more complicated. In January 1883, the Eastern & Midlands Railway was formed by the amalgamation of the Lynn & Fakenham, Yarmouth & North Norfolk and Yarmouth Union railways with the intervening gap between Melton Constable and North Walsham being opened in April of the same year. In July, the fledgling Eastern & Midlands also absorbed the Midland & Eastern Railway and the Peterborough, Wisbech & Sutton Bridge Railway. The new railway went on to open the 15-mile branch from Melton Constable to Cromer in 1887. What would become the Midland & Great Northern Joint Railway was now complete.

FREIGHT AND THE 'DOODLE-BUGS'

Local traffic on the Eastern & Midlands Railway or the later M&GN was never heavy but where the company achieved a major advantage was by moving large amounts of freight into and out of the system via the Midland Railway at Peterborough and the

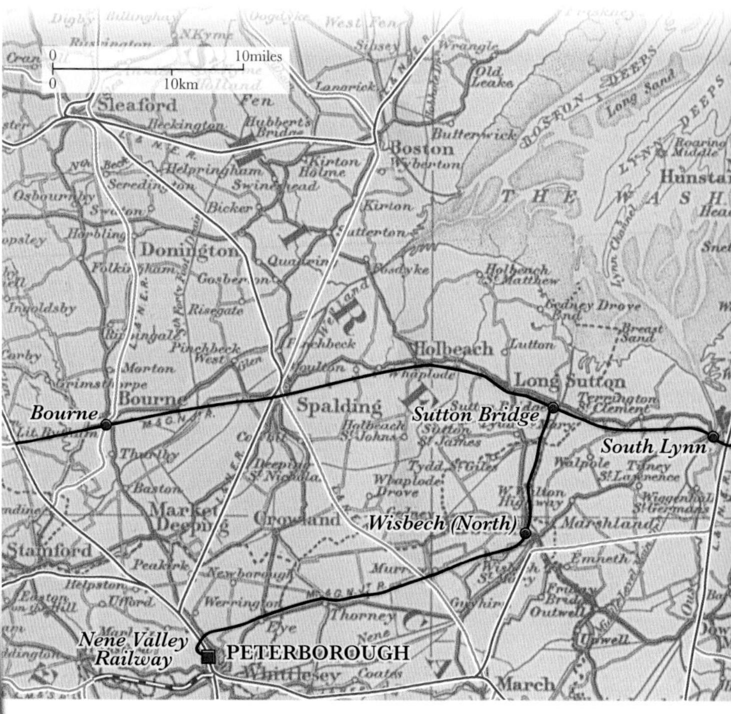

◀ **The M&GN met the Midland Railway's line from Saxby at Little Bytham Junction. Holidaymakers to Norfolk on Summer Saturday trains were taken from Birmingham New Street on a slow and convoluted journey to their destination. Here, the 1.45pm from Birmingham to Yarmouth, Cromer and Norwich heads through Castle Bytham station in August 1957.**

▲ Nearing the end – Ivatt Class 4MT 2-6-0 No. 43065 heads an M&GN train at Spalding on 21 February 1959, less than two weeks before the whole system closed. Affectionately known as 'mucky ducks' or 'doodle-bugs', these rather less-than-beautiful locos were the mainstay of the M&GN in the 1950s.

Great Northern Railway at Spalding, Bourne and Peterborough. Summer holiday traffic from outside the system also later became important, although the preponderance of single-track main line was not conducive to a speedy service.

The Eastern & Midlands Railway soon fell on hard times and, on 1 July 1893, it was taken over by the Midland Railway and Great Northern Railway to form the Midland & Great Northern Joint Railway. Connections with the Midland Railway were greatly improved by the opening of a direct route from Bourne to Saxby in Leicestershire in 1898. While owned equally by the

▲ Ivatt Class 4MT 2-6-0 No. 43094 clanks across the swing bridge over the River Nene at Sutton Bridge with the 12.58pm Peterborough to Yarmouth train on 30 August 1958. Once carrying both rail and road, the bridge survives today.

◀ The Midland & Great Northern Joint Railway Preservation Society ran a railtour over parts of the closed system on 27 May 1961. Here, spotlessly clean Ivatt Class 4MT 2-6-0 No. 43151 halts at Wisbech North on the Peterborough to Sutton Bridge line.

MR and GNR, the new joint railway remained autonomous until 1936 – it had its headquarters in King's Lynn, its own locomotive and wagon works at Melton Constable (where it employed several hundred men), its own coat of arms and its own livery, with locomotives painted a light golden brown. Despite a rather eclectic mix of locomotives from the various constituent companies, the mainstay of motive power on the M&GN were the 15 handsome Beyer-Peacock 4-4-0s that had been introduced in 1881 and remained in service until 1936 when LNER locos such as Class K2 2-6-0s and ex-GER 'Claud Hamilton' 4-4-0s took over. From nationalisation in 1948 to closure in 1959 these were replaced by the ex-LMS Ivatt Class 4 2-6-0s or 'doodle-bugs', as they were affectionately known.

FINAL YEARS OF THE M&GN

Until the 1940s, the M&GN system saw fairly substantial amounts of freight traffic including fish from Great Yarmouth, cattle and agricultural produce such as grain, sugar beet, potatoes, cabbages, flowers and fruit. Passenger traffic was very heavy during the summer months with through workings to Cromer and Yarmouth from King's Cross, Manchester, Sheffield, Birmingham, Leicester and Nottingham. In 1923, the M&GN

◀ A group of schoolboys are instructed in the fine art of trainspotting at Melton Constable station as ex-LNER Class B17/6 4-6-0 No. 61654 'Sunderland' prepares to leave in 1956. The hub of the system, Melton Constable closed in 1936.

▼ Ex-LNER Class D16/3 4-4-0 No. 62533 departs from West Runton with a Melton Constable to Cromer Beach train in September 1953. The section from Cromer to Sheringham via West Runton is the only surviving stretch of the M&GN still open for regular passenger services.

▲ End of the line at Yarmouth – Ivatt Class 4MT 2-6-0 No. 43108 departs from Beach station with the 6.02pm train to South Lynn on 28 August 1958. Yarmouth Beach station closed on 2 March 1959 along with most of the M&GN system.

passed into the joint ownership of the newly formed LMS and LNER but by the 1930s competition from road traffic was starting to take its toll. The LNER took over railway operations in 1936, introducing economies and closing the locomotive works at Melton Constable and the admin headquarters in King's Lynn. Losses were mounting and, while the Second World War brought a reprieve, the end was in sight for this straggling, mainly single-track, rural railway. Under the new cost-cutting British Railways' management, closure of almost the whole system came on 2 March 1959. The only lines to escape were those from Spalding to Sutton Bridge (retained for freight until 1965), Murrow to Eye Green (retained for freight until 1966), Cromer to Sheringham (still open for passenger traffic), Sheringham to Melton Constable (which closed to passengers in 1964) and from Melton Constable to Norwich (City), which continued to see freight until 1960 when the Themelthorpe Curve was opened near Whitwell & Reepham. This allowed freight traffic to travel via the former GER Bure Valley route and then down the remaining M&GN section to Norwich. The line was cut back to Lenwade in 1969 where a concrete works continued to be served by rail until 1982.

▲ **With a sea of caravans in the distance, ex-GER Class B12/3 No. 61540 approaches Yarmouth, south of Caister-on-Sea, with a train from Melton Constable and beyond in the late 1950s. One member of this class, No. 61572, has been preserved and can be seen on the North Norfolk Railway.**

THE LINE TODAY

Much of the M&GN's route across the Fens has long ago disappeared beneath ploughed fields, although many of the former station buildings are now private residences. At Sutton Bridge, the famous 1897-built road-rail swing bridge over the River Nene still stands in all its glory, although today it carries only road traffic.

The trackbed of the Norwich (City) to Melton Constable section northwards from Hellesdon to the site of the 1960 Themelthorpe Curve now forms part of the Marriott's Way footpath and cycleway. At Themelthorpe this continues eastwards along the former Great Eastern Railway's line to Reepham.

On the Melton Constable to Yarmouth section, the 61-mile Weavers' Way long-distance path between Cromer and Yarmouth uses the trackbed of the M&GN between Aylsham, North Walsham and Honing.

On the Melton Constable to Cromer branch, the section from Cromer to Sheringham is still open with trains operated by National Express East Anglia (marketed as the 'Bittern Line'). The 5¼-mile section between Sheringham and Holt was reopened as the North Norfolk Railway in 1989 (see below).

HERITAGE RAILWAYS

NORTH NORFOLK RAILWAY

Sheringham Station, Station Approach,
Sheringham, Norfolk NR26 8RA

Website: www.nnrailway.co.uk

Tel: 01263 820800

Route: Sheringham to Holt

Length: 5½ miles

Nearest main-line station: Sheringham

The steeply-graded North Norfolk Railway route was originally part of the meandering Midland & Great Northern Joint Railway that linked the Midlands and Peterborough with Cromer, Great Yarmouth and Norwich. The majority of this cross-country line was closed in 1959. The present NNR is on the trackbed of the Melton Constable to Cromer Beach branch of the MGNJR, which was closed in 1964. After several rather optimistic preservation plans on other parts of the system were rejected as impractical, the preservation group moved in, initially at Weybourne, now based at Sheringham. In 1969, the year John Betjeman became the NNR's president, the railway became the first of the preservation societies to be floated as a public company, and by 1989 the present route was fully reopened. The restored period stations, particularly at Weybourne, have often been used as TV and film locations. A large collection of restored steam and diesel locomotives and ex-LNER rolling stock operate the trains. The current star is ex-LNER Class B12 4-6-0 No. 8572, built in 1928, which was returned to traffic in early 1995 after a major rebuild at Mansfeld locomotive works in Germany. Other steam locomotives include Great Eastern Railway Class J15 0-6-0 No. 564, built in 1912, and several industrial examples built by Hunslet, Andrew Barclay and Bagnall. A railway museum and museum signalbox are open to the public at Sheringham.

▲ Visiting ex-GWR 'City' Class 4-4-0 No. 3717 'City of Truro' approaches Weybourne on the North Norfolk Railway. Part of the National Railway Museum collection, this loco is normally based at Toddington on the Gloucestershire Warwickshire Railway.

WELLS & WALSINGHAM LIGHT RAILWAY

Wells-next-the-Sea, Norfolk NR23 1RB

Website: www.wellswalsinghamrailway.co.uk

Tel: 01328 711630

Route: Wells-next-the-Sea to Little Walsingham

Length: 4 miles

Nearest main-line station: none in area

The longest 10¼in-gauge railway in the world also operates the most powerful steam locomotive of that gauge – a 20ft-long 'Garratt' 2-6-0+0-6-2 'Norfolk Hero', built in 1986. This unique little line, owned, built and operated by retired naval commander Roy Francis, opened in 1982 on the trackbed of the old standard gauge Wells & Fakenham Railway, which opened in 1857 and was closed by BR in 1964. An 0-6-0 tank engine, 'Pilgrim', operated services from opening until 1986. Intermediate halts are provided at Warham St Mary and Wighton, and a former Great Eastern Railway signalbox, originally sited at Swainsthorpe, has been preserved at Wells station and is now a shop and tea room.

MID-NORFOLK RAILWAY

Dereham Station, Station Road, Dereham, Suffolk NR19 1DF

Website: www.mnr.org.uk

Tel: 01362 690633

Route: Wymondham Abbey to Dereham

Length: 11½ miles

Nearest main-line station: Wymondham

Formerly part of the Great Eastern Railway's line from Wymondham to King's Lynn, which was closed in stages between 1964 and 1989. Opening as a tourist line in 1997, the railway operates mainly diesel services between Wymondham and Dereham with intermediate stations at Yaxham (where there is also a short 2ft-gauge line), Thuxton and Kimberley Park. Visiting steam locomotives can occasionally be seen at work on the line. The railway also owns a further 6 miles of track northwards from Dereham to the restored County School station; once this opens the Mid-Norfolk Railway will be the third longest heritage railway in England. Charter and excursion trains along with commercial freight traffic and MOD military traffic also use the line via the connection with the national rail network at Wymondham. Numerous special events such as vintage rallies are also held by the railway.

BURE VALLEY RAILWAY

Aylsham Station, Norwich Road, Aylsham, Norwich NR11 6BW

Website: www.bvrw.co.uk

Tel: 01263 733858

Route: Aylsham to Wroxham

Length: 9 miles

Nearest main-line station: Wroxham

The Bure Valley Railway runs along part of the trackbed of the branch line from Wroxham to Aylsham, opened by the East Norfolk Railway in 1878 and extended to County School in 1880. It was finally closed by BR in 1982. The 15in-gauge line cost £2.5 million to build and was opened by author and broadcaster Miles Kington as a miniature passenger-carrying line in 1990. Since then it has had no fewer than five owners. The Bure Valley station at Wroxham is adjacent to that of the main network, connected by a footbridge, and has a three-track layout with a turntable. As the line meanders along the valley of the River Bure, alongside the Bure Valley Walk, it passes through three other stations, at Coltishall, Brampton and Buxton, before arriving at Aylsham through a ¼-mile long tunnel, where the railway has its overall-roofed terminus, engine sheds and workshops. Five steam locomotives and one diesel operate the line and visiting engines from the Romney, Hythe & Dymchurch Railway and the Ravenglass & Eskdale Railway can occasionally be seen at work. Combined rail and Broads boat excursions are available in the summer.

▼ Based on the Indian railways' 'ZB' Class, 2-6-2 'Spitfire' prepares to leave Aylsham station with a train for Wroxham on the 15in-gauge Bure Valley Railway.

GREAT NORTHERN

King's Cross to Doncaster

Despite the underhand activities of its rivals at Euston (in particular, the financier George Hudson), the Great Northern Railway (GNR) succeeded in building a world-beating railway that, through peacetime and wartime, has stood the test of time.

Although it was possible to travel by train from London to York by 1840, the journey was always very indirect and time consuming. Passengers first had to travel from the London & Birmingham Railway's new terminus at Euston to Hampton-in-Arden, then on the Birmingham & Derby Junction Railway to Derby, followed by the North Midland Railway to Leeds and finally the York & North Midland Railway (part of it over the metals of the Leeds & Selby Railway) to York. Much of this journey was travelled over railways owned by George Hudson, the wealthy but corrupt Mayor of York, railway financier and later politician who became known as 'The Railway King'.

Ex-LNER Class 'A4' 4-6-2 No. 60025 'Falcon' of King's Cross shed (34A) gets ready to leave King's Cross station with a northbound express in 1953. The culmination of Nigel Gresley's tenure as Chief Mechanical Engineer of the LNER, the 'A4s', or 'Streaks' as they are known, live on with the preservation of no fewer than four examples in the UK and two others as static exhibits in Canada and the USA.

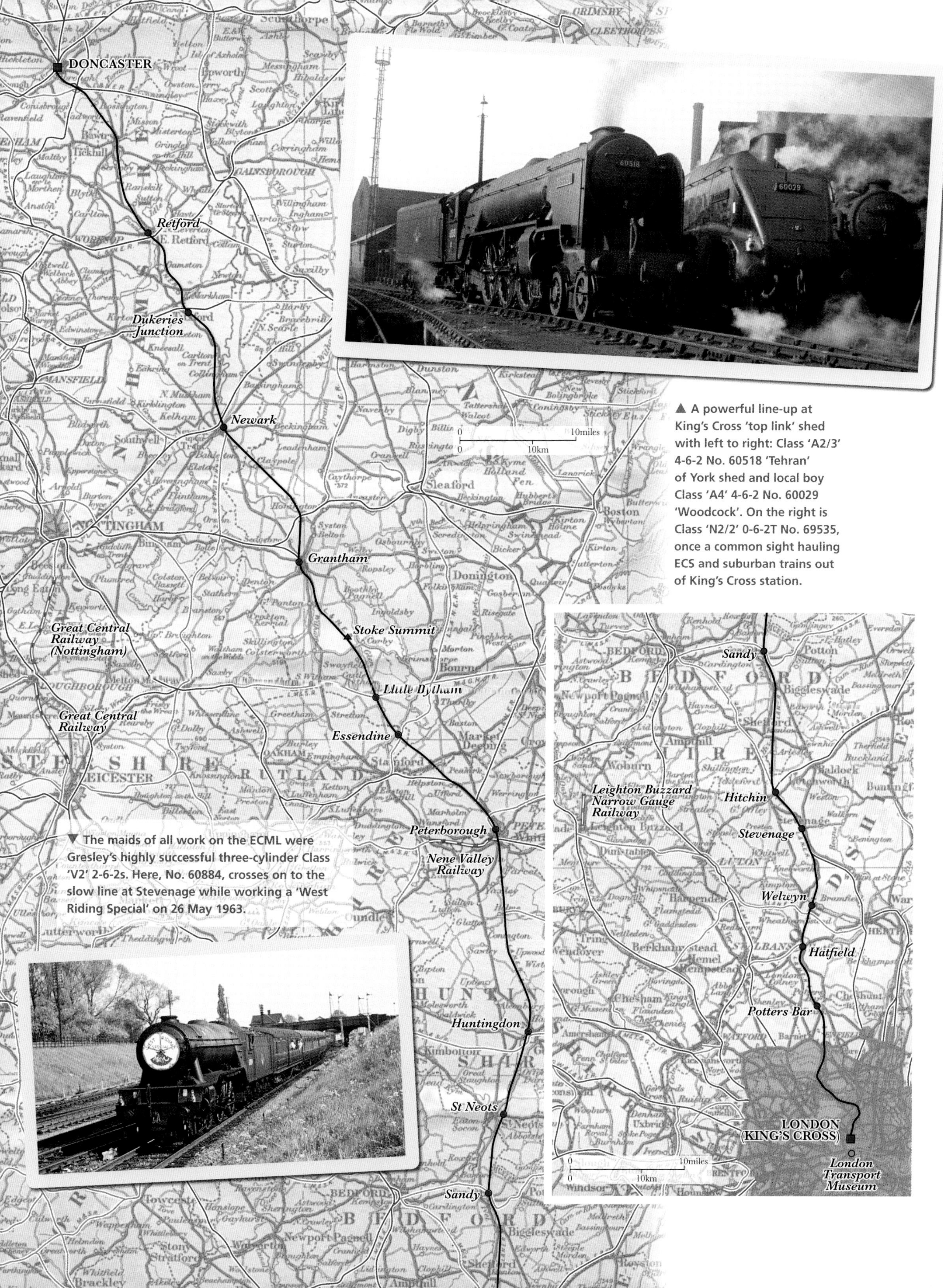

▲ A powerful line-up at King's Cross 'top link' shed with left to right: Class 'A2/3' 4-6-2 No. 60518 'Tehran' of York shed and local boy Class 'A4' 4-6-2 No. 60029 'Woodcock'. On the right is Class 'N2/2' 0-6-2T No. 69535, once a common sight hauling ECS and suburban trains out of King's Cross station.

▼ The maids of all work on the ECML were Gresley's highly successful three-cylinder Class 'V2' 2-6-2s. Here, No. 60884, crosses on to the slow line at Stevenage while working a 'West Riding Special' on 26 May 1963.

UNDERHAND HUDSON

George Hudson inherited a fortune from his great uncle, became Mayor of York and helped establish York Union Banking. He became the largest shareholder in many new railway schemes and built up a railway empire (including the Midland Railway) that by 1844 controlled 1,000 miles of line. He became known as the 'railway king' but he employed underhand tactics to prevent the building of competitive lines (such as the Great Northern) – bribing MPs to vote against various railway Acts of Parliament (or to vote for his schemes) was one of his crimes. Despite this he remained MP for Sunderland until 1859. He was ruined when large-scale fraud was discovered in one of his railways (the Eastern Railway) and he fled the country. On his return, in 1865, he was jailed for three months and spent the rest of his life in Europe with financial support from friends.

In the early 1840s the route from London to York was clearly useless, and, in 1846, the Great Northern Railway was authorised to build a direct line from London to York via Peterborough, Grantham and Doncaster, with a loop line from Peterborough to Retford via Lincoln. By that date, George Hudson controlled over 1,000 miles of railway stretching from Birmingham to Newcastle and he was furious about the new scheme, which threatened to strike into the heart of his railway empire.

Despite Hudson's underhand tactics to try and delay the new railway, William Cubitt was appointed as chief engineer for the fledgling GNR and work started on the London to Peterborough section with Thomas Brassey acting as main contractor. Work was slow due to the terrain north of London, which required the building of two viaducts at Welwyn and nine tunnels. Meanwhile, the Peterborough to Retford loop line via Lincoln was forging ahead across flat lands and this opened as far

◀ Fitted with German-type smoke deflectors, ex-LNER Class 'A3' 4-6-2 No. 60062 'Minoru' looks in fine fettle as it heads the down 'The Yorkshire Pullman' express to Leeds, Bradford and Harrogate through Wood Green station in June 1961.

▶ Peppercorn Class 'A1' 4-6-2 No. 60136 'Alcazar' approaches Sandy station with the 7.43am York to King's Cross express on August Bank Holiday, 7 August 1961. The lines on the right are the ex-LNWR cross-country route between Cambridge and Bedford.

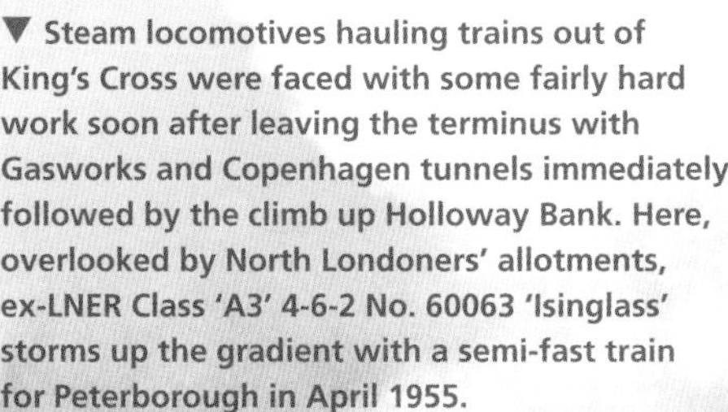

▼ Steam locomotives hauling trains out of King's Cross were faced with some fairly hard work soon after leaving the terminus with Gasworks and Copenhagen tunnels immediately followed by the climb up Holloway Bank. Here, overlooked by North Londoners' allotments, ex-LNER Class 'A3' 4-6-2 No. 60063 'Isinglass' storms up the gradient with a semi-fast train for Peterborough in April 1955.

as Lincoln in 1848. The intervening section of the loop was provided by the Manchester, Sheffield & Lincolnshire Railway's line from Lincoln to Retford over which the GNR obtained running powers. The Retford to Doncaster section was opened by the GNR in 1849.

At the southern end the railway opened from Peterborough to a temporary terminus at Maiden Lane in 1850 and to King's Cross in 1852. In the same year, the direct main line north of Peterborough opened to Retford, and the GNR main line to Shaftholme Junction north of Doncaster was complete. Until 1871, through running to York was achieved only by running powers between Burton Salmon and Knottingly over George Hudson's York & North Midland Railway and the Wakefield, Pontefract & Goole Railway. Matters greatly improved in 1871, by which time Hudson had died in disgrace, when the North Eastern Railway opened a direct line (via Selby) from Shaftholme Junction, north of Doncaster, to Chaloner's Whin Junction, on the Leeds line south of York. The East Coast Main Line to York was now in place and the route remained unchanged until the opening of the Selby cut-off in 1983.

The success of the Great Northern Railway in generating traffic also brought the problem of congestion north of King's Cross. The original double track was already proving insufficient only 15 years after opening, so a long process of widening the line to provide four tracks was instigated. This was not an easy task as extra tunnels had to be built alongside existing ones with the last, at Potters Bar, not being completed until 1959. Welwyn Viaduct was (and still is) a double-track bottleneck but, apart from this viaduct, by 1978 there was quadruple track stretching northwards

▲ Thompson Class 'B1' 4-6-0 No. 61406 of Immingham shed gets ready to leave Peterborough North station with the Summer Saturdays-only Skegness to King's Cross 'Butlins Express' on 18 July 1959.

▼ Probably the most famous locomotive in the world, ex-LNER Class 'A3' 60103 'Flying Scotsman' picks up water at speed at Werrington troughs, north of Peterborough, while hauling the down 'The Talisman' express to Edinburgh on 22 July 1959. This national treasure has recently been the subject of a major overhaul at the National Railway Museum, York.

King's Cross's Class 'A4' 4-6-2 No. 60028 'Walter K. Whigham' bursts out of the northern end of Stoke Tunnel south of Grantham with a down express on 2 August 1958.

from King's Cross to just south of Peterborough. The opening of the Hertford Loop from Wood Green to Stevenage in 1924 by the newly formed LNER also brought relief to the main line and still provides a useful diversionary route.

FAMOUS TRAINS

The Great Northern's locomotive, carriage and wagon works was established at Doncaster in 1853 and under successive chief mechanical engineers – Patrick Stirling, Henry Ivatt and Nigel Gresley – produced some of the finest steam locomotives in the world. Stirling Singles, Ivatt Atlantics and Gresley Pacifics were all world-beaters culminating in Gresley's 'A4' Pacifics built for the LNER and 'Mallard's' record-breaking run of 126mph down Stoke Bank in 1938. Doncaster went on to build over 2,000 steam, diesel and electric locomotives, celebrating its 150th anniversary in 2003.

Traffic on the Great Northern out of King's Cross was initially slow to develop thanks in the main to the spoiling tactics employed by George Hudson and his successors at Euston Square. However, by 1860 this had all been put to rest and the Great Northern was enjoying a massive surge in both freight and passenger traffic along its main line. By then, through trains were being run from King's Cross to Edinburgh and the three companies involved, the GNR, the North Eastern Railway and the North British Railway, developed special rolling stock for this service, known as East Coast Joint Stock.

Introduced in 1862, the 10am 'Special Scotch Express' departure from King's Cross to Edinburgh was the forerunner of the LNER's 'Flying Scotsman', the famous train introduced in 1924 and initially hauled by Gresley's new 'A1' Pacifics – the fitting of corridor tenders allowed the first non-stop run between the capitals in 1928. The heyday of LNER expresses came in 1935 with the introduction of the non-stop streamlined 'Silver Jubilee' express between King's Cross and Newcastle. This was hauled by Gresley's new 'A4' Pacifics, which achieved a 99 per cent reliability record until it ceased to run at the start of the Second World War.

The outbreak of war saw Government control of Britain's railways and the Great Northern main line stretched to the limit – that it coped so well is testament to the founding fathers of the GNR and the far-sightedness of the LNER. Following nationalisation in 1948 it took some years before normal service was resumed, but by the 1950s a steady stream of named expresses was making its way northwards daily from King's Cross. Even in the twilight of steam the list was impressive: 'The Flying Scotsman', 'The Elizabethan', 'The Talisman' 'The Heart of Midlothian' and 'The Night Scotsman' to Edinburgh; 'The Queen of Scots' to Glasgow; 'The Aberdonian' to Aberdeen; 'The Northumbrian', 'The Tees-Tyne Pullman' and 'The Tynesider' to Newcastle; 'The Tees-Thames' to Saltburn; 'The Master Cutler' to Sheffield; 'The Yorkshire Pullman' to Harrogate; 'The West Riding' and 'The White Rose' to Bradford.

The introduction of 'Deltic' diesels in 1961 soon saw an end to steam traction on the Great Northern main line and by June 1963 the 'top link' steam shed at King's Cross had been closed. The 'Deltics' were replaced by HST sets between 1976 and 1981 and the opening of the Selby cut-off north of Doncaster in 1983 saw further improvements to train times. Electrification to Edinburgh was completed in 1990 and now the 10am departure from King's Cross takes less than 4½ hours to reach Edinburgh.

▼ One of Edinburgh Haymarket's Class 'A4s', No. 60009 'Union of South Africa' (fitted with a corridor tender) heads the up non-stop 'The Elizabethan' express through the centre road at Doncaster station on 31 August 1961. Introduced in 1953, this famous train, which features in the 1954 British Transport Films documentary *Elizabethan Express*, ceased running at the end of the 1961 summer timetable.

THE LINE TODAY

Trains along the East Coast Main Line (ECML) between King's Cross and Doncaster are operated by East Coast (the temporarily nationalised franchise), First Hull Trains and Grand Central. Suburban services out of King's Cross are operated by First Capital Connect.

The original Great Northern Railway main line to York (1848–1852) via the Lincoln Loop has become the Water Rail footpath and cycleway (part of National Cycle Network/NCN Route 1) between Lincoln (Waterside South) and Woodhall Junction.

Until the opening of the Selby cut-off in 1983, the ECML between Doncaster and York went via Selby and York. Once the cut-off had opened the original line between Chaloner's Whin and Selby was closed and its trackbed used as the York to Selby Railway Path (part of NCN Route 65).

▲ Resplendent in LNER apple-green livery, visiting Class 'B1' 4-6-0 No. 1306 pollutes the skies while hauling a rake of 'blood and custard' coaches on the Nene Valley Railway.

HERITAGE RAILWAY

NENE VALLEY RAILWAY
Wansford Station, Stibbington, Peterborough PE8 6LR

Website: www.nvr.org.uk

Tel: 01780 784444

Route: Yarwell Junction to Peterborough

Length: 7½ miles

Nearest main-line station: Peterborough

Originally part of the London & North Western Railway's route from Peterborough to Market Harborough, opened in 1845 and closed by BR in 1966, the Nene Valley Railway is now well known for its international flavour and location filming for TV and cinema. Since 1974, with assistance from Peterborough Development Corporation, the Peterborough Railway Society has had its headquarters at Wansford, which has become the main centre for foreign locomotives and rolling stock in Britain. Trains started operating in 1977 and a new NVR station at Peterborough (Nene Valley) was opened in 1986 adjacent to a site currently being developed into an international railway museum. From Peterborough the line runs through Nene Park along the banks of the River Nene, crossing the river twice, and into open countryside, before passing through Wansford and the 616yd Wansford Tunnel. Current restored stock on the NVR consists of examples from Germany, Denmark, Sweden, France and Belgium, as well as many from Britain, including the line's first locomotive, former BR Class 5MT 4-6-0 No. 73050 'City of Peterborough'. Film-makers have taken advantage of the continental flavour and the NVR stations have often been cleverly disguised as foreign locations for films such as *Octopussy* and *Goldeneye*, television dramas and commercials. A Travelling Post Office demonstration train with mailbag-exchange apparatus can also be seen in action. A new museum exhibiting the railway's extensive collection of Travelling Post Office and Wagons-Lit rolling stock is being built at Ferry Meadows. It will also feature materials from the Nene Valley Railway's collection of memorabilia.

MUSEUM

LONDON TRANSPORT MUSEUM
Covent Garden Piazza, London WC2E 7BB

Website: www.ltmuseum.co.uk

Tel: 0207 379 6344

Nearest London Underground station: Covent Garden (Piccadilly Line)

A large collection of public transport road and rail vehicles used in London from Victorian times to the present day is housed in the former Flower Market, which dates back to 1870. Included on display are a 1866-built Metropolitan Railway 4-4-0 condensing tank No. 23 and a 1922-built 1,200 horsepower Bo-Bo electric locomotive 'John Hampden', Wotton Tramway traction engine locomotive No. 807 built in 1872, as well as examples of early underground electric trains. Visitors to the museum can 'drive' an Underground train on a simulator and also take part in signals and points demonstrations. The museum has a large photographic and film archive section containing over 100,000 black and white photographs of London Transport and its predecessors.

THE LAST MAIN LINE

Marylebone to Sheffield

Built to the continental loading gauge, Edward Watkin's grand dream of reaching Europe via a Channel Tunnel failed to get beyond the bufferstops at Marylebone station. Its duplication of existing north–south routes led to the Great Central's early closure in 1966.

▲ **Happy days at Marylebone – until 1959 the Great Central's premier express was 'The Master Cutler' to and from Sheffield Victoria. Here, disembarked passengers admire the ex-LNER Class 'A3' 4-6-2 No. 60102 'Sir Frederick Banbury' of Leicester Central shed, after its arrival in London. 'The Master Cutler', upgraded as a Pullman train, was rerouted to King's Cross station in 1960.**

The last main line to be built into London, the Great Central Railway, had its roots in a much smaller company, the Manchester, Sheffield & Lincolnshire Railway. The MS&LR had existed since 1847 when it was formed by the amalgamation of four railway companies and the Grimsby Docks Company in order to improve communications across the Pennines between the important northern industrial centres of Manchester and Sheffield, the coalfields of South Yorkshire and the fast-growing port of Grimsby. The MS&LR, under its ambitious General Manager (and later Chairman) Edward Watkin soon flourished and expanded its territory through takeovers and the arrangement of joint running rights with other railways in the region. Up to that point, despite intense competition from its larger rivals, the MS&LR, a major coal carrier, was a thriving concern. However, Edward Watkin was never a man to sit on his laurels and, as part of his dream to build a railway tunnel under the English Channel, planned further expansion southwards to London.

WATKIN'S GRAND DREAM

The new railway, from Annesley in Nottinghamshire to a new London terminus at Marylebone, would transform Watkin's company from a regional player into a major north–south route of strategic importance that would compete head on with giants such as the Midland Railway and the Great Northern Railway. One section of the line, southwards from Quainton Road in Buckinghamshire to Harrow, was to be jointly run with the Metropolitan Railway, of which Edward Watkin was also Chairman, which had already started operating services on this route in 1892.

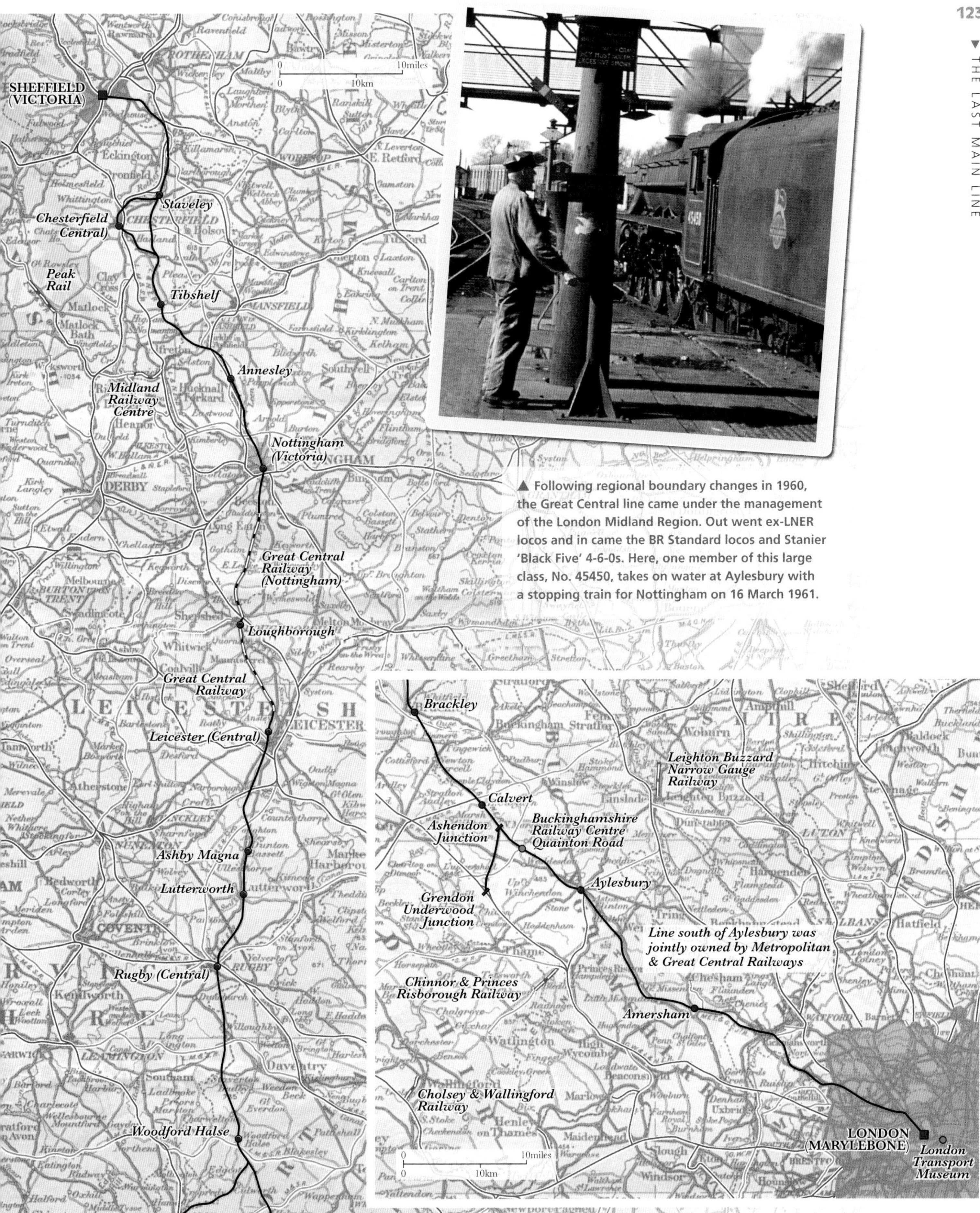

▲ Following regional boundary changes in 1960, the Great Central line came under the management of the London Midland Region. Out went ex-LNER locos and in came the BR Standard locos and Stanier 'Black Five' 4-6-0s. Here, one member of this large class, No. 45450, takes on water at Aylesbury with a stopping train for Nottingham on 16 March 1961.

The MS&LR obtained Parliamentary approval for the London Extension, as it was then known, in 1893 and, to crown his grand dream, Watkin changed the name of his company to the Great Central Railway in 1897. In anticipation of the London Extension, the company had already opened a new line south from Woodhouse Junction, south of Sheffield, to Staveley and Annesley with a loop serving Chesterfield.

Work started on the construction of the new 92-mile line in 1895 and it was opened for passenger traffic on 15 March 1899. From the outset, the line was designed for fast traffic with a continental loading gauge and no level crossings. Major towns and cities that were served by the Great Central included Nottingham, Loughborough, Leicester and Rugby. All of these destinations were already well served by other major railway companies and the company soon ran into trouble because the actual cost of building the new line was nearly double the original estimate of £6 million.

Before the new main line had been completed there was a major falling out between the GCR and the Metropolitan Railway and so an 'Alternative Route' was built from Grendon Underwood Junction on the GCR main line and Ashenden Junction on the GWR's line from Birmingham and Banbury. From Ashenden Juncton to Northolt Junction the line was jointly owned by the GCR and GWR. The 'Alternative Route' was opened in 1906 by which time the GCR and the Metropolitan had made friends again, making the new route rather superfluous!

THE FORTUNES OF THE GCR

Despite the main line reaching London, the most important part of the new Great Central was the 'branch' between Culworth Junction, south of Woodford & Hinton (renamed Woodford Halse in 1948), and Banbury, which carried enormous quantities of freight and coal traffic and also inter-regional cross-country passenger trains. Woodford, once a sleepy village, soon grew into a major railway junction that was further enhanced when a new spur was built linking it to another major freight-carrying line, the east–west Stratford-upon-Avon & Midland Junction Railway.

Edward Watkin retired as Chairman of the Great Central in 1899 and his place was taken by Alexander Henderson. Sam Fay

▼ Built to continental loading gauge standards, the Great Central was a highly successful freight route, moving vast quantities of coal from the Nottinghamshire coalfields 24 hours a day. Here, a 'windcutter' coal train is seen approaching Charwelton station, south of Rugby, behind BR Standard Class '9F' 2-10-0 No. 92031 on 2 March 1963.

▶ 'The Master Cutler', seen at full speed south of Rugby, c.1953, and unusually in the hands of ex-LNER 'B1' Class 4-6-0 No. 61376, a Leicester Great Central (38C) engine. This celebrated Great Central express, which paid tribute to the silver plate industry in Sheffield, was usually diagrammed for an 'A3' Pacific.

▼ The Woodford Halse to Banbury line was once an important route for cross-country passenger and freight services from the Great Central to the GWR/Western Region. Here, BR Standard Class '9F' heads a southbound freight near Thorpe Mandeville village, north of Banbury, on 12 October 1963.

THE
MASTER CUTLER
61376

The down 'The South Yorkshireman' from Marylebone to Bradford Exchange leaves Rugby Central behind Leicester Central's ex-LNER Class 'A3' 4-6-2 No. 60107 'Royal Lancer' in 1952. This loco was built in 1923 as an 'A1' Pacific, rebuilt as an 'A3' in 1946 and withdrawn in 1963.

With its connection to the Western Region at Banbury, the Great Central was a useful through route for cross-country inter-regional trains, often bringing 'foreign' locos that had strayed far from their territory. Here, begrimed ex-GWR 'Grange' Class 4-6-0 No. 6844 'Penhydd Grange' is seen at Leicester Central at the head of a train from Banbury and Oxford on 6 August 1955.

took over as General Manager in 1902 and, in the same year, John Robinson was appointed Chief Mechanical Engineer. The headquarters of the company moved to Marylebone in 1905. In Robinson the Great Central had found a very able locomotive and rolling stock designer and soon the company was living up to its publicity for 'Rapid Travel in Luxury'. Despite this, passenger traffic never lived up to expectations although the railway did achieve much success as a freight carrier, especially at moving coal, in which it excelled. In the 1923 amalgamation, the Great Central became part of the newly formed London & North Eastern Railway and, on nationalisation in 1948, was allocated to the Eastern Region of British Railways.

The Great Central's fortunes took a severe downturn in 1960 when it was transferred to the London Midland Region of British Railways. The Marylebone to Sheffield expresses were withdrawn and other services were placed in the hands of worn-out steam locomotives. At a time when railway rationalisation and full-scale closures were becoming a reality, the duplication of north–south routes into London soon brought about the GCR's demise. Through freight services were withdrawn on 14 June 1965 (when Woodford Halse shed closed) and the railway closed as a through route completely on 3 September 1966. Apart from the suburban services from Marylebone to Aylesbury and a short-lived section that was retained for passenger traffic between Rugby Central and Nottingham (closed 5 May 1969), the Great Central had ceased to exist. With hindsight the continental loading gauge of the Great Central could well have been adapted as a new high-speed railway linking the Midlands and North England with the Continent via the Channel Tunnel, exactly as Edward Watkin originally envisaged in his 'grand dream' over 100 years ago.

▲ **Watched by a couple of young trainspotters, an ex-LNER Class 'B17' 4-6-0 stands at Sheffield Victoria with a 'City of Leicester Holiday Express' for the Yorkshire coast in 1955.**

▼ **In its last year of operation, the up 'The South Yorkshireman' from Bradford Exchange to Marylebone heads south towards Annesley near Tibshelf behind a fairly clean Class 'B1' 4-6-0 No. 61380 on 29 September 1959. All through expresses from Yorkshire to Marylebone ceased following the transfer of the Great Central line from the ER to the LMR in 1960.**

▲ Newly built Class 'A1' 4-6-2 No. 60163 'Tornado' is put through its paces on the Great Central Railway.

▶ On loan from the National Railway Museum, the famous Great Northern Railway 'Stirling Single' 4-2-2 No. 1 makes a departs from Loughborough on the Great Central Railway.

THE LINE TODAY

Train services between Marylebone and Aylesbury are operated by Chiltern Railways. North of Aylesbury the line has been singled as far as Calvert and is used by freight trains carrying containerised domestic waste to one of the largest landfill sites in the UK. Northwards from Calvert the trackbed is intact as far as Rugby and part of this section may be used for the proposed high-speed railway from London to Birmingham. The section from Loughborough to Leicester has been reopened by the Great Central Railway as a heritage line. A more recent heritage line known as GCR Railway, Nottingham (below right) runs passenger trains between Ruddington, near Nottingham, to Loughborough.

HERITAGE RAILWAYS

GREAT CENTRAL RAILWAY

Great Central Station, Great Central Road,
Loughborough, Leicestershire LE11 1RW

Website: www.gcrailway.co.uk

Tel: 01509 230726

Route: Loughborough Central to Leicester North

Nearest main-line stations: Loughborough, Leicester

Length: 8 miles

Britain's last main line, the Great Central Railway, was opened in 1899 and linked Manchester, Sheffield and Nottingham with Marylebone station in London. Designed for fast traffic with a continental loading gauge and no level crossings, the railway was never a great success and was eventually closed throughout by BR in 1966 with the Rugby to Nottingham section remaining open until 1969. The section from Loughborough to Quorn & Woodhouse was reopened by the Main Line Steam Trust in 1973, to Rothley in 1976 and finally to Leicester North in 1991. Uniquely among heritage lines, it is double track throughout so that the railway can operate with the appearance of a main line. A very large collection of impressive main-line preserved steam and diesel locomotives is based on the GCR to provide a variety of train operations, and visiting engines can frequently be seen in action. Stations have been restored to different periods in the railway's history; Loughborough is typical of the 1960s, Quorn & Woodhouse recreates the 1940s, Rothley captures the Edwardian era and Leicester North a three-platform main-line terminus. Passengers are conveyed in traditional main-line style through delightful Leicestershire hunting countryside and, en route, cross Swithland Reservoir on two viaducts.

GREAT CENTRAL RAILWAY (Nottingham)

Ruddington Fields Station, Mere Way,
Ruddington, Nottingham NG11 6NX

Website: www.gcrn.co.uk

Tel: 0115 9405705

Route: Ruddington to Loughborough

Length: 9 miles

Nearest main-line station: Nottingham

Following closure of the Great Central main-line in 1966, a short section from Nottingham to an MOD ordnance depot at Ruddington was kept open until the early 1980s. On closure of the depot, the railway was reopened by a group of enthusiasts and now operates passenger trains between Ruddington and East Leake most weekends. A few trains continue to Loughborough but there are no facilities to leave or join the train here.

▼ A good head of steam at Quainton Road, from left to right: ex-LSWR 'Class '0298' 2-4-0 No. 30585; Andrew Barclay 0-4-0ST No. 699 'Swanscombe'; Peckett 0-4-0ST No. 2087.

MUSEUM

BUCKINGHAMSHIRE RAILWAY CENTRE

Quainton Road Station, Quainton,
Nr Aylesbury, Bucks HP22 4BY

Website: www.bucksrailcentre.org

Tel: 01296 655720

Route: within site

Length: ½ mile

Nearest main-line station: Aylesbury

A 25-acre railway centre incorporating two demonstration lines based on the former Metropolitan Railway country station at Quainton Road (where that railway originally met the Great Central Railway). The centre, opened in 1969, houses a very large collection of steam and diesel locomotives, which operate trains along two short sections of track within the site. Occasional specials also work from Quainton Road to Aylesbury Town along the freight-only line still owned by Network Rail. Both engines and rolling stock are restored to working order in well-equipped workshops, which are open to public viewing. Locomotives and rolling stock include Metropolitan Railway 0-4-4T No. 1, London & South Western Railway 2-4-0 well tank No. 0314, ex-GWR/London Transport 0-6-0 pannier tank No. L99, GWR 'Castle' Class 4-6-0 No. 5080 'Defiant', WR/BR 'Modified Hall' Class 4-6-0 No. 6989 'Wightwick Hall', a London & North Western Railway first-class royal dining car and vintage coaching stock examples from the London Chatham & Dover Railway, Great Northern Railway and Manchester, Sheffield & Lincolnshire Railway. Future plans include a proposed reconnection to the national network, which will enable steam trains to operate between Aylesbury and Calvert, via Quainton. The Centre is usually open at weekends and on some Wednesdays from April to October.

LONDON MIDLAND REGION

Happy days at Crewe as a large throng of trainspotters watch Polmadie's spotlessly clean ex-LMS 'Coronation' Class 4-6-2 No. 46221 'Queen Elizabeth' pass through on the fast line with the up 'Royal Scot', c.1955.

ROYAL SCOT
46221

WEST COAST MAIN LINE part 1

Euston to Crewe

By 1847, the West Coast Main Line, south of Crewe, as we know it today was in place. Under the London & North Western Railway, it soon became Britain's major trunk line and, under the LMS, the proving ground of some of Britain's most successful steam locomotive designs.

The southern section of what later became known as the West Coast Main Line (WCML) between Euston and Crewe was built by three different railway companies that in 1846 amalgamated to form the London & North Western Railway, or 'Premier Line' as it preferred to be called.

THE INITIAL LONG HAUL

Down at the London end, the London & Birmingham Railway (L&BR) was authorised in 1833 to build a 112-mile line from Camden, in north London, to Curzon Street in Birmingham via Rugby and Coventry. Engineered by Robert Stephenson, it became the first inter-city railway to serve London, but its opening was delayed in part due to the excavation of the long cutting near the summit of the line at Tring. It suffered with problems encountered

▶ **Green-liveried ex-LMS 'Coronation' Class 4-6-2 No. 46255 'City of Hereford' leaves the old Euston station with the down 'The Caledonian' express to Glasgow Central in March 1960. This restaurant car train left Euston at 3.35pm with stops en route at Stafford and Carlisle, arriving in Glasgow at 11pm.**

The clock is just coming up to 12.40pm and Stanier 'Black Five' 4-6-0 No. 45434 and 'Princess Royal' Class 4-6-2 No. 46205 'Princess Victoria' have just arrived at Euston with 'The Shamrock' from Liverpool Lime Street on 19 February 1957. This train carried passengers who had sailed overnight in ferries from Dublin and Belfast.

by landslips during the building of Wolverton Viaduct and with quicksand during the construction of the 2,432yd Kilsby Tunnel in Northamptonshire. An extension from Camden to Euston Square was authorised in 1835, although trains along this steep section of line were, at first, cable-hauled by a stationary steam engine at Camden because, believe it or not, steam locomotives were initially prohibited at the behest of local landowners.

With Kilsby Tunnel completed, the L&BR finally opened throughout on 17 September 1838, meeting the recently opened Grand Junction Railway (see pages 146–153), Britain's first trunk line, at Curzon Street station in Birmingham. Trains continued to be rope-hauled out of Euston up Camden Bank until 1844 and meanwhile Philip Hardwick's grand terminus at Euston and his imposing Doric Arch were taking shape. Designed by Hardwick's

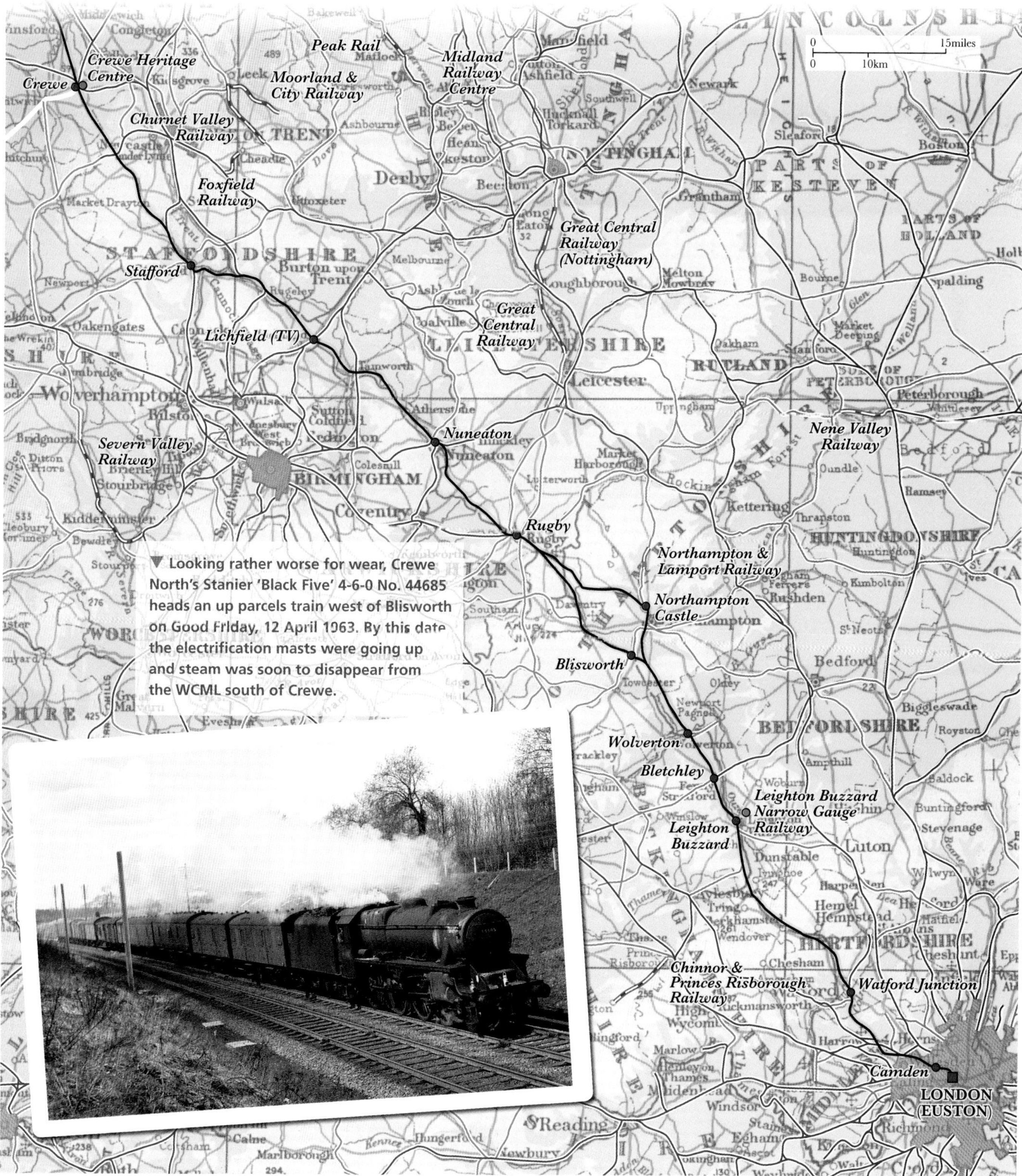

▼ Looking rather worse for wear, Crewe North's Stanier 'Black Five' 4-6-0 No. 44685 heads an up parcels train west of Blisworth on Good Friday, 12 April 1963. By this date the electrification masts were going up and steam was soon to disappear from the WCML south of Crewe.

▲ **Camden shed in June 1960 – on the left is 'Royal Scot' Class 4-6-0 No. 46153 'The Royal Dragoon' of Bushbury shed, while on the right, Camden-allocated 'Coronation' Class 4-6-2 No. 46242 'City of Glasgow' gets ready to haul 'The Ulster Express' to Heysham. Camden shed closed in September 1963.**

son, Euston's classical Great Hall was completed in 1849. Sadly, the station and arch were largely demolished in the early 1960s during an orgy of destruction by BR that was witnessed across Britain's rail network, and replaced by the current modern building.

OPENING UP THE MIDLANDS

The L&BR, along with the Grand Junction Railway (GJR) and the Manchester & Birmingham Railway, amalgamated in 1846 to form the London & North Western Railway. At Birmingham, the L&BR had shared a terminus at Curzon Street with the GJR, but this soon proved inconvenient and inadequate and, in 1854, the LNWR opened a new through joint station with the Midland Railway at New Street. Curzon Street, with its classically styled Hardwick-designed frontage, took a backstage position, used only by excursion trains until 1893 and as a goods station until the 1960s. Unlike Euston, which suffered

▲ **Overlooked by one of Rugby's landmarks, the AEI (Associated Electrical Industries) building to the east of the WCML, ex-LMS 'Jubilee' Class 4-6-0 No. 45615 'Malay States' heads a down express out of the station on 22 July 1961. Then allocated to Newton Heath (26A), this loco was withdrawn at the end of 1962.**

Holyhead-allocated BR Standard Class 7MT 'Britannia' No. 70047 (the only member of its class not to be named) pauses at Rugby Midland while heading the down 'The Irish Mail' to Holyhead in the winter of 1958.

the ignominy of total demolition, Curzon Street escaped the destruction by British Rail and the main entrance building is now Grade 1 listed.

Although by 1838 the railway route from Euston to the Midlands and the north was in place, the journey, which involved a change of trains at Curzon Street, was time-consuming. Enter the Trent Valley Railway, which was authorised in 1845 to build a 51-mile line from the L&BR at Rugby to the GJR at Stafford, via Nuneaton, Tamworth and Lichfield. Financially backed by the three constituent companies of the LNWR, the TVR was also designed by Robert Stephenson and built by Thomas Brassey. Opening in 1847, by which time it had become part of the newly formed LNWR, the Trent Valley route immediately proved its worth by bypassing Birmingham and thus cutting journey times dramatically between London, Manchester and Liverpool. The Northampton Loop Line was opened by the LNWR in 1881; previous to that date passengers to and from Northampton had had to change at Blisworth on the main line. Probably one of

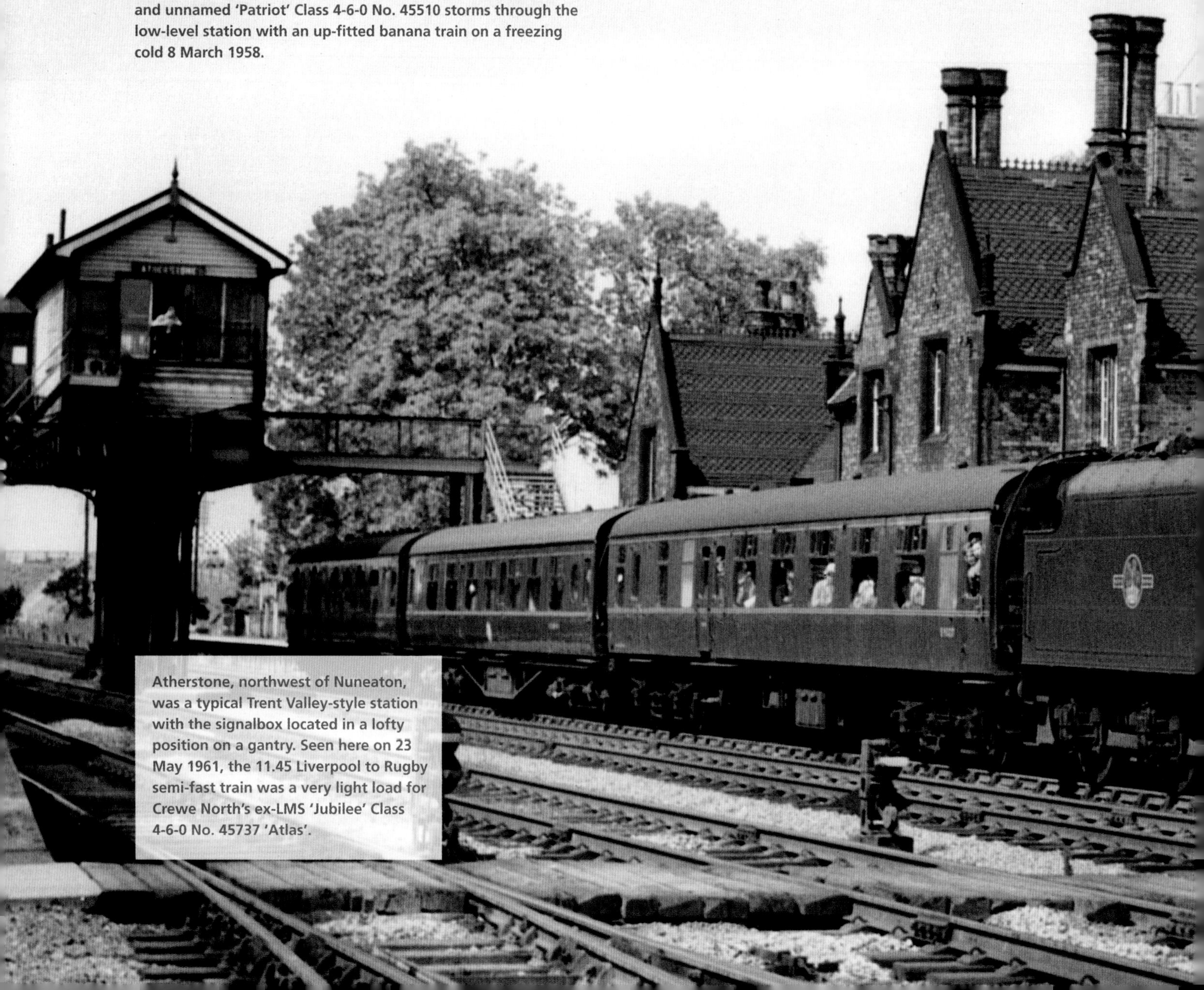

▲ Tamworth, where the Midland main line from Birmingham to Derby crossed over the WCML, was a favourite haunt of trainspotters in the 1950s and early 60s. Here ex-LMS unrebuilt and unnamed 'Patriot' Class 4-6-0 No. 45510 storms through the low-level station with an up-fitted banana train on a freezing cold 8 March 1958.

Atherstone, northwest of Nuneaton, was a typical Trent Valley-style station with the signalbox located in a lofty position on a gantry. Seen here on 23 May 1961, the 11.45 Liverpool to Rugby semi-fast train was a very light load for Crewe North's ex-LMS 'Jubilee' Class 4-6-0 No. 45737 'Atlas'.

the busiest main lines in the world, the direct route from Euston to Crewe was soon quadrupled along most of its length with water troughs being installed at three locations: at Castlethorpe, north of Wolverton; at Hademore, east of Lichfield, and at Whitmore, south of Crewe.

The London & Birmingham Railway had established its main works at Wolverton in 1838 and went on to build locomotives there for the LNWR until 1863, by which time all locomotive production was carried out at Crewe. Wolverton went on to become the company's Carriage and Wagon Works, producing the first sleeping cars in 1873, the first six-wheeled bogie coaches in 1893 and a sumptuous Royal Train for Edward VII in 1903. Rolling stock continued to be built here for the LMS and British Railways until 1962. Since then, although much reduced in size, it has continued to carry out rolling-stock maintenance and is also the home base for the current Royal Train.

▼ Stanier's 'Coronation' Class locos were magnificent beasts and were the mainstay of WCML express motive power for 25 years. Originally built in 1939 with a streamlined casing, No. 46239 'City of Chester' is seen here near Milford, east of Stafford, with the down Sunday 'Mid-Day Scot' on 14 September 1958.

▶ With modernisation of the station proceeding at a snail's pace, ex-LMS unrebuilt 'Patriot' Class 4-6-0 No. 45516 'The Bedfordshire and Hertfordshire Regiment' of Warrington Dallam shed (8B) takes on water at Stafford station while hauling an up part-fitted freight on Good Friday, 31 March 1961. The loco was withdrawn five months later.

Under LMS management, the West Coast Main Line soon became a test bed for the latest products rolled out from Crewe. Certainly the most famous must be Stanier's 'Coronation' Class 4-6-2s, introduced in 1937. Initially streamlined with matching articulated carriages and go-faster stripes, they were built to haul the 'Coronation Scot' express that ran between Euston and Glasgow until 1939. The first member of this class, No. 6220 'Coronation', achieved a British rail-speed record of 114mph in 1937 while on a test run south of Crewe, narrowly missing becoming derailed on the final approach to the station. Following the Second World War and nationalisation of the railways, many named expresses were either reinstated or newly introduced from Euston. By 1960, the romantic-sounding names of far-off places included 'The Caledonian', 'The Royal Scot', 'The Mid-Day Scot', 'The Royal Highlander' sleeper train, 'The Lancastrian', 'The Comet', 'The Red Rose', 'The Merseyside Express', 'The Shamrock', 'The Manxman', 'The Welshman', 'The Irish Mail' and 'The Lakes Express' – where have they all gone?

A veritable heaven for steam enthusiasts until the early 1960s, the Euston to Crewe line witnessed not only the daily procession of expresses, mail and sleeper trains between London, the Midlands, northwest England and Scotland but also an intensive 24-hour freight operation. Huge numbers of trainspotters with their notebooks, cameras and Ian Allan Locospotters books would gather at Euston, Rugby, Tamworth and Crewe to watch the cream of British steam at work – from Stanier's 'Princess' and 'Coronation' Pacifics and the later BR Standard 'Britannia' Pacifics to 'Royal Scot', 'Patriot', 'Jubilee' and 'Black Five' 4-6-0s, along with the ex-LNWR 0-8-0 'G2/2a' and Stanier 8F 2-8-0 workhorses. The only interlopers were the five prototype LMS and SR diesels, which started to appear in 1947, but this idyllic scene was all soon to end with Camden's top link shed closing to steam in September 1963. Willesden, Rugby and Stafford sheds struggled on until 1965 but by this time the diesels had taken over completely – even their reign was cut short by electrification of the WCML from Euston to Crewe in 1966.

▲ With the first part of the WCML electrification, from Crewe to Liverpool/Manchester, soon to be switched on, Edge Hill's 'Royal Scot' Class 4-6-0 No. 46132 'The King's Regiment Liverpool' enters Crewe station on 4 July 1959.

THE LINE TODAY

Passenger services between Euston and Crewe via the Trent Valley are currently operated by Virgin Trains and London Midland.

HERITAGE RAILWAYS

LEIGHTON BUZZARD RAILWAY

Page's Park Station, Billington Road,
Leighton Buzzard LU7 4TN

Website: www.buzzrail.co.uk

Tel: 01525 373888

Route: Page's Park to Stonehenge Works

Length: 2½ miles

Nearest main-line station: Leighton Buzzard

Built during the First World War to transport sand from pits near Leighton Buzzard, this former industrial 2ft-gauge line was saved from closure by a preservation group who started to operate trains in 1968. Now home to 11 steam and 40 diesel locomotives, originating from West Africa, India, Spain and Britain, trains operate from the railway's headquarters at Page's Park, running behind housing estates and into open country before arriving at Stonehenge Works, a former brickworks. It is here that many items of the railway's historic collection are housed. Sharp curves and steep gradients abound on this fascinating line. The oldest working locomotive on the railway is the 1877-built 0-4-0 vertical-boilered 'Chaloner', and visiting locomotives are a common sight on special events days. The Greensand Railway Museum houses narrow gauge railway artefacts from the First World War. Restoration of the ½-mile line to Double Arches is also a long-term objective.

▶ Built in Poland in 1959, Tkh 0-6-0T No. 5374 carries out a spot of shunting at Pitsford Sidings on the Northampton & Lamport Railway.

NORTHAMPTON & LAMPORT RAILWAY

Pitsford & Brampton Station, Pitsford Road, Chapel Brampton, Northampton NN6 8BA

Website: www.nlr.org.uk

Tel: 01604 820327

Route: Either side of Pitsford & Brampton station

Length: 1½ miles

Nearest main-line station: none in area

The Northampton to Market Harborough branch was opened by the London & North Western Railway in 1858 and included six stations and two tunnels. It was first closed to passengers in April 1960 but reopened to through traffic in January 1961, closed again in May 1961 and then reopened a second time in July 1972. The passenger service was finally withdrawn in August 1973 and the line closed completely in August 1981. The Society originally started around the same time as the line closure, moved once and changed its name twice before finally becoming the Northampton & Lamport Railway. The railway presently extends for ¾ mile with Pitsford & Brampton station roughly at the centre. The route shares the original track formation with the Brampton Valley Walk, a linear park operated by Northamptonshire County Council. The signalbox at Pitsford Ironstone exchange sidings is an example of a rare 10ft-square LNWR type, which was originally located at Wolverton works. Another LNWR signalbox, originally from Little Bowden level crossing, controls the station site. The first public steam train operated in 1995 and a Light Railway Order has been granted northwards to Spratton, which will allow the railway to extend to approximately 3 miles in length. In the more distant future it is hoped to extend to Lamport, giving a total run of 7 miles. A good collection of both steam and diesel main-line and industrial locomotives is based at the site.

◀ Getting up a full head of steam on the Leighton Buzzard Light Railway. On the left is 0-4-0ST 'Alice' while on the right is the 1877-built vertical-boilered 0-4-0 'Chaloner'.

FOXFIELD RAILWAY

Caverswall Road Station, Blythe Bridge, Stoke-on-Trent, Staffs ST11 9BG

Website: www.foxfieldrailway.co.uk

Tel: 01782 259667/396210

Route: Blythe Bridge to Dilhorne Park

Length: 2¼ miles

Nearest main-line station: Blythe Bridge

Operating on an old colliery line, opened in 1893 and closed in 1965, this railway is situated very close to Blythe Bridge station. After closure, a preservation group took over and passengers were first carried in 1967, with Caverswall station opening in 1982. Small and powerful industrial steam and diesel locomotives haul trains up fearsome gradients to a summit 705ft above sea level. The large collection of locos includes 15 steam, 12 diesel and 2 battery electric engines.

MUSEUM

CREWE HERITAGE CENTRE

Vernon Way, Crewe, Cheshire CW1 2DB

Website: www.creweheritagecentre.co.uk

Tel: 01270 212130

Nearest main-line station: Crewe

A standard gauge railway museum, opened in 1987 near Crewe station, houses a changing collection of mainly ex-BR main-line diesel and electric locomotives. Passenger rides are given at weekends in steam-hauled brakevans over the 300yd of track within the site. Steam locomotives are stabled here when working special trains to the North Wales coast. In addition there are three restored working signalboxes (Crewe Station A, Crewe North Junction and Exeter West), railway artefacts and a ½-mile long passenger-carrying 7¼in-gauge miniature railway.

THE NORTH WALES COAST

Chester to Holyhead

Featuring Robert Stephenson's famous Britannia Tubular Bridge over the Menai Strait, the Chester to Holyhead line marked the rebirth of Holyhead as the premier port for Ireland and the rapid development of resorts along the North Wales coastline.

BR Standard Class 7MT 'Britannia' 4-6-2 No. 70045 'Lord Rowallan' of Holyhead shed (6J) heads 'The Irish Mail' at Chester, c.1958. This famous overnight train from Holyhead to Euston was often the first introduction that Irish migrants had to their new homeland.

For hundreds of years the Irish Mail was carried between London and Dublin over rutted roads by horse and stagecoach to Holyhead and then by sailing ship over the stormy Irish Sea. This important route was vastly improved during the early 19th century when Thomas Telford upgraded what is now known as the A5 road across Snowdonia and built the Menai suspension bridge to Anglesey. Despite such great efforts and the introduction of steamships for the sea crossing, it was still a slow and lengthy journey by stagecoach and, by the 1830s, no match for the new-fangled railways, which were already spreading like tentacles across Britain. The opening of the railway route between London and the north in 1839 brought an end to Holyhead's importance when the Irish Mail service was rerouted to run via Liverpool.

▲ **Stanier 'Black Five' 4-6-0 No. 45094 hurries through Holywell Junction station on the fast line with a North Wales coast express on Saturday, 4 September 1954. This date is significant as the short branch line to Holywell Town, which had opened in 1912, saw its last passenger trains on that day.**

Chester had been reached in 1840 by the opening of the Chester & Crewe Railway and it wasn't long before proposals were put forward for a new railway along the North Wales coast and across Anglesey to Holyhead. Backed financially by the London & Birmingham Railway, the Chester & Holyhead Railway (C&HR) was incorporated in 1844, but the decision on how to cross the Menai Straits was put off until the following year. Engineered by Robert Stephenson, the railway was opened in two separate sections in 1848, namely Chester to Bangor and across Anglesey to Holyhead. The intervening gap was filled by a novel tubular bridge built of rectangular wrought-iron tubes through which trains could pass – named the Britannia Tubular Bridge, it opened in 1850.

▼ **In the days when Chester boasted a four track railway to the west, BR Standard Class 7MT 'Britannia' 4-6-2 No. 70045, 'Lord Rowallan' heads the down 'The Irish Mail' across the River Dee with the panorama of Chester racecourse in the background, c.1958.**

The building of the Chester to Holyhead Railway had left the company in dire financial straits and the line was worked from the outset by the newly formed London & North Western Railway (LNWR). Despite the growth of traffic along the line, including through expresses to and from Euston and the carrying of considerable amounts of coal, slate and Irish cattle, the company couldn't make ends meet and in 1858, to the LNWR's horror, approached the Great Western Railway for help. Not surprisingly, the LNWR's headquarters at Euston could not countenance this encroachment into their territory and made a counter offer that was accepted by the C&HR at the beginning of 1859.

RESORT GROWTH

The opening of the railway saw not only the renaissance of Holyhead (where the Great Breakwater was completed in 1870) as the premier port for Ireland but also brought about a massive development of resort towns along its route. Prestatyn, Rhyl, Colwyn Bay and Llandudno all owe their popularity as Victorian and 20th century destinations to the railway. Llandudno itself was connected to the main line in 1858 with a 3-mile branch from Llandudno Junction station.

In addition to the Llandudno branch, the Chester to Holyhead line spawned numerous other branch lines along its 84½-mile route. Westwards from Chester the 2-mile Holywell branch opened as a tramway in 1867 but was soon abandoned. It was later reopened by the LNWR in 1912 and closed to passengers in 1954. The 3-mile Dyserth branch from Prestatyn opened for freight in 1869 and for passengers in 1905. Passenger services ended in 1930 and the branch closed completely in 1964. At Foryd, west of Rhyl, the Vale of Clwyd Railway opened to Denbigh in 1858, closing to passengers in 1955 and completely in 1965. Llandudno Junction opened for the Llandudno branch in 1858 and the Conway & Llanrwst Railway opened southwards to Llanrwst in 1863. The company was taken over by the LNWR in 1867, which extended the line to Betws-y-Coed a year later and to Blaenau Ffestiniog through the 3,726yd Ffestiniog Tunnel in 1879; it is still open.

Continuing westwards, the 4½-mile Bangor to Bethesda branch opened in 1884, but closed to passengers in 1951 and completely in 1963. At Menai Bridge station, the 8½-mile branch to Caernarvon opened in 1852 and closed in 1970. On Anglesey, famous for having the longest station name in Britain – Llanfairpwllgwyngyllgogerychwyrndrobwllllantysiliogogogoch – a branch of approximately 17½ miles from Gaerwen to Amlwch opened in 1867 and closed to passengers in 1964. The line continued to serve a chemical works at Amlwch until 1993 and the track has since been mothballed.

▲ *Top* Llandudno Junction was, and still is, an important railway crossroads with lines radiating eastwards to Chester, westwards to Holyhead, northwards to Llandudno and southwards to Blaenau Ffestiniog. During steam days it saw a steady procession of holiday trains from all over northern England and the Midlands heading for the North Wales coast resorts. Here, Carnforth-based 'Jubilee' Class 4-6-0 No. 45592 'Indore' leaves the station with an up train on 22 June 1963.

▲ *Bottom* England's King Edward I would have turned in his grave when the North Wales Coast line was built through the ancient walls of the town of Conwy. Here, Stanier 'Black Five' 4-6-0 No. 45133 leaves Conwy station with an eastbound train on 22 July 1964. Closed in 1966, it was reopened as an unstaffed halt in 1987.

Saltley's Stanier 'Black Five' 4-6-0 No. 45349 heads the 4.05pm Llandudno to Birmingham New Street train past the sand dunes at West Shore, Deganwy, on 31 March 1963.

▲ Ex-LMS 'Coronation' Class 4-6-2s became regular performers on the North Wales Coast line following their relegation from duties on the WCML. Here No. 46254 'City of Stoke-on-Trent' makes steam and smoke as it is readied to haul the relief up 'The Irish Mail' at Holyhead shed in August 1964, only two months before withdrawal. The diagonal yellow stripe on the cabside indicates that it was banned from working under the wires south of Crewe.

The North Wales Coast line also saw the introduction of the first water troughs in Britain. The brainchild of the LNWR's locomotive superintendent John Ramsbottom, they enabled tender engines to pick up water without stopping and were first installed at Mochdre, west of Colwyn Bay, in 1860. Traffic eventually became so heavy that the line was quadrupled between Chester and Llandudno Junction in the early 20th century.

FURTHER GROWTH

The development of the resorts along the North Wales coast also brought heavy seasonal traffic to the line that continued well into the British Railways era in the 1950s. Along with the Holyhead expresses, mail trains and overnight sleeper trains from Euston, numerous Summer Saturday trains were run from London, the Midlands and the North to carry holidaymakers to the delights of Prestatyn (for the Butlin's holiday camp), Rhyl, Colwyn Bay and Llandudno. From the 1930s until the end of steam these were headed by 'Royal Scot', 'Patriot', Jubilee' and the go-anywhere Stanier 'Black Five' 4-6-0s, while trains such as the 'Irish Mail' saw haulage towards the end of steam by 'Coronation' and 'BR Standard 'Britannia' 4-6-2s. Even some of the 'Patriot' 4-6-0s were named after the seaside towns they served such as 'Holyhead', 'Llandudno', 'Rhyl' and 'Bangor'. Probably the most interesting summer weekday working was 'The Welshman' express from Euston, which, on Saturdays in the late 1950s ran as two separate trains, one to Llandudno and the other to Pwllheli (for Butlin's) via Bangor, Caernarfon and Afonwen. Steam workings along the coast line ended at the end of 1966 when the engine sheds at Llandudno Junction and Holyhead closed.

Freight traffic along the line was also very heavy and not only included freight and livestock to and from Ireland via Holyhead but also vast amounts of slate from Snowdonia and granite from the quarry at Penmaenmawr – the latter had its own narrow gauge rail system until the early 1960s. Crushed granite from the quarry for use as track ballast is still carried by rail today.

The major incident to affect the line to Holyhead occurred in 1970 when the Britannia tubular bridge was destroyed by fire. It was rebuilt as a two-level rail/road steel truss arch bridge and reopened for trains in 1972 and for motor vehicles in 1980.

▶ Ex-South African Railways 2-6-2+2-6-2 Garratt loco No. 87 heads for Aberglaslyn Pass on the newly reopened Welsh Highland Railway.

▶ *Inset* Built by Albert Barnes in 1920, 4-4-2 'Joan' hauls a train alongside Marine Lake on the Rhyl Miniature Railway. The loco was named after Joan Butler, the daughter of the then railway company's owner.

THE LINE TODAY

Passenger services between Chester and Holyhead are currently operated by Arriva Trains Wales, while trains between London Euston and Holyhead are operated by Virgin Trains. Trains from Llandudno Junction, northwards to Llandudno and southwards along the scenic Conwy Valley to Blaenau Ffestiniog, are also operated by Arriva Trains Wales.

HERITAGE RAILWAYS

WELSH HIGHLAND RAILWAY

Harbour Station, Porthmadog, Gwynedd, LL49 9NF

Website: www.welshhighlandrailway.net

Tel: 01766 516000

Route: Caernarfon to Porthmadog

Length: 23½ miles

Nearest main-line station: Porthmadog

Opened in stages from 1997, the ambitious 1ft 11½in gauge Welsh Highland Railway runs first along the trackbed of the closed Carnaerfon to Afonwen standard gauge line to Dinas then strikes off in an easterly direction along the route of the old Welsh Highland Railway (closed throughout in 1937) into the Snowdonia National Park to Rhyd Ddu, Beddgelert, Aberglaslyn Pass and Porthmadog. The steam locomotives hauling the trains are massive (by narrow gauge standards) Beyer-Garratt articulated locos rehabilitated from South Africa. At Porthmadog Harbour station the WHR connects with the narrow gauge Ffestiniog Railway to Blaenau Ffestiniog.

RHYL MINIATURE RAILWAY

Marine Lake, Rhyl, Clwyd, LL18 1LN

Website: www.rhylminiaturerailway.co.uk

Tel: 01352 759109

Route: around Marine Lake

Length: 1 mile

Nearest main-line station: Rhyl

Opened in 1911, this classic 15in gauge seaside miniature railway takes passengers on a route around the perimeter of the Marine Lake at Rhyl, and on its southern shore parallels the North Wales Coast main line, where the locomotive shed is situated. Steam motive power includes four 4-4-2 'Atlantics' built by Albert Barnes in the 1920s. A new Central station and museum was opened in 2007.

TRAMWAY

GREAT ORME TRAMWAY

Victoria Station, Church Walks, Llandudno, Gwynedd LL30 2NB

Website: www.greatormetramway.co.uk

Tel: 01492 879306

Route: Victoria Station to Great Orme Summit

Length: 1 mile, 8 chains

Nearest mainline station: Llandudno

Opened in 1902, the 3ft 6in-gauge Great Orme Tramway is the only cable-operated street tramway in Britain. Built to take passengers to the 679ft summit of the Great Orme, where there are magnificent views of Snowdonia, Anglesey and the Irish Sea, the line climbs gradients as steep as 1-in-4. The bottom terminus is at Victoria station, from which the line rises, first along the centre of the road, 400ft in 872yd. The upper section rises 150ft in 827yd along its own right of way. As the line is divided into two sections, passengers have to change cars at the halfway point, where there is a central winding house. The original steam-driven winding drums were replaced by electricity in 1958. Four original tramcars survive, all 30ft long with end balconies and seating 48 people, and are equipped with radio-telephone links to the winding house. Half Way station features interpretative material showing the history of the tramway.

MUSEUM

PENRHYN CASTLE INDUSTRIAL RAILWAY MUSEUM

Penrhyn Castle (NT), Bangor, Gwynedd LL57 4HN

Website: www.nationaltrust.org.uk

Tel: 01248 371337

Nearest main-line station: Bangor (3 miles away)

Situated in the former stables of this National Trust property is a large collection of industrial steam locomotives and rolling stock, both standard and narrow gauge, including exhibits from the Dinorwic Quarry and the Padarn and Penrhyn Railways. The oldest loco in the collection is the 4ft-gauge Padarn Railway 0-4-0 'Fire Queen' built in 1848. There is also a display of signs and models.

WEST COAST MAIN LINE part 2

Crewe to Carlisle

Forming the middle section of what became the West Coast Main Line, the Crewe to Carlisle railway route features the famous Shap Summit, a gruelling slog (1 in 75 gradient) for steam locomotives from 1846 until the end of steam in 1967.

▲ Acton Bridge, 173 miles north of Euston, is the station before the flying junction at Weaver, which separates the lines to Carlisle and Liverpool. Here a railtour in May 1958 during which 'Crab' No. 42939 and 'Jubilee' No. 45593 'Kolhapur' managed to occupy the up and down main lines.

The middle section of the West Coast Main Line (between Crewe and Carlisle) was built by four different railway companies, all but one of which had become absorbed by the London & North Western Railway (LNWR) by 1879. To the south, the London & Birmingham Railway (L&BR) had reached Birmingham (Curzon Street) via Rugby and Coventry in 1838. The more direct Trent Valley Railway via Tamworth and Lichfield opened from Rugby to Stafford in 1847, by which time it had been absorbed by the newly created LNWR (for more details see pages 132–139).

GREEN FIELDS TO GREAT ENGINES

Opening one year earlier than the L&BR, the Grand Junction Railway (GJR) was authorised in 1833 to build an 82-mile line from Birmingham (Curzon Street) to Warrington via Wolverhampton, Stafford and Crewe. Engineered by George Stephenson and Joseph Locke, it opened for business in 1837 at Warrington, making use of the Warrington & Newton Railway, which had opened in 1831 to gain access to the Liverpool & Manchester Railway at Newton Junction. One of the stations on the line served the village of Monks Coppenhall but was named Crewe because of its proximity to Crewe Hall – apart from the village everything there was just green fields. Crewe soon became an important railway junction with the opening of the Chester & Crewe Railway in 1840 and the Manchester & Birmingham Railway (M&BR) in 1842, and it was here that the GJR established its works in 1843. The London & North Western Railway was formed by an amalgamation of the Grand Junction, L&BR and

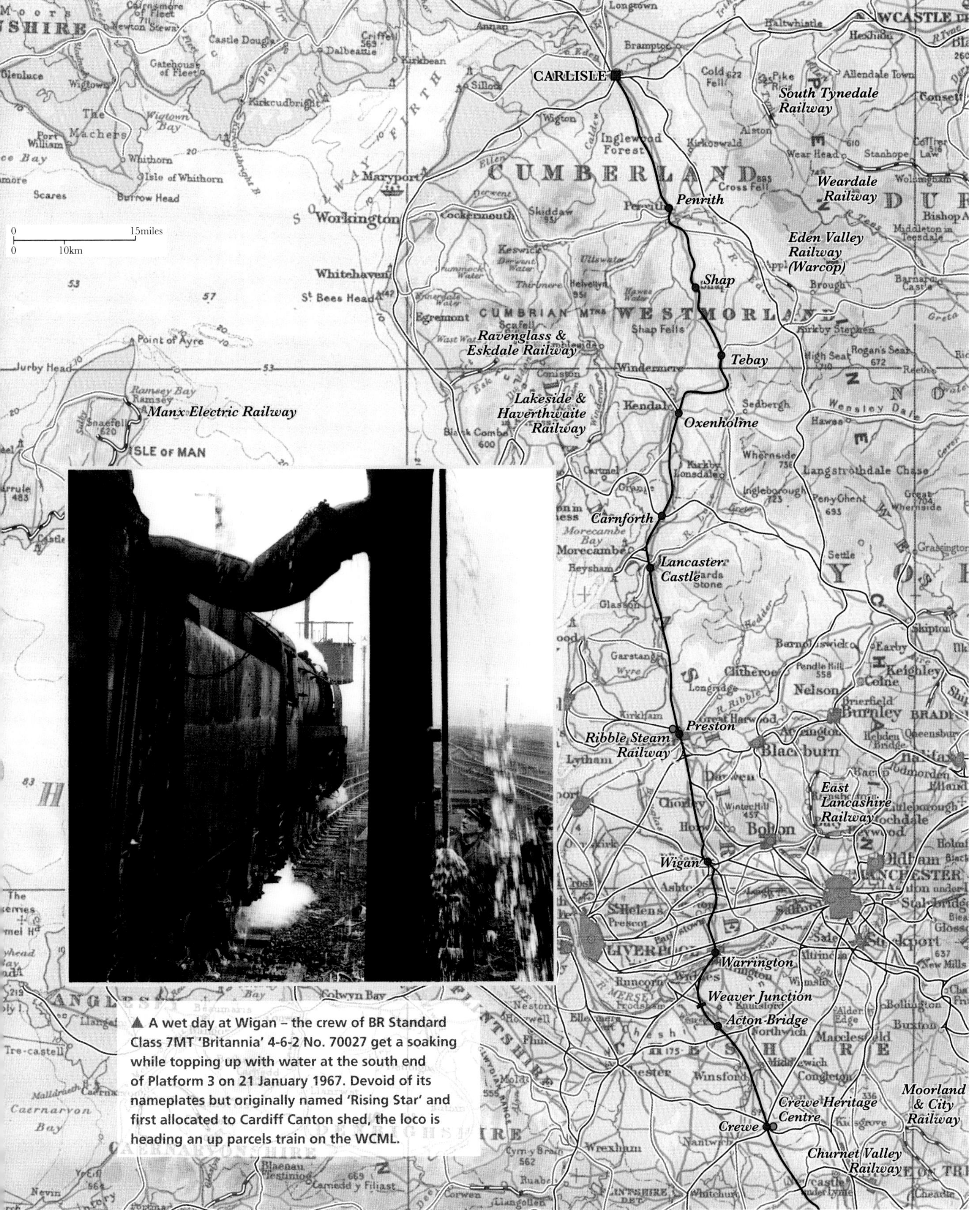

▲ A wet day at Wigan – the crew of BR Standard Class 7MT 'Britannia' 4-6-2 No. 70027 get a soaking while topping up with water at the south end of Platform 3 on 21 January 1967. Devoid of its nameplates but originally named 'Rising Star' and first allocated to Cardiff Canton shed, the loco is heading an up parcels train on the WCML.

▲ A group of young trainspotters gather at the north end of Lancaster Castle station to witness the departure of BR Standard Class 7MT 'Britannia' 4-6-0 No. 70012 on a Euston to Workington express on 9 October 1965. Once named 'John of Gaunt' (the nameplate had recently been removed to foil souvenir hunters), this loco spent its early life working on the Great Eastern main line between Liverpool St and Norwich.

◀ BR Standard Class 5MT 4-6-0 No. 73100 negotiates Lostock Hall Junction south of Preston with the Summer Saturdays Dundee to Blackpool train on 9 July 1966. To save running round the train at Preston, the passengers were treated to a circular tour, first entering the East Lancs side of the station from the north, then going round the junctions to the south of Preston before heading north again back through the station, then finally taking the Blackpool line.

▼ Dillicar water troughs were located to the south of Tebay. Here, two Stanier 'Black Five' 4-6-0s (leading engine No. 44778) send up a cloud of smoke, steam and spray as they pound northwards with an express on 5 August 1967.

Inset Unrebuilt ex-LMS 'Patriot' Class 4-6-0 No. 45513 waits for the road ahead at the north end of Preston station on 1 July 1961. Someone has obviously bothered to clean the lower cabside panel on this otherwise grimy and unnamed locomotive. Built in 1932, the loco was named 'Sir W. A. Stanier' in 1943 but lost its name when newly-built 'Coronation' Class 4-6-2 No. 46256 was named 'Sir William A. Stanier, F.R.S.' in 1947.

70027

the Manchester & Birmingham Railway in 1846, with Crewe becoming the main locomotive works of this now much enlarged company.

The population of Crewe grew from a few hundred in 1845 to 40,000 by 1901, when the railway employed 8,000 men and women. In 1848, it employed over 1,000 people and was turning out one locomotive a week. At its peak in the 1930s, Crewe Works employed over 20,000 people and under William Stanier turned out such classic LMS steam locomotives as the 'Princess' and 'Coronation' Class Pacifics and 'Jubilee' and 'Black Five' 4-6-0s. Under BR it built Riddles' 'Britannia', 'Clan' and the unique 'Duke of Gloucester' Pacifics and by 1990 it had built over 8,000 steam, diesel and electric locomotives. Most of the works have since been closed and the site redeveloped.

◀ BR Standard Class 7MT 'Britannia' 4-6-2 No. 70027 (once named 'Rising Star' but now devoid of nameplates) attacks Shap bank near Scout Green signalbox with the 1.27pm Liverpool to Glasgow express on 17 June 1967. This was the last summer of steam haulage on the WCML and the loco was withdrawn only three months later.

▼ A portrait of human activity and inactivity – in the days when nearly all mail was still carried by the railways ex-LMS 'Jubilee' Class 4-6-0 No. 45675 (formerly named 'Hardy' but now devoid of its nameplates) has its tender refilled at Carlisle before heading off with a northbound train on 30 July 1966.

A MAIN LINE FORMS

The West Coast Main Line north of Newton Junction to Preston was opened by the North Union Railway (NUR) in 1838. It was later leased jointly by the GJR and the Manchester & Leeds Railway (see pages 168–173) – their successors, the LNWR and Lancashire & Yorkshire Railway respectively, continued with this arrangement until the Big Four Grouping of 1923 when it became part of the LMS. To the north of Preston, the Lancaster & Preston Junction Railway (L&PJR) opened in 1840. This railway was first worked by the NUR but this arrangement ended in acrimony in 1842 and the L&PJR, in a fit of spite, leased itself to the Lancaster Canal Company. This arrangement continued until 1849, when it was leased by its new northern neighbour, the Lancaster & Carlisle Railway (L&CR). The latter company took over the L&PJR ten years later.

The final section of the major trunk route from London to Carlisle, the 69-mile Lancaster & Carlisle Railway was authorised in 1844. Engineered by Joseph Locke (the arch proponent of the power of steam) and built by Thomas Brassey, the railway took a route through the Lune Gorge before ascending the final 3 miles from Tebay to Shap Summit on a gradient of 1 in 75. From the north, Shap was approached along a 10-mile climb on a gradient of 1 in 125. The line was built by 10,000 navvies and opened in 1846, taking only 2½ years to complete. Worked from the outset by the newly formed LNWR, it remained independent until 1879 when it was taken over by the former company.

▲ Stanier 'Black Five' 4-6-0 No. 45290 of Newton Heath shed (26A) has a light load to haul up Shap Bank as it starts the climb north of Tebay with a Manchester Victoria to Glasgow Central train on 26 May 1958. The wagons in the background are on the former NER line to Kirkby Stephen and Darlington.

With the opening of the Caledonian Railway's main line from Glasgow to Carlisle (see pages 230–235) in 1848, the West Coast Main Line as we know it today was complete. Along with its 'branches' to Birmingham, Liverpool, Manchester, Leeds and Holyhead, the WCML was by far the most important trunk route in Britain, serving Britain's major centres of population and industry. It was described, justifiably, as the 'Premier Line' and was one of the most successful companies in Britain. In 1923 it became a main constituent company of the newly formed LMS.

The route of the famous Anglo-Scottish expresses such as the 'Royal Scot', the streamlined but short-lived 'Coronation Scot' and the post-war 'Caledonian', the WCML between Crewe and Carlisle included water troughs along its 141-mile route. First introduced by the LNWR in North Wales in 1860, the troughs allowed many of these expresses to run non-stop between Euston and Carlisle and were located at three locations: between Brock and Garstang; north of Hest Bank; at Dillicar south of Tebay.

During the BR era, the Crewe to Carlisle section of the WCML became something of a mecca for steam enthusiasts. Despite creeping dieselisation and electrification and the extinction of Stanier's 'Princess' and 'Coronation' Class Pacifics by 1964 and the dieselisation of Anglo-Scottish expresses, steam in the form of Stanier 'Black Five' 4-6-0s and 8F 2-8-0s, and newer BR Standard types including 'Britannia' Pacifics and 9F 2-10-0s continued to hold sway on most freight and parcels trains until the bitter end. By 1967, Shap had become a major draw for railway photographers eager to record their last sights of steam trains struggling up the long gradient, assisted in the rear by banking engines from Tebay. This all ended at midnight on 31 December, when both Carlisle Kingmoor and Tebay engine sheds were closed to steam. In the south, Crewe South shed had already closed on 6 November and all that was left were a few pockets of steam in the Manchester area and at Carnforth; these had all closed by 5 August 1968. The reign of steam in Britain was finally over. Following this there was a short diesel interregnum until electrification took over in 1974.

THE LINE TODAY

Passenger services between Crewe and Carlisle are currently operated by Virgin Trains. Parts of the route also see trains run by First TransPennine Express. The West Coast Main Line is also the principal freight corridor between England and Scotland.

HERITAGE RAILWAYS

CHURNET VALLEY RAILWAY

Kingsley & Froghall Station, Froghall, Staffordshire ST10 2HA

Website: www.churnet-valley-railway.co.uk

Tel: 01538 750755

Route: Leekbrook Junction to Kingsley & Froghall

Length: 5¼ miles

Nearest main-line station: none in area

Situated on the former North Staffordshire Railway line from Rocester to North Rode, opened in 1849 and completely closed by BR in 1988, the Cheddleton Railway Centre is housed in Cheddleton station building and yard in the picturesque Churnet Valley. It was originally opened by a group of preservationists in 1973, who restored the ornate station building, installed a museum and gave steam-train rides along the short length of track. In 1994 the Society signed a contract to purchase the 7 miles of redundant trackbed between Oakamoor and Leekbrook Junction and launched a share issue in 1995 to raise capital for the reopening of the line. Since then the railway has opened between Leekbrook Junction (no road access) to Kingsley & Froghall via Cheddleton and Consall stations. The line south of Kingsley to Oakamoor has been reopened but there is currently no station here. Locomotives based at Cheddleton include former Eastleigh-built Stanier Class 8F 2-8-0 No. 8624, BR Standard 9F 2-10-0 No. 92134 and several main-line diesels and DMUs. Future plans include a northward extension to Leek. Trains from the Churnet Valley also operate over the newly-opened Moorland and City Railway to Cauldon Low.

RIBBLE STEAM RAILWAY

Chain Caul Road, Preston PR2 2PD

Website: www.ribblesteam.org.uk

Tel: 01772 728 800

Route: Preston Riverside Strand Road Crossing

Length: 1½ miles

Nearest mainline station: Preston (2 miles)

Home to the railway collection from the now-closed Southport Railway Museum, the Ribble Steam Railway opened in 2005 and runs steam-hauled trains along part of the standard gauge Preston Docks line, crossing Preston Marina on a swing bridge, during summer months. The adjoining museum includes a large collection of industrial steam and diesel locomotives.

EAST LANCASHIRE RAILWAY

Bolton Street Station, Bury, Lancashire BL9 0EY

Website: www.east-lancs-rly.co.uk

Tel: 0161 764 7790

Route: Heywood to Rawtenstall

Length: 12 miles

Nearest main-line station: Bury Interchange (Manchester Metrolink)

The original East Lancashire Railway came into being as early as 1846 to serve cotton mills in the Irwell Valley north of Bury. The line was extended to Bacup in 1852 and the railway was absorbed by the Lancashire & Yorkshire in 1859 and then the LNWR in 1922, before becoming part of the LMS in 1923 and closing to all traffic in 1980. A preservation group had previously moved in to Bury and subsequently opened a transport museum in 1969. After receiving financial assistance, exceeding £1 million, from the local councils and county council, the first public trains started running between Bury and Ramsbottom in 1987, with Rawtenstall being reached in 1991. The eastward link from Bury to Heywood connects with the main rail system. Trains are operated along the picturesque Irwell Valley, with its several viaducts, by a variety of preserved main-line steam and diesel locomotives. Steam locomotives include LMS Class 3F 0-6-0 No. 47324, LMS 'Black Five' 4-6-0 No. 5337 and BR Standard Class 8 4-6-2 No. 71000 'Duke of Gloucester. Visiting locomotives from other railways can frequently be seen in action and the ELR has built up a reputation for its varied collection of preserved diesels, which can be seen in action on several diesel weekends. Preserved main-line diesels include examples from Classes 01, 05, 08, 20, 24, 33, 37, 40, 50 and 55.

MUSEUM

BURY TRANSPORT MUSEUM

Castlecroft Goods Warehouse, Castlecroft Road, Bury BL9 0LN

Website: www.burytransportmuseum.org.uk

Tel: 0161 763 7949

Nearest main-line station: ELR Bury Bolton Street station

The museum houses a collection of historic road vehicles and railway vehicles.

▼ Preserved ex-LNER Class 'A4' 4-6-2 No. 60007 'Sir Nigel Gresley', finished in early BR lined blue, crosses the river at Summerseat on the East Lancashire Railway.

THE LONG DRAG

Leeds to Carlisle

Initially unwanted by the Midland Railway, the Settle–Carlisle line is now a living memorial to Victorian engineering skills. As the third Anglo-Scottish trunk route, it could never compete with its rivals but after overcoming several closure proposals its recent renaissance can only be welcomed.

The southern section of the Leeds to Carlisle line started life as the Leeds & Bradford Railway, which opened between Leeds and Shipley in 1846 and was extended by the Leeds & Bradford Extension Railway to Skipton in 1847. Both of these companies were promoted by the financier George Hudson (see page 116) and taken over by the Midland Railway (MR) in 1851. The route was further extended by the North Western Railway (NWR) in 1849 when it opened between Skipton and Ingleton. Northwards from Ingleton, the NWR had planned to extend its line to Low Gill where it would meet the Lancaster & Carlisle Railway (worked by the London & North Western Railway) but work was halted. The railway between Ingleton and Low Gill was built finally by the Lancaster & Carlisle and opened in 1861, by which time the MR had taken over working the NWR. In theory offering a through route for MR trains to Scotland, the Ingleton line was beset by operating problems, exacerbated initially by the fact that the LNWR and MR stations at Ingleton were a mile apart and separated by a viaduct. Through running was deliberately discouraged by the LNWR so the Midland was forced to reconsider. Thus was the Settle to Carlisle railway born.

FORCEFUL CONSTRUCTION

Surveying for the new 71¼-mile line from Settle Junction to Carlisle started in 1865 and the project received authorisation a year later, but a national financial crisis soon put a stop to any progress on this £2.3 million project. In 1869 the Midland Railway

▼ Holbeck's ex-LMS 'Royal Scot' Class 4-6-0 No. 46145 'The Duke of Wellington's Regt. (West Riding)' prepares to leave Leeds City station with the down 'The Thames-Clyde Express' on 28 February 1960.

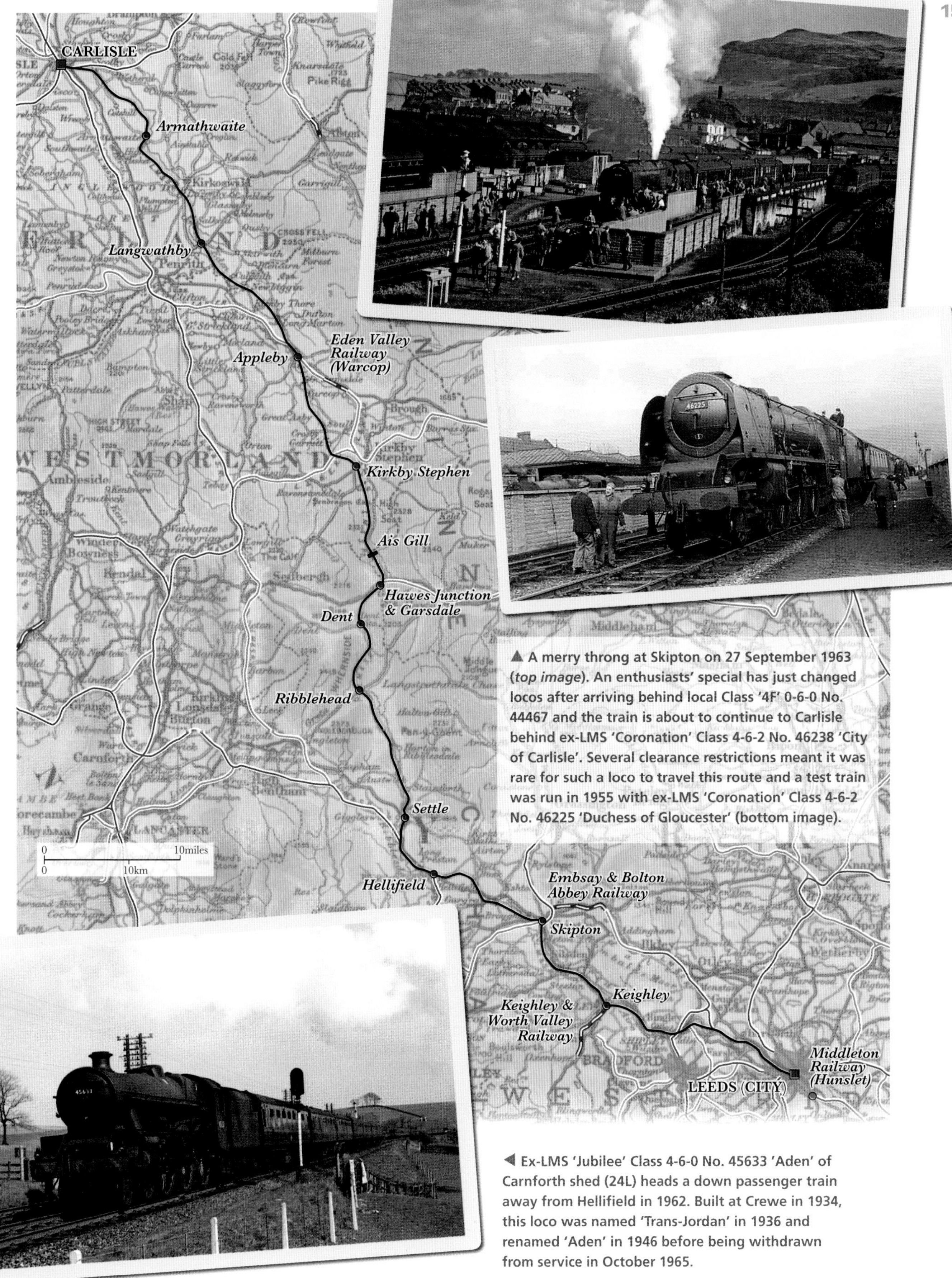

▲ A merry throng at Skipton on 27 September 1963 (*top image*). An enthusiasts' special has just changed locos after arriving behind local Class '4F' 0-6-0 No. 44467 and the train is about to continue to Carlisle behind ex-LMS 'Coronation' Class 4-6-2 No. 46238 'City of Carlisle'. Several clearance restrictions meant it was rare for such a loco to travel this route and a test train was run in 1955 with ex-LMS 'Coronation' Class 4-6-2 No. 46225 'Duchess of Gloucester' (bottom image).

◀ Ex-LMS 'Jubilee' Class 4-6-0 No. 45633 'Aden' of Carnforth shed (24L) heads a down passenger train away from Hellifield in 1962. Built at Crewe in 1934, this loco was named 'Trans-Jordan' in 1936 and renamed 'Aden' in 1946 before being withdrawn from service in October 1965.

▲ A BR Standard Class 9F 2-10-0 hauls a northbound empty anhydrite train across the 24-arch Ribblehead Viaduct on 14 October 1966. Until 1976 these trains, diesel-headed after 1967, were a common sight on the Settle–Carlisle, carrying anhydrite from a gypsum mine at Long Meg near Little Salkeld, northwest of Appleby, to a plant at Widnes in Cheshire.

▼ The long drag up to Ais Gill Summit – amid the bleak Pennines a BR Standard Class 4MT 4-6-0 climbs towards Ribblehead Viaduct with a northbound freight on 4 February 1967. This wonderfully evocative scene was to disappear in less than a year.

sought to abandon the scheme but Parliament refused permission on the grounds that other railway companies would suffer and the company was forced to start construction work. The statistics for this line are mind-boggling, especially as it was built through the wild Pennine Hills without the aid of mechanical excavators. Using temporary tramways, picks, shovels, wheelbarrows and horsedrawn carts, more than 6,000 navvies blasted their way across the landscape (assisted by recently invented dynamite), building 23 viaducts (the longest at Ribblehead has 24 arches) and 13 tunnels (the longest, Blea Moor, is 1½ miles long). The summit of the line, at Ais Gill, is 1,169ft above sea level and this is reached on a 15-mile-long ruling gradient of 1 in 100.

The workforce lived in temporary encampments along the line; the largest at Ribblehead, housing 2,000, including accompanying wives and children, had all the amenities of a small town. The weather was frequently atrocious with gales, snowstorms and heavy rain often dampening the navvies' spirits. Drunken behaviour in scenes reminiscent of the Wild West was rife and both local police and preachers were called in to deal with this problem. Many navvies also died, either from work-related accidents or in drunken brawls, and local cemeteries were enlarged to cope with the influx of bodies.

◀ The loops at Blea Moor allowed slow-moving goods trains to replenish water supplies. Here, on 28 July 1966, BR Standard Class 9F 2-10-0 No. 92004 heads through with a southbound anhydrite train from Long Meg to Widnes, while BR standard Class 7MT 'Britannia' No. 70032 'Tennyson' rests in the northbound loop with a freight from Skipton. Farther up is No. 92114 with a return anhydrite empties train.

The railway was finally opened to goods traffic in 1875 although passengers had to wait a further year before making the epic journey. The Settle–Carlisle line (the line that the Midland Railway didn't want to build) was completed three years late and had cost 70 per cent more than the original estimate. To cope with the extra traffic generated by the Settle–Carlisle, the station at Carlisle Citadel was considerably enlarged and, for the first time, allowed Midland Railway trains to run directly from London St Pancras to Glasgow St Enoch via the Glasgow & South Western Railway and to Edinburgh via the North British Railway's Waverley Route – the third Anglo-Scottish trunk line was open for business.

Soon, newly introduced Pullman car trains double-headed by Midland Railway crimson lake locomotives were a regular sight on the line. Prior to the Big Four Grouping of 1923, the timetable shows three stopping trains that covered the whole route each way on weekdays, along with two through expresses from St Pancras to and from Glasgow and two expresses to and from Edinburgh. In addition there were daily sleeping car trains to and

Despite the use of snow fences along the line, the Settle–Carlisle was often closed following heavy snowfalls. The winter of 1962/63 was particularly harsh and the line had been closed for several days before snowploughs broke through the drifts. Here, on 26 January 1963, the line had just been reopened at Dent station where Kingmoor's Stanier 'Black Five' 4-6-0 No. 44669 storms through with a northbound freight.

▼ **Remote Blea Moor could be a wild, wet and windy place – BR standard Class 4MT 4-6-0 No. 75041 pauses in the loop with a short northbound freight (one coal wagon and a guard's van) on 27 July 1966 as the driver passes the time of day with the signalman.**

from Glasgow and Edinburgh. The two principle expresses of the day were 'The Waverley' (St Pancras to Edinburgh) and 'The Thames-Clyde Express' (St Pancras to Glasgow St Enoch) – both were introduced by the LMS in 1927, although the former was named the 'Thames-Forth Express' until the Second World War. Water troughs installed at Garsdale avoided a time-wasting stop to replenish water. Despite this and compared to the alternative East Coast and West Coast routes, the journey times were slow and by the BR era these expresses' days were numbered. During this post-war period they were usually headed by 'Royal Scot' or 'Jubilee' 4-6-0s, although there was a period when ex-LNER 'A3' 4-6-2s also put in appearances. Dieselisation followed in the early 1960s and in 1968 'The Waverley' was withdrawn. 'The Thames-Clyde' soldiered on until 1976 when it was also withdrawn following the electrification of the West Coast Main Line. Despite dieselisation of these expresses, the Settle–Carlisle line saw steam workings until the end of 1967 when Carlisle Kingmoor shed was closed.

◀ **An ex-LMS Hughes 'Crab' 2-6-0 raises a pall of smoke over the Pennine fells as it struggles up to the summit of the line at Ais Gill with a freight on 26 May 1961.**

Frequently blocked by snowfall in winter, expensive to maintain and operate, not serving any major centres of population, with little local traffic and paralleled by the West Coast Main Line, it was hardly surprising that the Settle to Carlisle line was listed for closure in the 1963 Beeching Report. In the end, the line's usefulness as a diversionary route when the WCML was closed probably saved the day, although all stations along the line apart from Settle and Appleby were closed in 1970. Another scare came in the early 1980s when the majestic Ribblehead Viaduct was deemed unsafe and closure loomed again. By this time there were only two return trains each day but after sustained organised opposition the closure was refused in 1989. Since then there has been a transformation of the line's fortunes, helped in no small way by the Friends of the Settle–Carlisle Line, who have improved facilities with eight stations reopened and signal boxes at Armathwaite and Settle restored. There has also been major investment in the infrastructure, viaducts have been restored, passenger train services improved, through freight workings reintroduced and steam charter trains regularly make appearances. After years of uncertainty the future looks good for the Settle–Carlisle line.

Despite its length the Settle–Carlisle line gave birth to only one branch line (the trans-Pennine line from Darlington to Tebay and the Penrith line via Kirkby Stephen had already opened in 1861 and 1862 respectively) – the 5¾-mile branch from Hawes Junction to Hawes was opened in 1878. At Hawes it made an end-on connection with the North Eastern Railway's 34-mile branch from Northallerton via Leyburn. The line closed to passengers in 1954 and completely in 1959, leaving Hawes at the end of a long freight-only branch line from Northallerton until 1964.

▲ Leaking steam, BR Standard Class 7MT 'Britannia' 4-6-2 No. 70014 'Iron Duke' approaches Birkett Tunnel south of Kirkby Stephen with a southbound football special on 5 February 1967. The train of newly painted blue and white Mk 1 coaches looks slightly garish among the Pennine fells, while the 'Brit' seems to have lost its original nameplate (replaced by a painted version).

▼ In the brief period when 'The Thames-Clyde Express' was hauled by ex-LNER 'A3' 4-6-2s, No. 60070 'Gladiateur' enters Carlisle station with the southbound train from Glasgow St Enoch on 27 May 1961. The loco would have continued to haul the train over the Settle–Carlisle before an engine change at Leeds for the journey south to St Pancras.

THE LINE TODAY

Passenger services between Leeds and Carlisle are operated by Northern Rail. The line is also an important diversionary route for West Coast Main Line traffic. Lancashire DalesRail operates a return train service for ramblers on Sundays (Easter to October) from Blackpool to Carlisle via Clitheroe and the Settle–Carlisle. The SettleCarlisle Partnership promotes the scenic Settle to Carlisle railway (see www.settle-carlisle.co.uk).

▲ Middleton Railway's ex-NER Class Y7 0-4-0T No. 1310 of 1891 vintage emerges from a short tunnel under the motorway in South Leeds.

▶ The joy of steam – preserved ex-GWR 'Hall' Class 4-6-0 No. 4953 'Pitchford Hall' puts on a spectacular display on the Keighley & Worth Valley Railway.

HERITAGE RAILWAYS

MIDDLETON RAILWAY TRUST

Moor Road, Hunslet, Leeds LS10 2JQ

Website: www.middletonrailway.org.uk

Tel: 0845 680 1758

Route: Moor Road to Park Halt

Length: 1¼ miles

Nearest main-line station: Leeds

The Middleton Railway operates at weekends on the site of the first railway to obtain an Act of Parliament, in 1758. Originally built to a gauge of 4ft 1in, it was also the first railway to use steam haulage commercially and became, in 1960, the first standard gauge line to be run by volunteers. An interesting collection of steam and diesel locomotives and rolling stock is housed on the line and in the museum, including North Eastern Railway Class Y7 0-4-OT No. 1310, built in 1891, and LNER Class Yl 0-4-0 vertical boiler Sentinel No. 54, built in 1933.

KEIGHLEY & WORTH VALLEY RAILWAY

The Railway Station, Haworth, Keighley, West Yorkshire BD22 8NJ

Website: www.kwvr.co.uk

Tel: 01535 645214 (01535 647777 talking timetable)

Route: Keighley to Oxenhope

Length: 5 miles

Nearest main-line station: Keighley

This was one of the earliest preserved standard gauge railways, reopened by a preservation society in 1967. The railway still serves the community of the Worth Valley as originally intended. The former Midland Railway branch from Keighley, on the main Leeds to Skipton line, to Oxenhope opened in 1867 to serve the large number of local mills, and was closed to passengers by BR in 1962. The line, although short, offers much to the visitor, together with its associations with the Brontës at Haworth and the filming of E. Nesbit's *The Railway Children* at Oakworth. A large collection of nearly 40 steam and diesel locomotives has been built up over the years and the railway is also home to two museums, The Vintage Carriage Trust at Ingrow and the Railway Museum at Oxenhope, and extensive workshop facilities. Passenger services are usually operated by Lancashire & Yorkshire Railway 0-6-0 No. 957 (built in 1887), former BR Standard Class 4MT 2-6-4 tank No. 80002, WD 2-8-0 No. 90733 (built in 1945) and a Class 101 DMU. Steam trains operate most of the services along this picturesque route, calling at carefully restored award-winning gas-lit stations. Tiny Damems station is reputably the smallest in Britain.

EMBSAY & BOLTON ABBEY STEAM RAILWAY

Bolton Abbey Station, Bolton Abbey, Skipton, North Yorkshire BD23 6AF

Website: www.embsayboltonabbeyrailway.org.uk

Tel: 01756 710614

Route: Embsay to Bolton Abbey

Length: 4 miles

Nearest main-line station: Skipton

The former Midland Railway branch from Skipton to Ilkley opened in 1888 and was closed to passengers by British Rail in 1965. The Yorkshire Dales Railway obtained a Light Railway Order in 1979 and since then has reopened 4 miles of track from Embsay, with its original Midland Railway buildings, to a new award-winning terminus at Bolton Abbey. The railway owns and operates a very large collection of finely restored industrial steam locomotives, vintage carriages and diesels.

THE CUMBRIAN COAST

Carlisle to Barrow-in-Furness

Built to serve some of the world's largest haematite iron-ore mines, the scenic coastal railway route from Carlisle to Barrow-in-Furness, built by four separate companies, was completed in 1850 and narrowly escaped closure in the 1960s.

The southern section of the railway along the Cumbrian Coast had its beginnings in the presence of haematite iron ore, mined near Barrow-in-Furness for hundreds of years. The ore was originally carried by packhorse to Ulverston, from where it was shipped out to furnaces in South Wales. However, tidal conditions at Ulverston were not ideal and soon the ore was being sent via the then small harbour village of Barrow.

THE FURNESS RAILWAY

By the early 19th century schemes were being put forward to link the mines with Barrow by means of a railway. So the Furness Railway (FR) was born – isolated initially from other railways and, despite scathing criticism from the poet William Wordsworth, it opened between Barrow and Lindal in 1846 along with a branch northwards to slate mines at Kirkby. The latter was extended to serve copper mines near Broughton in 1848. The Furness Railway remained isolated until 1854 when the Ulverstone & Lancaster Railway (taken over by the FR in 1862) opened for goods traffic in August 1857. At Carnforth this railway met the London & North Western Railway's West Coast Main Line.

Meanwhile to the north, the Maryport & Carlisle Railway (M&CR) had opened throughout in 1845, the company also remaining independent until 1923. To the south of Maryport, the Whitehaven Junction Railway, supported by the Maryport

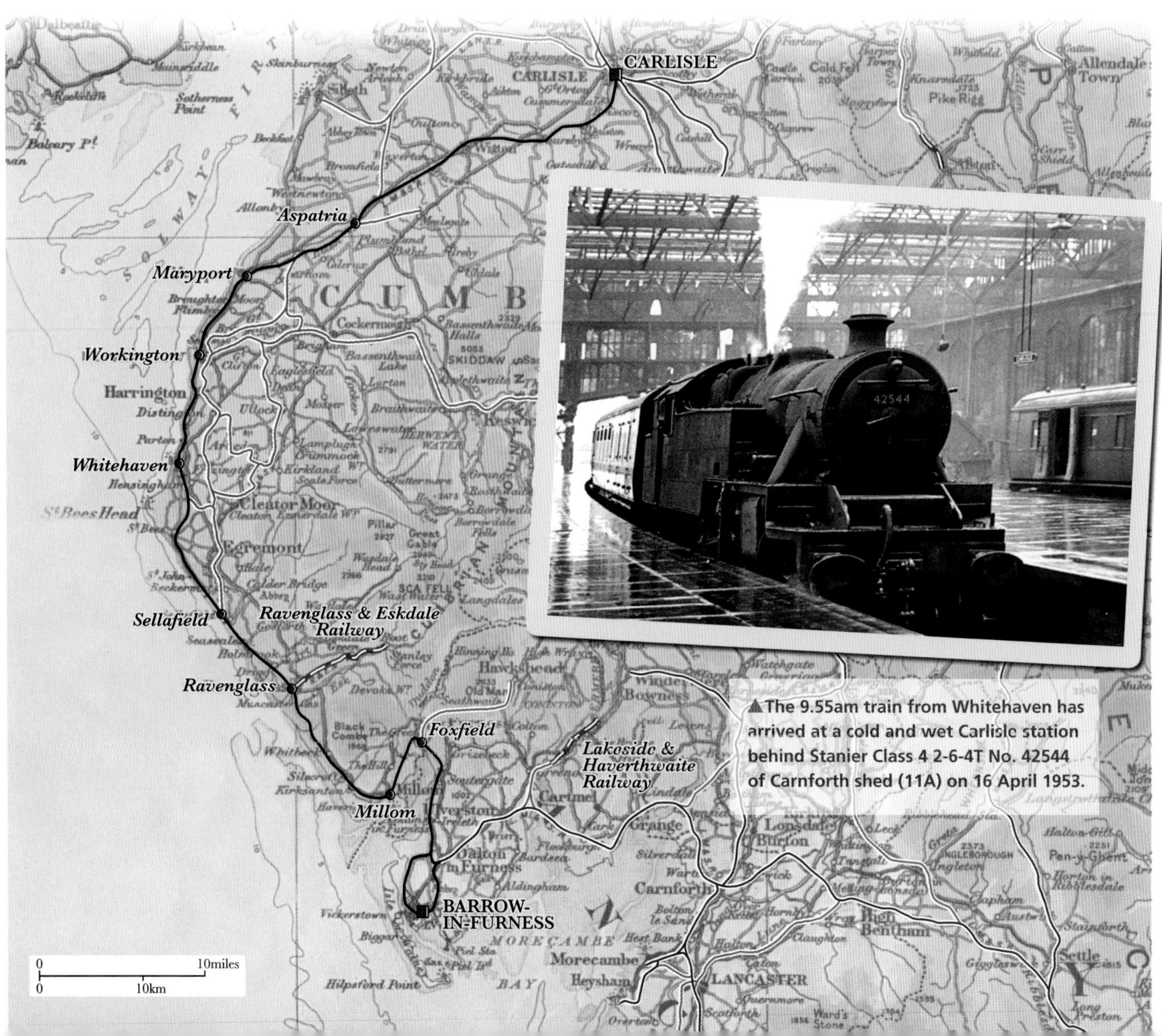

▲The 9.55am train from Whitehaven has arrived at a cold and wet Carlisle station behind Stanier Class 4 2-6-4T No. 42544 of Carnforth shed (11A) on 16 April 1953.

& Carlisle, opened its coast-hugging route to Whitehaven via Workington in 1847. The missing link in the coastal chain was provided by the Whitehaven & Furness Junction Railway, which opened throughout via Ravenglass in 1850 and was later absorbed by the Furness Railway in 1866.

Although the M&CR and the FR remained independent until the 1923 Grouping, the coastal section of railway from Maryport to Whitehaven (the Whitehaven Junction Railway) was taken over by the London & North Western Railway (LNWR) in 1866. This blocking movement by the LNWR was only possible after the Cockermouth, Keswick & Penrith Railway had opened through the Lake District in 1865 – the latter railway was worked from the outset by the LNWR.

The Furness Railway was therefore caught in a pincer movement by the LNWR until the Furness & Midland Joint Railway was opened from Carnforth to the Midland Railway's line at Wennington in 1867, thus allowing haematite iron-ore trains to travel unhindered from the FR to furnaces in Yorkshire.

Carrying vast amounts of haematite, the FR was a highly profitable railway for many years and one of the first to promote tourism successfully, remaining independent until 1923 when it became part of the newly formed London, Midland and Scottish (LMS). During its life the FR had turned what was once a small village into a thriving dock and steel town – Barrow-in-Furness also went on to become a major shipbuilding centre and was the focus of Luftwaffe bombing attacks in the Second World War when Central station was destroyed.

▲ A rope-worked incline once connected a coal mine on the clifftop at Whitehaven with the harbour below. Steam haulage, in the form of NCB saddle tanks, continued to operate around the harbour sidings well after the end of main-line steam in Cumbria. Here NCB 0-4-0ST No. 8 shunts a rake of coal wagons in 1968.

AFTER AMALGAMATION

Until the 1923 Grouping, most passenger services along the Cumbrian Coast Line from either Carlisle in the north or Barrow in the south terminated at Whitehaven, with only two through trains each weekday running along the whole route. This pattern continued under the LMS but by the 1950s, under British Railways, most Barrow-bound trains originated at Workington while trains from Carlisle terminated at Whitehaven. Even as late as the early 1960s Workington was still well served by

Perched high on the clifftops overlooking the Irish Sea at Lowca Washery, north of Whitehaven, Giesl-chimneyed Hunslet NCB 0-6-0ST 'Warspite' performs its humble duties with coal wagons in the summer of 1968.

▼ *Main image* **The Stephenson Locomotive Society's 'Furness Rail Tour' visited Millom Steelworks on 2 September 1967 – a year before closure. Here the tour engine, Stanier 'Black Five' 4-6-0 No. 45134 meets up with the works' diminutive 0-4-0ST No. 2 'Prince John'. Along with Millom, the West Cumbrian steelworks at Barrow and Workington (the latter famous for the manufacture of railway lines) have long since closed.**

through trains using the coastal route, including through carriages to Liverpool Exchange, Birmingham New Street and London Euston.

Despite the early introduction of diesel multiple units, this nearly all came to an end in 1963 when the line from Whitehaven to Barrow was listed in Dr Beeching's report. Fortunately it was saved, no doubt helped by its strategic importance serving the Sellafield nuclear processing facility. Freight trains continued to be steam-hauled for a few more years until Barrow shed closed at the end of 1966 and Workington at the end of 1967.

With the coming of the railway to Whitehaven in 1847, a whole collection of feeder lines sprouted up to serve haematite and coal mines in the foothills of the Lake District. These included the Whitehaven, Cleator & Egremont Railway, which opened in 1856 and lost its passenger trains in 1935; the Rowrah & Kelton Fell Mineral Railway, which opened in 1877 (closed 1927); and the Cleator & Workington Junction Railway, opened 1879 (closed 1928). Numerous colliery and harbour networks continued to use steam, in the form of NCB saddle tanks, long after it had been eradicated on the main rail network. At Ravenglass the 3ft-gauge Ravenglass & Eskdale Railway opened in 1875. Regauged as a 15in miniature railway in 1915, it is still open as a passenger-carrying line (see page 167). Farther south at Foxfield, the 9½-mile branch to Coniston opened in 1859, and closed to passengers in 1958 and to goods in 1962.

▲ Stanier 'Black Five' 4-6-0 No. 44671 passes through Ravenglass station with a coal train bound for Barrow, c.1960. On the right is the 15in-gauge Ravenglass & Eskdale Railway terminus with a couple of old Pullman coaches in the sidings.

▼ Hauled by ex-LMS Fowler Class 4 2-6-4T No. 42393, the 9.49am train from Millom to Barrow pauses at Foxfield station on 14 September 1950.

◀ The 9½-mile branch line from Foxfield to Coniston Lake lost its passenger service on 8 October 1958 and closed to goods on 30 April 1962. Here, Ivatt Class 2 2-6-2T No. 41221 waits to depart with a train to Foxfield on 16 July 1957.

THE LINE TODAY

Passenger services between Carlisle and Barrow-in-Furness via Whitehaven and Ravenglass are operated by Northern Rail. There is no Sunday service.

HERITAGE RAILWAYS

RAVENGLASS & ESKDALE RAILWAY

Ravenglass, Cumbria,
CA18 1SW

Website: www.ravenglass-railway.co.uk

Tel: 01229 717171

Route: Ravenglass to Dalegarth

Length: 7 miles

Nearest main-line station: Ravenglass

The Ravenglass & Eskdale Railway opened in 1875 as a 3ft-gauge line to carry haematite iron ore from mines in Eskdale to the Furness Railway at Ravenglass. The first locomotive was Manning Wardle 0-6-0 'Devon'. Passenger services started in 1876 but the company became bankrupt and was managed by a receiver. Passenger trains stopped in 1908 and goods services ceased in 1913. However, W. J. Bassett-Lowke, the famous manufacturer of model railways, came to the rescue and regauged the line to 15in. The first locomotive was 'Atlantic' 4-4-2 'Sans Pareil' and in 1915 trains ran again on what was the 'World's Smallest Public Railway'. A daily train service operated and an additional locomotive, 0-8-0 'Muriel' (later to become 'River Irt' and converted to 0-8-2), was purchased from Sir Arthur Heywood. The line flourished with the growth of granite traffic, and a new locomotive, 2-8-2 'River Esk', was built. In 1925, the line was purchased by Sir Aubrey Brocklebank, who enlarged the quarries and stone-crushing plant. Following the end of the Second World War, the Ravenglass & Eskdale Railway was purchased by the Keswick Granite Company in 1948, who closed the quarries in 1960 and put the line up for sale by auction. However, an eleventh-hour rescue operation was mounted by railway enthusiasts and the line was saved again. In 1967 another locomotive, 2-8-2 'River Mite', entered service and with improved revenues the railway has been progressively restored. The railway workshops constructed 2-6-2 'Northern Rock' in 1976 and have also built new diesel and steam locomotives for Blackpool Pleasure Beach and a Japanese leisure park. The RER also pioneered the use of radio for operation of their trains, a system that is now widely used by the main-line railways. The headquarters of the line at Ravenglass, also home to the railway-owned 'Ratty Arms' public house and an interesting railway museum, is situated adjacent to the main-line railway station on the Cumbrian Coast Line. Six steam and six diesel locomotives operate on the line, and coaching stock consists of a mixture of open, semi-open and closed saloons.

LAKESIDE & HAVERTHWAITE RAILWAY

Haverthwaite Station, Nr Ulverston, Cumbria LA12 8AL

Website: www.lakesiderailway.co.uk

Tel: 015395 31594

Route: Haverthwaite to Lakeside

Length: 3½ miles

Nearest main-line station: none in area

The former Furness Railway branch from Ulverston to Lakeside opened in 1869, and was finally closed by BR in 1967. A preservation group took over the steeply graded section from Haverthwaite and steam trains started running again in 1973 when the line was opened by the Bishop of Wakefield, the Rt Rev. Eric Treacy. The short but highly scenic journey can be taken in conjunction with a 10½-mile trip along Lake Windermere as trains connect with steamers at Lakeside terminus. A collection of restored industrial and ex-BR steam and diesel locos are used on the line, with the main power being two LMS-designed and BR-built 2-6-4 tank engines, Nos 42073 and 42085, dating from 1950 and 1951 respectively

▼ Ravenglass & Eskdale Railway's 0-8-2 No. 4 'River Irt' arrives at Ravenglass station with a train from Dalegarth. The loco was originally built by Sir Arthur Heywood in 1894 for his Eaton Hall Railway in Cheshire.

THROUGH THE PENNINES

Manchester to Bradford

The earliest of three trans-Pennine railway lines, the Manchester & Leeds Railway along the Calder Valley brought growth and prosperity to the world-leading cotton industry of east Lancashire when it opened and later, in the British Railways era, also witnessed the final days of steam haulage in the UK.

◀ It's the final week of steam on British Railways and the clock is inexorably ticking away at Manchester Victoria. Here, on 4 August 1968, Stanier 'Black Five' 4-6-0s Nos 44871 and 44894 wait for the arrival of the 'Bahamas Special' for a final trip across the Pennines. The former loco has been preserved and has recently returned to main-line working.

Until the late 18th century, transporting goods over the Pennines between Lancashire and Yorkshire had been a time-consuming business, the centuries-old rutted tracks impeding the progress of the Industrial Revolution. This all changed in 1776 when a group of Rochdale businessmen proposed a canal from Manchester to Sowerby Bridge, where it would meet the Calder & Hebble Navigation. Engineered by James Brindley, the Rochdale Canal and its 92 locks opened throughout in 1804, and linked up with the Bridgewater Canal in Manchester. Built as a wide canal, it had serious advantages over its rival, the Huddersfield Narrow Canal, which burrowed under the Pennines through the 5,696yd-long Standedge Tunnel.

WATER VERSUS RAIL

The Rochdale Canal was a success from the start and, until the coming of the railways, became the premier route for trade between Lancashire and Yorkshire, carrying vast amounts of coal, cotton, wool, salt, timber and limestone, along with finished goods from hundreds of textile mills.

The canal's supremacy was short-lived when the Liverpool & Manchester Railway (L&MR) opened in 1830. This revolutionary new transport system enabled vast quantities of raw materials and finished goods to be transported cheaply and quickly between the port of Liverpool and east Lancashire. Soon there were schemes put forward to build railways from Manchester to the textile mills in the Pennine foothills and farther afield across the Pennines to Yorkshire. In the end three major railway routes were built, all tunnelling through the hills, but the first to see the light of day was the Manchester & Leeds Railway (M&LR), which received authorisation in 1836.

Engineered by George Stephenson and Thomas Gooch (brother of GWR locomotive superintendent Daniel Gooch), the railway was opened in stages: from Oldham Road station in Manchester to Littleborough in 1839; from Normanton (where it met the North Midland Railway's line to Leeds) along the Calder Valley to Hebden Bridge in 1840; the intervening gap between Littleborough and Hebden Bridge involved the excavation of Summit Tunnel, which opened in 1841. At its western end the line was extended to meet the L&MR's new station at Hunt's Bank (later renamed Manchester Victoria) in 1844.

At just over 1½ miles long, Summit Tunnel was, for a short period, the longest railway tunnel in the world. Excavated through treacherous seams of shale, sandstone and coal by a team of navvies using just picks, shovels and wheelbarrows, the tunnel was lined with over 23 million bricks and took three years to complete. Since its opening in 1841 the tunnel has been closed only once, when a derailed petrol train caught fire inside it on 20 December 1984.

MANCHESTER & LEEDS RAILWAY

Following the course of the River Calder, the newly opened Manchester & Leeds Railway had naturally bypassed the important and growing cotton town of Halifax, itself located up a narrow tributary of the river. Local mill owners were furious and it wasn't until 1844 that the M&LR opened a short branch from Greetland to the town. Two years later the West Riding Union Railway was authorised to build a line from Sowerby Bridge (on the M&LR's main line) to Halifax (where it met the branch from Greetland) and up the Hebble Valley to Low Moor and the Yorkshire wool capital of Bradford. Involving the boring of five tunnels, the West Riding Union Railway opened throughout in 1852, by which time the line had already amalgamated with the newly formed Lancashire & Yorkshire Railway.

Bradford had already been reached from the north by the Leeds & Bradford Railway in 1846 with trains terminating at what later became known as Forster Square station. Trains from

▶ **Stanier 'Black Five' 4-6-0 No. 44729 emerges from the eastern end of Summit Tunnel with a Liverpool Exchange to Leeds/Bradford express on 14 June 1961. The site of a serious fire in 1984, the tunnel at 1½ miles long and took 3 years to build.**

▼ **The Liverpool Exchange to Newcastle express is seen here heading east of Hebden Bridge on 27 February 1960 led by ex-LMS 'Jubilee' Class 4-6-0 No. 45698 'Mars'. At the narrowest part of the valley, to the right of the railway is the River Calder, the Rochdale Canal and the road.**

Main image Witnessed by a throng of well-dressed railway photographers perched on their vantage points, this Summer Saturdays steam spectacular at Bradford was soon to end. Seen here on 26 August 1967, the simultaneous departure from Exchange station at 8.20am of two trains: 'Black Five' 4-6-0 No. 44694 (left) heading for Bridlington via Low Moor and Halifax has rear end assistance, while No. 44662 (right) tackles the 1 in 50 gradient unaided with a Skegness train. Both engines were allocated to Low Moor shed (55J).

▲ **Out of all of Stanier's 842 'Black Five' 4-6-0s No. 44767 was unique, being the only one fitted with the Stephenson link motion – apparently it was a fine performer and a regular on the Calder Valley route. Here the loco is seen ready to leave Halifax station with the 5.49pm train to Liverpool Exchange on 17 August 1959.**

Halifax first terminated at Adolphus Street station, but this soon proved to be inadequate and a new joint terminus, named Exchange, was opened in 1867. The Leeds, Bradford & Halifax Junction Railway (later absorbed by the Great Northern Railway) had already reached Bradford from Leeds in 1854 and its trains also terminated at Exchange station. Even this was proving inadequate by the 1880s when it was rebuilt in the style of King's Cross station with two arched roofs and ten platforms. Sadly, this grand building was demolished in 1976 and replaced by the modern four-platform Interchange station located farther south.

THE CREATION OF THE L&YR

The Lancashire & Yorkshire Railway had been formed by the amalgamation of several Lancashire and Yorkshire railway companies, including the M&LR, in 1847; by taking over other railways in the region, it went on to build an unparalleled east–west railway empire stretching from Liverpool to Goole. Manchester Victoria station with its 17 platforms was one of the largest in the UK and the company also went on to own the largest fleet of ships of any pre-Grouping railway company. Previously located at Miles Platting, its main railway works at Horwich, near Bolton, opened in 1887 and at its peak employed around 1,500 men who went on to build hundreds of steam locomotives for the L&YR and later the LMS and British Railways. Perhaps the most famous of these is the ugly but practical 'Horwich Crab' 2-6-0, which was designed by the

The chalked message on the smokebox door says it all. The date is 1 October 1967, the very last day of steam haulage in the West Riding of Yorkshire and, despite this, Holbeck's 'Black Five' 4-6-0 No. 45428 is ready to tackle the 1 in 50 gradient out of Exchange station with the Bradford portion of an up express to King's Cross via Leeds. Bradford Exchange station was demolished in 1976 and a modern 'interchange' station was opened farther south.

Lancashire & York Railway's chief mechanical engineer, George Hughes. Introduced by the LMS in 1926, 245 of these powerful mixed-traffic locos were built and could be seen hard at work all over the LMS system between Ayr and Bristol. Horwich Works closed in 1983.

Freight traffic over the Calder Valley line became so heavy that it was quadrupled from Hebden Bridge to Luddendon Foot, just west of Sowerby Bridge, and between Brighouse and Wakefield in the late 19th and early 20th centuries. Water troughs were also installed on the line between Rochdale and Smithy Bridge and at Luddendon Foot. Steam held sway here until Low Moor engine shed, south of Bradford, closed in October 1967, while in Manchester, the premier L&YR engine shed at Newton Heath, once home to a large number of Stanier 'Black Five' and 'Jubilee' 4-6-0s, 'Crab' 2-6-0s and ex-WD 2-8-0s, closed to steam in February 1968. Founded in 1878, the football team from Newton Heath engine shed, known as Newton Heath LYR Football Club, changed its name to Manchester United in 1902.

Westwards from Todmorden, the line through Burnley and Blackburn to Preston witnessed the very last days of steam on British Railways with Rose Grove shed closing on 5 August 1968 – gone are the days of grimy ex-WD 2-8-0s clanking along the Calder Valley with their loaded coal trains from the Yorkshire coalfields. By then freight and passenger traffic had dropped considerably along the line and the former L&YR main line east of Milner Royd Junction (a mile east of Sowerby Bridge) to Heaton Lodge Junction (one mile west of Mirfield) lost its passenger service in 1970 when Brighouse station closed. However, the line was still utilised by freight and diverted passenger trains and in 2000 regular trains recommenced between Manchester Victoria and Leeds via the Calder Valley with Brighouse station reopening.

THE LINE TODAY

Passenger services between Manchester Victoria and Bradford via Todmorden and Halifax are operated by Northern Rail. Additionally, a new Bradford to King's Cross express service via Halifax, Brighouse, Wakefield Kirkgate and Pontefract Monkhill has recently been introduced by Grand Central.

HERITAGE RAILWAY

KIRKLEES LIGHT RAILWAY

The Railway Station, Park Mill Way, Clayton West, Nr Huddersfield, West Yorkshire HD8 9XJ

Website: www.kirkleeslightrailway.com

Tel: 01484 865727

Route: Clayton West to Shelley (via 511yd Shelley Woodhouse Tunnel)

Length: 3¾ miles

This 15in-gauge miniature railway operates every weekend along part of the trackbed of the former Lancashire & Yorkshire Railway's branch from Clayton West Junction to Clayton West, opened in 1879 and finally closed by BR in 1983. The Kirklees Light Railway was the brainchild of Brian Taylor, who was also involved in the building of a 10¼in-gauge miniature steam railway at Shibden Park, Halifax. After several years of searching for a suitable site, work started on the present line in 1990 and the first train ran to Cuckoo's Nest in 1991 and to Skelmanthorpe in late 1992. Locomotives operating on the line include Hunslet-type 2-6-2 tank 'Fox', articulated 0-4+4-0s 'Hawk' and 'Owl' and 0-6-4 saddle tank 'Badger'. Rolling stock consists of nine 20-seat carriages, the fully enclosed examples being heated. All locomotives and rolling stock were produced for the railway by Brian Taylor, who has built and continues to supply equipment for other railways. Clayton West is also home to the Barnsley Society of Model Engineers, who operate a passenger-carrying miniature railway on most weekends.

▲ A working replica of Stephenson's 'Rocket' at work at the Manchester Museum of Science and Industry

MUSEUM

MUSEUM OF SCIENCE & INDUSTRY

Liverpool Road, Castlefield, Manchester M3 4FP

Website: www.mosi.org.uk

Tel: 0161 832 2244

Nearest main-line station: Deansgate

A science and industry museum situated in the original station buildings of the Liverpool & Manchester Railway, which were opened in 1830. In addition to the many and varied railway exhibits, there is much to interest everyone, with displays on cotton mills, aviation, gas, electricity, space, water supply and sewage disposal. Railway exhibits, all built in Manchester, include sectioned Isle of Man Railway 2-4-0 tank No. 3 'Pender', built by Beyer-Peacock in 1873, a working replica (with some original parts) of the 1829 'Novelty', South African Railways Class GL 3ft 6in-gauge Garratt 4-8-2+2-8-4 No. 2352 and ex-BR Class EM2 electric Co-Co No. 1505 'Ariadne' built in 1954. Steam trains, hauled by a replica of Robert Stephenson's 'Planet' loco, provide rides at weekends along nearly one mile of track within the museum complex and run past the original booking halls, waiting room and warehouse. The latter is the oldest railway building in the world and houses various displays on Manchester's industrial and social history.

◀ Hunslet-style 2-6-2T 'Fox' heads a train at Clayton West station on the 15in-gauge Kirklees Light Railway.

69865
E 88467 E

NORTH EASTERN REGION

A scene at at Whitby West Cliff looking towards Whitby Town on 4 September 1957. Class 'A8' 4-6-2T No. 69865, a Whitby (50G) engine, stands waiting for a fellow class member to clear the way.

THE RACE TRACK

York to Newcastle

Originally forming part of the vast railway empire of the disgraced 'Railway King' George Hudson, the route of the East Coast Main Line north of York as we know it today evolved over the course of nearly 50 years before it was finally completed in 1872.

On 27 September 1825, northeast England saw the opening of the world's first public railway, the Stockton & Darlington. Primarily designed to carry coal, it was extended to Middlesbrough in 1830. For a few years this modern mode of transport, along with a few other early colliery tramways, remained isolated until the building of the major Anglo-Scottish trunk line now known as the East Coast Main Line. A vital part of this route, from Newcastle to York, was built by the Great North of England Railway (GNoER). This company obtained authorisation first in 1836 to construct a railway from Newcastle to Croft, 5 miles south of Darlington to meet a branch of the Stockton & Darlington Railway. A year later, the GNoER was authorised to continue the railway southwards to York. Here it was proposed to connect with the planned York & North Midland Railway (Y&NMR), one of the many railways financed at this time by George Hudson, 'The Railway King' (see pages 116–117).

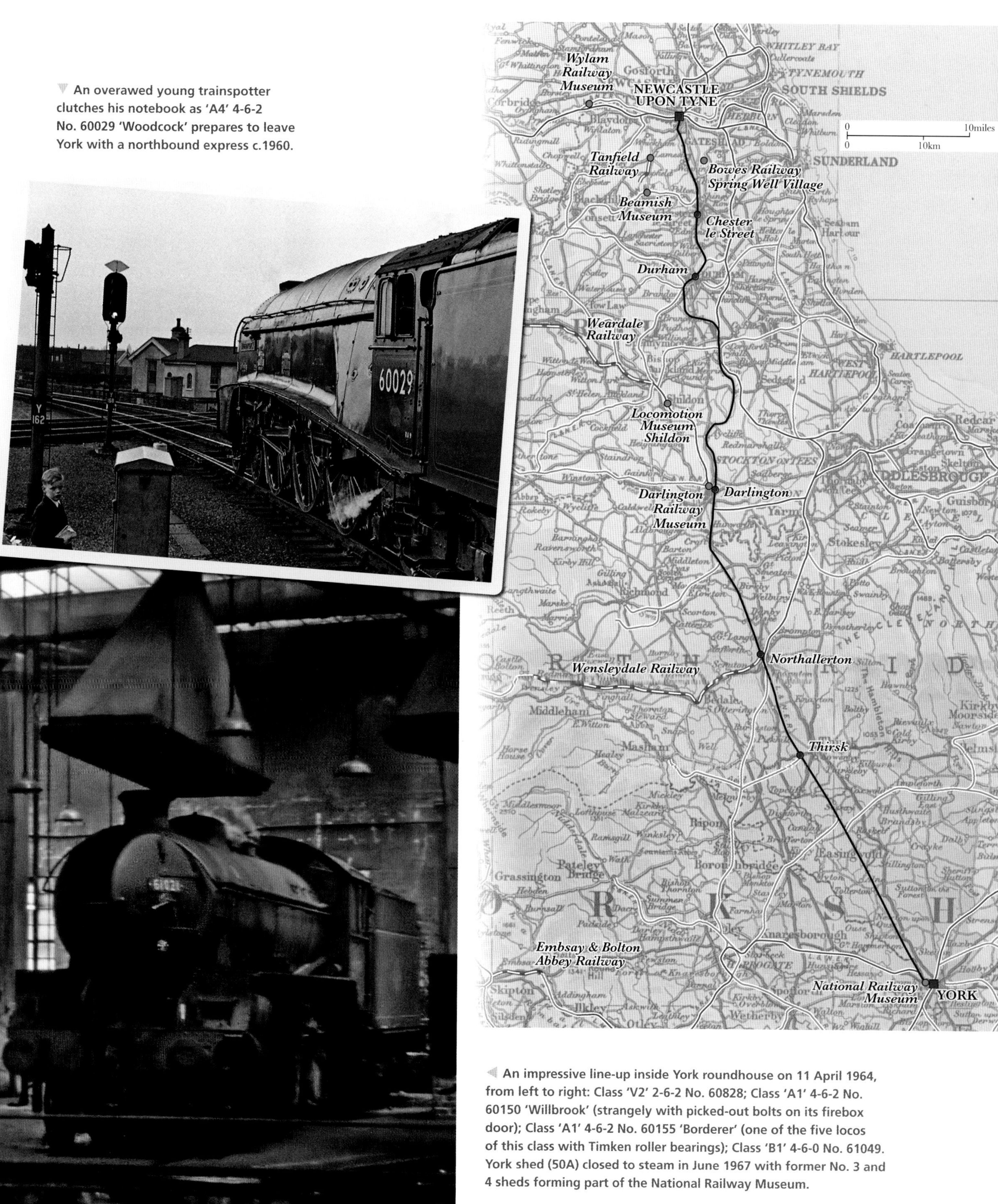

An overawed young trainspotter clutches his notebook as 'A4' 4-6-2 No. 60029 'Woodcock' prepares to leave York with a northbound express c.1960.

An impressive line-up inside York roundhouse on 11 April 1964, from left to right: Class 'V2' 2-6-2 No. 60828; Class 'A1' 4-6-2 No. 60150 'Willbrook' (strangely with picked-out bolts on its firebox door); Class 'A1' 4-6-2 No. 60155 'Borderer' (one of the five locos of this class with Timken roller bearings); Class 'B1' 4-6-0 No. 61049. York shed (50A) closed to steam in June 1967 with former No. 3 and 4 sheds forming part of the National Railway Museum.

▼ **With admiring glances from a group of schoolchildren, King's Cross's Class 'A4' 4-6-2 No. 60003 'Andrew K. McCosh' pauses at Darlington with an up express on 17 August 1961.**

TO DARLINGTON WITH HUDSON

Despite the original engineer being replaced by George Stephenson, the southern end of the line from Darlington to York presented no major engineering problems and was opened in 1841. However, the northern end from Darlington to Newcastle was a completely different situation. Although it received receiving authorisation to build the line in 1837, the GNoER had second thoughts and the incomplete section north of Darlington was taken over by George Hudson's newly incorporated Newcastle & Darlington Junction Railway (N&DJR) in 1843. Work on this progressed rapidly, in parts taking over existing east–west railways such as Durham Junction, with the line opening in 1844. The only drawback was that the railway had no rolling stock or locomotives and, in a strange twist of fate, had to lease these initially from the GNoER. In spite of this early setback, the N&DJR went from strength to strength, taking over several other northeastern railways before changing its name to the York & Newcastle Railway (Y&NR) in 1846. By then George Hudson's railway empire had grown to an extent of 1,000 miles but he was soon ruined by accusations of corruption and bribery.

THE NORTH EASTERN RAILWAY

A year later, the Y&NR amalgamated with the Newcastle & Berwick Railway, which had just opened its line northwards from Newcastle to Tweedmouth (see pages 200–205), becoming the York, Newcastle & Berwick Railway (YN&BR) – today's East Coast Main Line was gradually taking shape. The new company opened a new line from Northallerton to Leeming Bar

Class 'A3' 4-6-2 No. 60069 'Sceptre' belches out acrid smoke as it streaks along the ECML just south of Pilmoor, 16 miles north of York. The 11-coach train is the 4.48pm (ex-Darlington) Newcastle to Birmingham service, which was allowed 42 minutes to cover the 44 miles from Darlington to York.

in 1848 and planned to build a more direct route to Gateshead via the Team Valley. This far-reaching plan was put on hold following George Hudson's downfall in 1849 and in 1854 the North Eastern Railway (NER) was formed by the amalgamation of the Y&NMR, the YN&BR, the Leeds Northern Railway and the Malton & Driffield Junction Railway. At its formation, the NER was the largest railway company in Britain, owning more than 700 route miles along with various canals and dock installations. The route northwards from Darlington to Gateshead via the Team Valley was reinstated by the NER in 1865 and opened throughout in 1872 and the ECML between York and Newcastle was complete. At its northern end, Newcastle Central station, reached over the Tyne via Robert Stephenson's High Level Bridge, had already been opened in 1850 by the YN&BR and the Newcastle & Carlisle Railway. However, the small terminus station at York was woefully inadequate, with trains from London to Newcastle required to reverse out of the station before continuing their journey northwards. With its 13 platforms and overall curving arched roof, the present station at York was opened by the NER in 1877. It was the largest station in the world at the time.

From its inception in 1854, the NER had set up its headquarters at Gateshead in Newcastle where the company established its own locomotive, carriage and wagon works. Under successive locomotive superintendents – chiefly Edward Fletcher and Wilson Worsdell – the works turned out many classic steam locomotive types and in 1904 introduced the ground-breaking electrified North Tyneside suburban railway. Worsdell was replaced by Vincent Raven in 1910 by which time locomotive construction had been transferred to Darlington. Gateshead Works closed completely in 1932.

▲ Class 'B1' 4-6-0 No. 61338 heads a southbound train of Benzole tankers under the mixed upper/lower quadrant signal gantry at King Edward Bridge West Junction, Newcastle, on 22 June 1960.

RAVEN'S VISION

Vincent Raven's tenure as chief mechanical engineer for the NER was marked by several impressive steam locomotive designs including his Class 'Z' 4-4-2s and his five Pacific locos (three built under LNER management in 1924), which were all named after northeastern cities. Heavy freight locomotives also featured prominently as the NER carried more coal (and much iron ore and steel) than any other British railway. His development of Worsdell's 0-8-0s (LNER Class 'Q6' and 'Q7') stood the test of time, surviving well into the British Railways era. What is not so

Class 'A1' 4-6-2 No. 60139 'Sea Eagle' passes the 200-mile post just south of Beningbrough, north of York, on a Glasgow Queen Street to King's Cross express on 10 August 1957.

▲ **Fitted with German-style smoke deflectors, Heaton shed's Class 'A3' 4-6-2 No. 60051 'Blink Bonny' emerges light engine from the gloomy depths of Newcastle Central station on 1 August 1964. Built as an 'A1' Pacific in 1924 and rebuilt as an 'A3' in 1945 this handsome loco had only just over three months left before being despatched to the scrap yard.**

well known is that Raven advocated the electrification of the York to Newcastle main line, having already electrified the Shildon to Newport coal-carrying line in 1915. Years ahead of its time, a prototype main-line electric loco was built at Darlington in 1922, but Raven's plan was dropped by the LNER the following year.

Raven lost his job following the 'Big Four Grouping' of 1923 and with Nigel Gresley as Chief Mechanical Engineer of the LNER, the former NER works at Darlington continued to play an important role turning out Class 'K3' and 'K4' 2-6-0s, 'J39' 0-6-0s, 'B17' 4-6-0s, 'V2' 2-6-2s and later Thomson 'A2/1' and Peppercorn 'A1' Pacifics. Under British Railways management, Darlington turned out Standard Class 2 2-6-0s and 2-6-2Ts followed by various diesel classes until its closure in 1966.

Of course, the York to Newcastle line is best known for its world-famous named trains that thundered daily along the level race track north of York behind Gresley's 'A3' and 'A4' Pacifics. Pride of place must go to the 'Flying Scotsman', which was introduced in 1924 and survived into 'Deltic' days after the end of steam, and the short-lived streamlined 'Silver Jubilee', which provided a showcase for the world-beating 'A4' Pacifics before the Second World War brought this to an abrupt end. During the early years of the BR era, Gresley's Pacifics, along with Peppercorn 'A1' Pacifics, were the mainstay of motive power for a proliferation of named trains along this stretch, including 'The Queen of Scots Pullman', 'The Tees-Tyne Pullman', 'The Talisman', the summer-only non-stop 'Elizabethan', 'The Heart of Midlothian', 'The Northumbrian' and 'The North Briton'. All of this soon came to an end in the early 1960s with the introduction of the 'Deltic' and English Electric Type 4 diesels, but steam lingered on for some years with Gateshead closing in the autumn of 1965, Darlington in spring 1966 and York in the summer of 1967. Now even the 'Deltics' are a fading memory, replaced first by HST sets and then full electrification of the East Coast Main Line in 1990.

THE LINE TODAY

Passenger services between York, Darlington and Newcastle are operated by CrossCountry, First TransPennine Express and the recently nationalised East Coast.

HERITAGE RAILWAY

WENSLEYDALE RAILWAY

Leeming Bar Station, Leases Road, Leeming Bar, Northallerton, North Yorkshire DL7 9AR

Website: www.wensleydalerailway.com

Tel: 08454 505474

Route: Leeming Bar to Redmire

Length: 16 miles

Nearest main-line station: Northallerton

This rural line through the Yorkshire Dales was opened by the North Eastern Railway between Northallerton and Hawes in 1878. The line westwards from Hawes to Garsdale was also opened by the Midland Railway in 1878. Passenger traffic between Northallerton and Hawes ceased in 1954 and from Garsdale to Hawes (along with freight traffic) in 1959. The remaining branch from Northallerton was cut back to Redmire in 1964 and the line remained active for stone trains to Redmire Quarry until 1992. Since then the Wensleydale Railway Association, with financial help from the Ministry of Defence (who use the line to transport military vehicles), has reintroduced passenger trains between Leeming Bar and Redmire. A bus service links Northallerton station with Leeming Bar. Trains are normally operated by diesel multiple units but steam can also be seen in action on certain weekends during the summer. A restored 1960s single-decker bus operates a vintage bus service between Redmire station and Aysgarth Falls on Tuesdays, Fridays, Saturdays and Sundays between April and October.

▼ **The recently streamlined ex-LMS 'Coronation' Class 4-6-2 No. 6229 'Duchess of Hamilton' is one of the main exhibits at the National Railway Museum in York.**

MUSEUMS

BOWES RAILWAY CENTRE

Springwell Village, Nr Gateshead, Tyne & Wear NE9 7QJ

Website: www.bowesrailway.co.uk

Tel: 0191 416 1847

Nearest main-line station: n/a

One of the last steam locomotives built by Andrew Barclay, 0-4-0ST 'WST' (short for William Steuart Trimble, the deputy chairman of the locomotive's original owners, Long Meg Plaster & Mineral Company) in action on the Bowes Railway.

The Bowes Railway was designed by George Stephenson as a colliery line and opened in 1826. It was built to carry coal from collieries along its length to Jarrow on the River Tyne for shipment. The line passed into the ownership of the Bowes family in 1850, which operated it until collieries were nationalised in 1947. It used a mixture of rope-worked inclines and locomotive-hauled sections, and operated virtually unchanged until 1974. It is now a scheduled Ancient Monument and the centre at Springwell includes the only working rope-hauled standard gauge incline in the world. Preservation began in 1975 and visitors can now travel in steam-hauled brakevans along a short length of track from the engineering centre and up the east incline to Blackham's Hill, where they alight to visit the rope haulage buildings and watch rope demonstrations. An extension was opened in 1996 from Blackham's Hill to Wrekenton along the line's old Pelaw main railway branch. The centre also houses the largest collection of colliery rolling stock in the country, several steam and diesel locomotives and the restored 19th-century railway workshops.

NATIONAL RAILWAY MUSEUM

Leeman Road, York YO26 4XJ

Website: www.nrm.org.uk

Tel: 08448 153139

Nearest main-line station: York

The National Collection, formed from the Clapham Collection and the North Eastern Railway Museum Collection at York, opened in 1975 and is housed in two large halls (formerly York locomotive sheds), with the Great Hall opening in 1992. Railway technology is displayed around a central turntable in the Great Hall and exhibits range from the very early days of rail transport to the present with over 60 restored British-built, steam, diesel and electric locomotives on view. The South Hall contains 130 exhibits that illustrate travel by train with both passenger and goods trains lined up at platforms. These range from Queen Adelaide's royal saloon, built in 1842, a Lynton & Barnstaple Railway coach, built in 1897, a Wagons-Lits Night Ferry sleeping car, built in 1936, to numerous goods vehicles dating from 1815 to 1970. In addition, there is a hands-on children's centre and an extensive library with posters, photography and drawing collections. Numerous other locomotives, some in full working order, and rolling stock are on loan to other museums and preserved railways throughout Britain. The museum's conservation workshops now have a public viewing area while a miniature railway operates outside.

NATIONAL RAILWAY MUSEUM – 'LOCOMOTION'

Shildon, Co Durham DL4 1PQ

Website: www.nrm.org.uk

Tel: 01388 777999

Nearest main-line station: Shildon

An offshoot of the NRM at York, Shildon has rotating display of historic locos and rolling stock. The site includes the Welcome Building containing Timothy Hackworth's 'Sans Pareil', the Hackworth Museum, the Collection Building with its conservation workshop, a display of more than 70 railway heritage vehicles, prototype 'Deltic' and the LNER 'V2' 2-6-2 'Green Arrow', the record-breaking 'A4' 4-6-2 'Mallard' and the Soho railway workshop. Shildon includes a site railway that links all of these attractions and offers steam-train rides on special event days.

THE YORKSHIRE COAST

Scarborough to Middlesbrough

Beset by incompetent construction and financial difficulties, the two separate railways that made up the coastal route from Middlesbrough to Scarborough almost failed to open. The end came for the northern section in 1958, while the southern section closed in 1965 and is now a footpath and cycleway.

The construction of the northern end of the scenic coast-hugging railway from Middlesbrough to Scarborough started with the opening of the Middlesbrough to Saltburn line by the Stockton & Darlington Railway in 1861. South of here, construction of a railway was started by the Whitby, Redcar & Middlesbrough Union Railway (WR&MR – incorporated in 1866) but the company soon came to grief when part of the line slipped into the sea north of Sandsend. Unable to complete the heavily engineered line that included five large viaducts, the WR&MR had to ask the North Eastern Railway to complete the task. The line opened in 1883 and the company was taken over by the NER in 1889. A zig-zag branch, operating on the same principle as the South American railways in the Andes, connected the line to ironstone mines near Loftus and the gasworks at Skinningrove. North of Loftus, one of the original steel viaducts was found unsafe and replaced by an embankment in 1913 – but it wasn't removed and still lies buried beneath hundreds of thousands of tons of earth.

At the southern end, the York & North Midland had already opened its railway from York to the town of Scarborough in 1845. A year later the company opened the line from Seamer Junction, west of Scarborough, to Filey, Bridlington and Hull. Both of these lines are still open.

North of Scarborough, the Scarborough & Whitby Railway also almost failed to be completed. Work started on this scenic coastal line in 1872 but progress was slow and six years later it was nearly abandoned when the company ran into financial

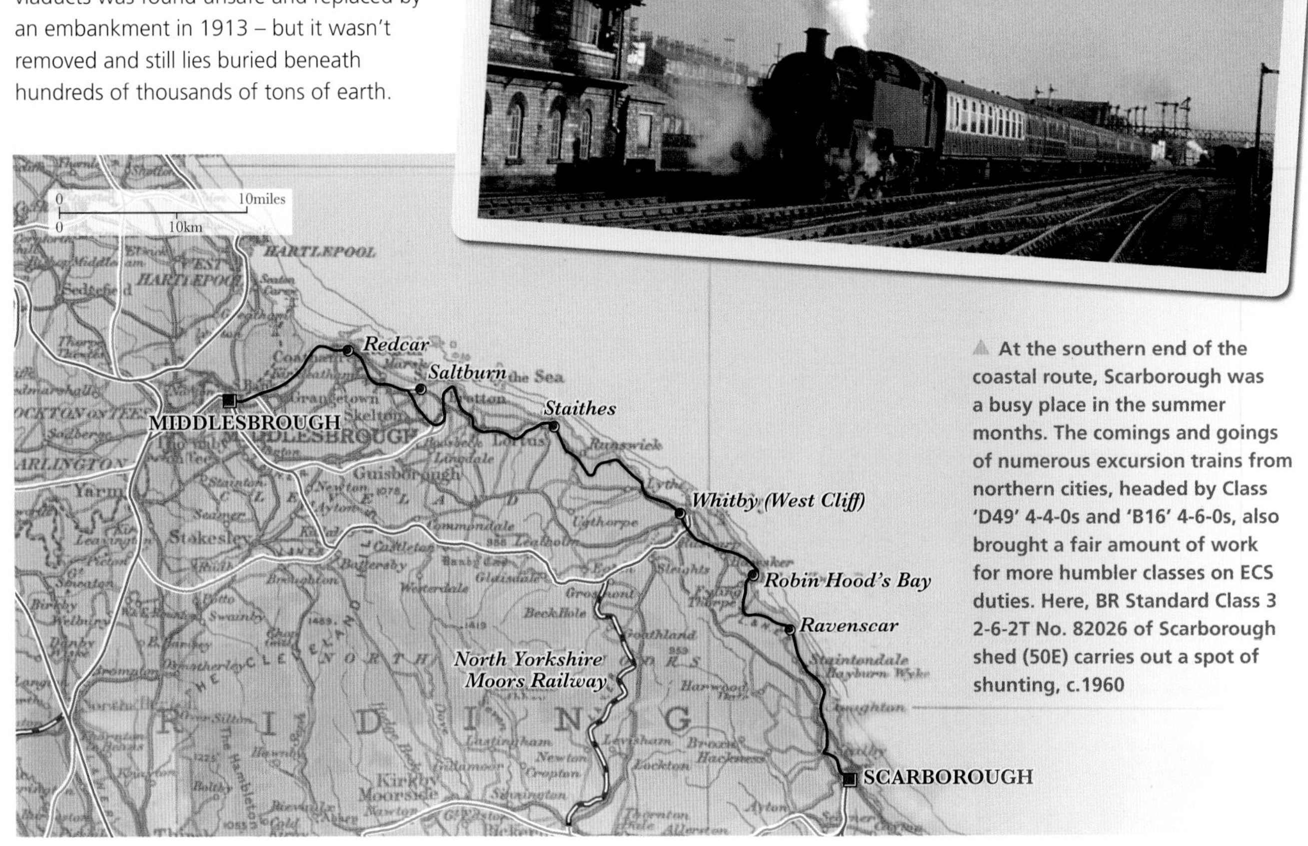

▲ At the southern end of the coastal route, Scarborough was a busy place in the summer months. The comings and goings of numerous excursion trains from northern cities, headed by Class 'D49' 4-4-0s and 'B16' 4-6-0s, also brought a fair amount of work for more humbler classes on ECS duties. Here, BR Standard Class 3 2-6-2T No. 82026 of Scarborough shed (50E) carries out a spot of shunting, c.1960

◄ A busy scene at Whitby (Town) station on 26 July 1958 – from left to right: 2 x 3-car Metropolitan Cammell DMUs about to leave on the 4.25pm Scarborough to Middlesbrough (via the Esk Valley); BR Standard Class 3 2-6-0 No. 77012 on empty stock; Class 'L1' 2-6-4T No. 67754 on the 6pm to Middlesbrough.

The last full year of regular steam operations between Scarborough and Whitby – BR Standard Class 4 2-6-4T No. 80120 is seen arriving at Ravenscar station with the 4.20pm Whitby (Town) to Scarborough train on 13 July 1957.

The cost of maintaining the coastal railway and its many viaducts north of Whitby led to its early demise. Here, less than a year before closure, ex-LNER Class 'L1' 2-6-4T No. 67766 crosses Newholm Beck Viaduct, south of Sandsend, with the 9.07am Middlesbrough to Whitby (Town) train on 16 July 1957.

Loftus station seen from a northbound train headed by an Ivatt Class 4MT 2-6-0 on 4 September 1957. The line through Loftus was reopened in 1974 for trains to and from the nearby Boulby potash mine.

BR Standard Class 4MT 2-6-4T No. 80116 heads across Staithes Viaduct with the 11.20am Scarborough to Middlesbrough train on the last day of services north of Whitby, 3 May 1958. A 20mph speed restriction was in force over the viaduct due to the strong winds experienced along this stretch of coastline. The viaduct was demolished in 1960.

Ex-LNER Class 'V3' 2-6-2T No. 67688 heads out of Middlesbrough station with a Saltburn to Darlington train on 27 April 1954. From 1933, trains from Whitby were routed to Middlesbrough via Guisborough but on closure of the line north of Whitby in 1958 all Whitby to Middlesbrough trains ran via the Esk Valley line.

difficulties. At the last minute the owner of Raven Hall, an 18th-century mansion overlooking Robin Hood's Bay, stepped in and rescued the company. Construction work recommenced and the line was opened for business in 1885. Worked from the outset by the North Eastern Railway, the steeply graded line was linked at its southern end to the grand Scarborough station via a tunnel. Arrangements at Whitby were much more complicated , with the 120ft-high Larpool Viaduct – built from over five million bricks – carrying the line over the River Esk to Whitby West Cliff station. From here a steeply graded reverse spur linked the line down under the viaduct to the Whitby & Pickering Railway station in the town. The latter railway had opened across the North Yorkshire moors as early as 1836, initially using horse power.

AN EXPENSIVE BUSINESS

Whitby West Cliff was also served by trains from the north by the Whitby, Redcar & Middlesbrough Union Railway that was also worked by the North Eastern Railway from the outset. From the 1930s, trains from Middlesbrough to Scarborough were routed away from Redcar to run via Nunthorpe and Guisborough. The tortuous journey for the passengers involved reversing at Guisborough and Whitby. However, with its numerous viaducts and tunnels, the line north of Whitby was very expensive to maintain and it closed beyond Guisborough on 5 May 1958. The remaining branch from Nunthorpe to Guisborough closed in 1964.

In steam days normal services between Middlesbrough and Scarborough were handled by a variety of locomotives, including powerful ex-NER 'A8' Class 4-6-2 tanks, ex-LNER 'V1' Class 2-6-2 tanks, ex-LMS Ivatt Class 4 2-6-0s and BR Standard Class 4 2-6-4 tanks. Diesel multiple units were introduced in 1958, and in May 1958 (on closure of the line north of Whitby) trains were rerouted via Battersby Junction and the Esk Valley line to Whitby, the 58½-mile scenic journey from Middlesbrough to Scarborough taking around 2½ hours. The Scarborough to Whitby line struggled on for a few more years until it closed completely on 6 March 1965. Today only the Esk Valley line to Whitby is still open for passenger traffic.

THE LINE TODAY

Passenger services between Middlesbrough, Redcar and Saltburn are operated by Northern Rail. South of Saltburn the meandering line is still used by freight trains to the special section steel mill at Skinningrove steelworks and the Boulby potash mine east of Loftus – the latter is the second deepest mine in Europe (4,600ft) and home to the ZEPLIN-III dark matter detector.

Services between Middlesbrough and Whitby via the Esk Valley are also operated by Northern Rail. Scarborough is served by trains from York operated by First TransPennine Express and from Hull and Bridlington by Northern Rail. The trackbed of the Scarborough to Whitby line is now a 23-mile footpath and cycleway known as the Scarborough to Whitby Railway Path and now forms part of National Cycle Network Route 1 and the Moor to Sea Cycle Route. The railway path crosses the 13-arch Larpool Viaduct, owned by Sustrans, at Whitby.

▼ *Heartbeat* country in the depths of winter – preserved ex-SR Class 'S15' 4-6-0 No. 825 hard at work as it leaves Goathland on the North Yorkshire Moors Railway.

HERITAGE RAILWAY

NORTH YORKSHIRE MOORS RAILWAY

Pickering Station 12 Park Street, Pickering, North Yorkshire YO18 7AJ

Website: www.nymr.co.uk

Tel: 01751 472508 (01751 473535 talking timetable)

Route: Grosmont to Pickering

Length: 18 miles

Nearest main-line station: Grosmont

The present North Yorkshire Moors Railway (NYMR) was one of the earliest railways built in Britain. Engineered by George Stephenson, it opened in 1836, along the route of an old turnpike road, and initially featured horse drawn trains and a rope-hauled inclined plane. In 1845 it was taken over by George Hudson's York & North Midland Railway and was rebuilt and enlarged for steam operation. The North Eastern Railway bought the line in 1854, and in 1865 a new route was opened to bypass the I,500yd-long I-in-15 Beck Hole Incline, which was replaced by the 1-in-49 gradient between Grosmont and Goathland. Absorbed into the LNER in 1923 it was eventually closed by BR as a through route to Malton and York in 1965. The North Yorkshire Moors Railway Preservation Society took over part of the line in 1967 and in 1973 trains started running again on what is now the second-longest preserved railway in the country. A workshop and engine sheds have been established at Grosmont and trains are operated by a large collection of powerful main-line steam and diesel locomotives. Locomotives include NER Class 'T3' 0-8-0 No. 63395, SR 'Schools' class 4-4-0 No. 30926 'Repton', two LMS Class 5 4-6-0s, SR Class 'S15' 4-6-0 No. 30825, LNER Class 'A4' No. 60007 'Sir Nigel Gresley' and ex-S&DJR 2-8-0 No. 53809, as well as several ex-BR diesels. A large and varied collection of rolling stock includes a Pullman set. NYMR trains connect with the main network at Grosmont, on the scenic Whitby to Middlesbrough Esk Valley line. Some NYMR steam-hauled trains continue their journey to Whitby. A journey on the railway across the wild grandeur of the North Yorkshire Moors National Park to Pickering involves a steep climb to Goathland, the fictional Aidensfield in the television series *Heartbeat*, before entering the picturesque Newtondale Gorge. The railway is frequently host to visiting locomotives from other preserved railways across the country.

ACROSS THE PENNINES

Darlington to Penrith

Where heavily laden steam-hauled mineral trains to Barrow and holiday trains to Blackpool once laboured over the bleak Pennine Hills, all that remains today is the sound of silence broken only by the thundering noise of juggernauts on the A66.

The railway route across the bleak northern Pennines was the brainchild of the Stockton & Darlington Railway (the world's first public railway, opened in 1825), which was eager to provide a through route for coal and coke from the Durham coalfields to the ironworks of Barrow and for iron ore in the reverse direction. The easterly part of what eventually became the through route to Darlington, the Darlington & Barnard Castle Railway, opened in 1856 before becoming part of the Stockton & Darlington Railway (St&DR) two years later. Meanwhile the South Durham & Lancashire Railway (SD&LR) was authorised in 1857 to build a line from West Auckland, where it met the St&DR, to Tebay on the West Coast Main Line. The route, engineered by Thomas Bouch (designer of the ill-fated Tay Bridge), took it via Barnard Castle, Stainmore Summit (1,370ft above sea level) and Kirkby Stephen, the latter town not reached by the Midland Railway's Settle & Carlisle line until 1876.

A HARD-WORKING LINE

The major engineering features on the single-track line were three iron viaducts at Barnard Castle, Deepdale and the iconic Belah Viaduct. The latter structure, built in only four months, was an engineering masterpiece, with a 1,040ft span across the valley of the River Belah and a height of 196ft making it the tallest railway bridge in England. The line, worked from the outset by the St&DR, opened in 1861 with the SD&LR becoming part of the St&DR early in 1862. The railway was an instant success, there being such vast quantities of coke and

◀ New kid on the block, brand new out of Darlington Works, Ivatt Class 2 2-6-0 No. 46501 arrives at Barnard Castle with the 4.10pm Darlington to Penrith train on 30 April 1952. Diesel multiple units replaced these steam-hauled trains in 1959. Once a busy junction, the station site at Barnard Castle has long ago disappeared without trace.

Following decades of the class working the Stainmore line, the final working of an ex-NER Class 'J21' 0-6-0 finally happened on 7 May 1960 when No. 65033 (now preserved) worked a special train organised by the Railway Correspondence & Travel Society (RCTS). Here the train is seen heading west near Bowes on its journey from Darlington to Tebay.

The Stainmore line was used as a through route from the northeast to Blackpool during the summer weekends. Here, BR Standard Class 4MT 2-6-0 No.76050 of West Auckland shed (51F) breasts Stainmore Summit heading east on 5 August 1961.

Closure of the famous Stainmore line was on 22 January 1962. However, as there was no Sunday service, the last trains ran on 20 January. A special was organised by the RCTS to be the last train to traverse the route and was double-headed by BR Standard Class 3MT 2-6-0 No. 77003 and BR Standard Class 4MT 2-6-0 No. 76049. The westbound special is seen here crossing the famous Belah Viaduct.

iron ore carried that the line was doubled by the North Eastern Railway in 1870. Despite this, working heavy trains up the steeply graded line to Stainmore Summit from both east and west was no mean feat and necessitated double heading and/or banking in the rear right through to the British Railways era. The line was also at the mercy of winter weather, with snowdrifts often blocking the line near Stainmore. The extreme winter of 1947 blocked the line for two months and was cleared only with help from the army. These harsh winters on the line were recorded for posterity by British Transport Films in their superb 1955 10-minute film *Snowdrift at Bleath Gill*.

While trains heading for Barrow travelled via Tebay, those heading for the ironworks of West Cumbria were soon able to travel via the single-track line from Kirkby Stephen to Clifton, south of Penrith, which opened in 1862. Known as the Eden Valley Railway, it was also worked from the outset by the Stockton & Darlington Railway and taken over by that company a year later. A spur south of Penrith linked the Eden Valley Railway to the Cockermouth, Keswick & Penrith Railway when that railway opened in 1865, enabling St&DR coke trains to travel across the Lake District to ironworks at Workington.

The St&DR became part of the newly formed North Eastern Railway in 1863 and passenger services through this sparsely populated region soon settled down to three or four return journeys each day between Darlington and Tebay while passengers for Penrith changed trains at Kirkby Stephen. During the summer months special trains were laid on from the northeast

Last day at Kirkby Stephen – the RCTS special last train pauses at Kirkby Stephen East on 20 January 1962 to water the two locomotives before the train departs for Tebay. A small group of local people pay their last respects.

to Blackpool and, even after regular trains were taken over by diesel multiple units in 1959, the North Eastern Region timetable shows three Saturdays-only steam-hauled trains (by then double-headed by BR Standard Class 3 and 4 2-6-0s or Ivatt Class 4 2-6-0s) running between South Shields, Darlington, Newcastle and Blackpool.

UNPOPULAR CLOSURES

While the Kirkby Stephen to Tebay 'branch' closed to passengers in 1952, it was still used by the Summer-Saturday special trains to Blackpool. Despite dieselisation of the regular services in 1959, the future looked bleak for the main line over Stainmore Summit. Freight was diverted via Carlisle and closure of the whole line occurred in early 1962 in the face of strong local opposition. The last train between Barnard Castle and Penrith ran over Belah Viaduct on 20 January (see pages 190–191). Goods trains were also withdrawn at the same time including those along the Tebay line. British Railways were so keen to rid themselves of this route that they lifted the track and demolished most of the viaducts with indecent haste, including the famous Belah Viaduct. All that was left was a short section between Appleby East (where there was a connection to the Settle & Carlisle line) and to an army training centre at Warcop and to Hartley Quarry. The latter closed in 1975 while the former was last used in 1989 when the track was mothballed. The line from Darlington to Barnard Castle, for the branch to Middleton-in-Teesdale, remained open until 30 November 1964.

▲ Ex-Great Northern Railway Class 'D3' 4-4-0 No. 4077 gets ready to leave Kirkby Stephen East with the 4.20pm Penrith to Darlington train on 7 June 1935. The last 'D3' was withdrawn by BR in 1951 but none of this class has been preserved.

▼ The end of the Eden Valley line from Kirkby Stephen – BR Standard Class 3MT 2-6-2T No. 82029 heads out past Penrith shed towards Clifton with the 10.32am train to Darlington in June 1957.

THE LINE TODAY

Following closure in 1962, British Railways lifted the line and dismantled its engineering features. Westwards from Darlington, the stations at Piercebridge and Gainford have been demolished, although at Winston the goods shed, stationmaster's house and crossing keeper's cottage have survived with different uses. At Broomielaw the station and signalbox are more or less intact, but at Barnard Castle all reminders of the station have gone. To the west of the town, Lartington station building is now a private residence, while Bowes station is partly derelict with the signalbox awaiting re-erection on the Eden Valley Railway.

For 8 miles to the west of Bowes, the trackbed across Stainmore Summit has been swallowed up by A66 road 'improvements'. The platforms at Barras survive, while the station building is now in pieces at Kirkby Stephen East awaiting re-erection. Only the stone abutments of Belah Viaduct survive on either side of the valley and the derelict signalbox still exists at the western end.

Kirkby Stephen East station has been restored and is now home to a railway heritage centre. Future plans include reopening the railway to Appleby East. To the north Musgrave station is now a private residence, while Warcop is now the headquarters of the Eden Valley Railway. From here to Appleby East the track is still *in situ*, and the station building (now a private residence), platform and goods shed still survive. Beyond Appleby the station buildings at Temple Sowerby, Cliburn and Clifton all survive in good order.

On the Tebay 'branch', the station at Ravenstonedale is now a private home, although much of the trackbed west of here to Tebay has been swallowed up by improvements to the A685. The Northern Viaduct Trust has saved three viaducts, including the magnificent 14-arch Smardale Viaduct, between Appleby and Ravenstonedale.

While Tebay station on the West Coast Main Line closed on 1 July 1968, Penrith station is still open and served by trains between Oxenholme and Carlisle operated by Virgin Trains and First TransPennine Express. At the eastern end, Darlington Bank Top station is served by trains operated by CrossCountry, First TransPennine Express, East Coast and Northern Rail, while Darlington North Road is served by Northern Rail trains to Bishop Auckland.

HERITAGE RAILWAYS

DARLINGTON RAILWAY CENTRE AND MUSEUM

North Road Station, Darlington, Co Durham DL3 6ST

Website: www.darlington.gov.uk/Culture/headofsteam

Tel: 01325 460532

Nearest main-line station: Darlington North Road

North Road station was built in 1842 for the Stockton & Darlington Railway. Now known as 'Head of Steam', the railway museum and restoration centre is housed in the restored station building, goods shed and the Hopetown Carriage Works. Exhibits include the original SDR 'Locomotion' built in 1825 and 0-6-0 'Derwent' built in 1845, as well as historic rolling stock including an SDR coach built in 1846 and an NER example built in 1860. The Centre also houses the Ken Hoole Study Centre with its large collection of railway photographs, archive material and the library collection of the North Eastern Railway Association. North Road station, with its overall roof, is still used by Regional Railways trains operating on the Darlington to Bishop Auckland service.

WEARDALE RAILWAY

Stanhope Station, Station Road, Stanhope, Bishop Auckland, Co Durham DL13 2YS

Website: www.weardale-railway.org.uk

Tel: 01388 526203

Route: Bishop Auckland (West) to Stanhope

Length: 18 miles

Nearest main-line station: Bishop Auckland

The Weardale Railway Preservation Society was formed in 1993 to assist with the campaign to reopen the mothballed railway line from Bishop Auckland to Eastgate in the scenic Wear Valley. Originally opened in stages between 1843 and 1895 to serve the local limestone quarries, the passenger service ceased in 1953 with freight lingering on until 1961 when the line was cut back to St John's Chapel. The present terminus is at Eastgate where, until 1993, bulk cement trains operated to serve the Lafarge factory. Now owned by the Weardale Railway Trust, daily train services on the line are normally operated by a Class 141 railbus with heritage steam or diesel traction running at weekends and on special events days. With a main-line connection at Bishop Auckland, the line's future appears secure as there are also now plans to run coal and stone trains along it once more.

EDEN VALLEY RAILWAY

Warcop Station, Warcop, Appleby, Cumbria CA16 6PR

Website: www.evr-cumbria.org.uk

Route: Warcop to Sandford

Length: 1 mile

Nearest main-line station: Appleby

The Eden Valley Railway opened between Kirkby Stephen and Clifton, south of Penrith, in 1862. Passenger services were withdrawn in 1962 but goods continued for a few more years until only the Appleby to Warcop section was left open for military trains to an army training centre. These ceased in 1989 but the track was mothballed and the Eden Valley Railway Society was formed in 1995 with the aim of restoring the line. In 2004, the Eden Valley Railway Trust was given permission to reopen the railway. Trains have recently started running again (Sundays only April to September), but at present only along the short section between Warcop and Sandford.

▲ Preserved Class 'K4' 2-6-0 No. 3442 'The Great Marquess' heads an RCTS special through Stanhope station on 11 June 1965 on the Weardale Railway.

HADRIAN'S WALL

Newcastle upon Tyne to Carlisle

Overcoming an early fundamental setback forbidding the use of locomotives, the Newcastle & Carlisle Railway became one of the earliest main lines in Britain, linking several late 18th-century colliery wagonways along its 60-mile route.

By the late 17th century, numerous wooden wagonways had been built to link the coalfields around Newcastle with the River Tyne where coal was loaded onto sailing ships for distribution around the coast of Britain. By the early 19th century, iron rails had replaced wood and soon steam power was replacing horse power. The region also witnessed one of the earliest schemes for a passenger-carrying main-line railway in Britain – the Newcastle & Carlisle Railway (N&CR) was incorporated in May 1829, five months before the famous Rainhill Trials for the Liverpool & Manchester Railway.

OFF TO A SHAKY START

While the railway had been chosen in favour of a canal, the Act authorising the N&CR had one serious flaw, namely that it forbade the use of locomotives. Despite this drawback the building of the line proceeded apace and the first section from Blaydon to Hexham opened in 1835. The problem over the use of steam locomotives reared its ugly head when an objecting landowner brought a temporary halt to proceedings, but this was soon overcome by an amendment to the original Act. The line was opened throughout from Carlisle Canal Basin in Carlisle to a temporary station in Newcastle on the south bank of the Tyne at Redheugh in 1837.

In 1851, the building of a timber bridge over the Tyne at Scotswood allowed the N&CR to reroute its trains from Carlisle along the north bank of the river through Elswick and into the newly opened Newcastle Central station. Scotswood Bridge had a fairly chequered

◄ **Thompson Class 'B1' 4-6-0 No. 61064 enters Prudhoe (for Ovingham) station with the 7.30am Carlisle to Newcastle train on 6 September 1955. The famous railway photographer Henry Casserley is watching the scene from the footbridge.**

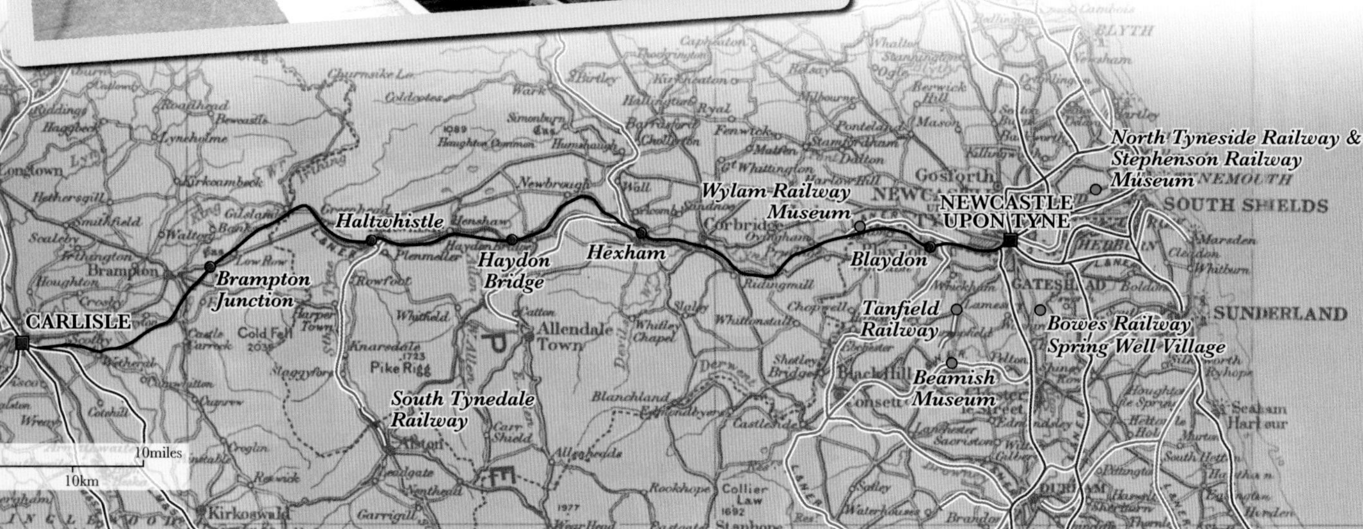

▲ **The typical rural railway – ex-North Eastern Railway Class 'J21' 0-6-0 No. 65033 heads one Gresley 'blood-and-custard' BSK coach with a train from Reedsmouth over the decrepit Borders Counties Bridge at Hexham in 1953. The loco was later preserved and spent most of its years at Beamish Museum, until moving to the North Norfolk Railway in 2007 so it could be restored to working order.**

early history – the first wooden structure was destroyed in a fire in 1860 and its (wooden) replacement lasted until 1865 when a temporary single-track bridge was opened. This in turn was replaced by a six-span wrought-iron bridge in 1871 but was closed permanently in 1982 when trains were diverted via Dunston-on-Tyne and over the King Edward VII bridge to Central station. The rusting bridge still stands today.

To the west the N&CR opened a 13-mile branch line from Haltwhistle to Alston in 1852. Designed primarily to serve the lead-mining industry, the branch continued in use until it was closed by British Railways in 1976. The trackbed of the southern section from Alston to Kirkhaugh is now used by a narrow gauge railway, the South Tynedale Railway (see page 199).

The N&CR remained independent until 1862 when it was absorbed by the North Eastern Railway. The town of Hexham soon became an important junction with the opening throughout of the North British Railway's meandering cross-border line to Reedsmouth and Riccarton Junction in the same year and the Hexham & Allendale Railway's 12¼-mile branch to Allendale in 1869. Passenger services on the former route were withdrawn in 1956 and the line had closed completely by 1963, while the Allendale branch lost its passenger service as early as 1930, closing entirely in 1950.

At its western end the N&CR was just a new kid on the block when it opened the section of its line between Carlisle and Greenhead in 1836 as Lord Carlisle had already opened a horsedrawn wooden wagonway in the area around Brampton as early as 1799. The wagonway, with an inclined plane, linked the town with coal mines on his estate at Blacksdyke, Howgill, Gairs, Roachburn, Bishop Hill, Midgeholme and Lambley – the latter later connected to the Haltwhistle to Alston branch via a spur. The wagonway was relaid with iron rails in 1809 and, on the opening of the N&CR, rerouted to run via Brampton Junction. Here, a horsedrawn railway coach conveyed passengers the short distance to Brampton Town, the service only adopting steam haulage in 1881. This branch was taken over by the North Eastern Railway in 1912 but closed to passengers as early as 1923. The rest of the colliery line remained open, and even saw Stephenson's famous 'Rocket' working on it between 1837 and 1840, but it was closed by the National Coal Board in 1953.

RECENT ACTIVITY

The pattern of train services along the Newcastle and Carlisle line has remained constant since NER days – consisting of a fairly regular all-stations stopping service between Newcastle and Hexham (many of these now originating from farther afield), interspersed with the full service to Carlisle, some of these trains continuing to Silloth (now closed) or Whitehaven. For over 100 years there was also one train each Saturday/Sunday to and

The return of steam – resplendent in LNER blue, preserved Gresley 'A4' 4-6-2 No. 4498 'Sir Nigel Gresley' stands in the centre road at the south end of Carlisle station, waiting to take over a special train to Newcastle on 6 October 1973.

THE
TYNESIDER
N° 4498
A 4
KINGS +

from Stranraer Harbour, but this ceased in December 2009. The majority of the passenger trains along the route were taken over by diesel multiple units in 1960 with some of them including a miniature buffet car. Ex-LNER steam continued to be seen on goods trains until the closure of Carlisle Canal shed in June 1963. The line fortunately escaped the attentions of Dr Beeching and has proved its worth over the years as an important diversionary route during engineering work on the WCML or ECML. Today it still sees the occasional passage of steam charter trains.

▼ The BLS/SLS special arrives at Alston behind Ivatt Class 4MT 2-6-0 No. 43121 of Carlisle Kingmoor shed on 26 March 1967. Kingmoor shed closed to steam at the end of the year. By then Alston was just a shadow of its former self, served only by a DMU shuttle from Haltwhistle until closure on 3 May 1976.

▲ Brampton Town was once connected to Brampton Junction by a short branch line. The passenger service was horsedrawn until 1881 when steam haulage was introduced. Here Brampton Railway No. 6, built by Neilson in 1881, stands at Brampton Town in 1922, just a year before the line closed.

THE LINE TODAY

Passenger services between Newcastle upon Tyne and Carlisle are operated by Northern Rail with some trains (operated by First ScotRail) continuing to Glasgow via Dumfries and Kilmarnock.

HERITAGE RAILWAYS

TANFIELD RAILWAY

Marley Hill Engine Shed, Old Marley Hill, Gateshead, Tyne & Wear NE16 5ET

Website: www.tanfieldrailway.co.uk

Tel: 0845 4634938

Route: Sunniside to East Tanfield

Length: 3 miles

Nearest main-line station: Newcastle Central and Durham

Situated on the site of one of the oldest railways in the world, the wooden-railed Tanfield Wagonway opened in 1725. The Tanfield Railway also boasts an early 18th-century railway bridge and an engine shed dating from 1854. The colliery line was eventually closed by BR in 1968, and by 1977 a group of preservationists had reopened the first section to the public. The line was extended to Sunniside in 1981 and East Tanfield in 1982. Beautifully restored vintage four-wheeled coaches are hauled by a very large collection of small, mainly steam, industrial locomotives. Causey station is the start of a woodland walk where the famous Causey railway arch, the world's first railway bridge, built in 1727, can be seen.

▼ Built in 1919, 'Renishaw Ironworks No. 6 0-6-0ST heads a train of vintage carriages on the Tanfield Railway.

Built in 1863, Furness Railway 0-4-0 No. 20 heads a short train at the reconstructed Rowley station at Beamish Open Air Museum.

SOUTH TYNEDALE RAILWAY

The Railway Station, Alston, Cumbria CA9 3JB

Website: www.strps.org.uk

Tel: 01434 381696

Route: Alston to Kirkhaugh (no road access at latter)

Length: 2¼ miles

Nearest main-line station: Haltwhistle

The former North Eastern Railway branch line along the South Tyne valley was opened from Haltwhistle, on the Carlisle to Newcastle route, to Alston in 1852 and closed by British Rail in 1976. Initially, preservation of this scenic branch in its standard gauge form was planned but this scheme failed. A new proposal for a 2ft-gauge line was put forward and, in 1983, a short length of narrow gauge track was opened from Alston. Gilderdale Halt was opened in 1987 and Kirkhaugh in 1996. Future plans for the South Tyndale Railway include extending the line still farther to Slaggyford, giving a total distance of 5 miles. It is possible that in the future the railway may extend even farther northwards towards Lambley, but in the meantime a footpath follows the route and crosses Knar Burn on a high viaduct. Many of the steam and diesel locomotives used on the railway have been obtained from a wide variety of sources, both in the UK and abroad. Much of the equipment is second-hand and many items have been rebuilt before being used on the railway. Included at the railway are 0-6-0 well tank No. 3 'Sao Domingos', built in Germany in 1928, 0-4-0 tank No. 6 'Thomas Edmondson', built in Germany in 1918, 0-6-0 tender engine No. 10 'Naklo', built in Poland in 1957 and 0-4-2 tank No. 12 'Chaka's Kraal', No. 6, built by Hunslet in 1940 for a South African railway, as well as many industrial diesel locomotives.

MUSEUMS

WYLAM RAILWAY MUSEUM

Falcon Centre, Falcon Terrace, Wylam, Northumberland NE41 8EE

Website: www.wylamparishcouncil.org

Tel: 01661 852174/01661 853520

Nearest main-line station: Wylam

This attractive small museum (open on Tuesday and Thursday afternoons and Saturday mornings) illustrates Wylam's unique place in railway history through a series of interesting exhibits about the work and achievements of the local pioneers and local railway projects. It was opened in 1981 to celebrate the 200th anniversary of the birth of George Stephenson. Born in Wylam, his birthplace, owned by the National Trust, it is open to the public (Tel. 01661 853457). Other notable Wylam residents included William Hedley, who was Wylam Colliery Manager, and Timothy Hackworth who was the colliery blacksmith.

BEAMISH OPEN AIR MUSEUM

Beamish, Co Durham, DH9 0RG

Website: www.beamish.org.uk

Tel: 0191 370 4000

Opened in 1970, Beamish is a very large, 200-acre, open-air award-winning museum of late 19th-century life in Northern England. Exhibits include recreated houses and shops, and a school, farm and colliery. There is much of railway interest such as a range of typical North Eastern Railway buildings, including the 1867 Rowley station (reconstructed after being moved from its site near Newcastle), goods shed and signalbox and a short length of line. Locomotives on display include a full-size replica of the famous Stockton & Darlington Railway 'Locomotion', NER Class 'Cl' 0-6-0 No. 876 built in 1889, and several industrial steam examples. A 1½-mile electric tramway runs through the site.

NORTHUMBRIAN COAST

Newcastle upon Tyne to Berwick-upon-Tweed

While the final section of the West Coast Main Line between Carlisle and Glasgow was forging ahead, the completion of the rival East Coast Main Line between Newcastle and Edinburgh was hampered by the crossing of two major rivers – the Tyne and Tweed.

▲ Sporting a 52B (Heaton) shedplate and fitted with German-style smoke deflectors, ex-LNER Class 'A3' No. 60080 'Dick Turpin' passes Manors on the outskirts of Newcastle on 1 August 1964. This loco was withdrawn two months later.

Although there had been various proposals to link Newcastle-upon-Tyne with Berwick by railway, the scheme that eventually received the green light was George Hudson's Newcastle & Berwick Railway (N&BR), which received authorisation in 1845. At its southern end, the new railway made use of existing lines, namely Hudson's Brandling Junction Railway (this was later renamed the Newcastle & Durham Junction Railway) at Gateshead and the Newcastle & North Shields Railway (already opened in 1839) to Heaton. From here, the new railway struck northwards to Morpeth, approached from the south by a dangerously sharp curve, before paralleling the North Sea coastline through Alnmouth to Tweedmouth, south of Berwick. The line opened throughout on 1 July 1847. One week later the Newcastle & Berwick Railway merged with Hudson's York & Newcastle Railway to form the York, Newcastle & Berwick Railway. Despite the opening of this railway, the crossing of the two rivers (Tyne and Tweed) took a while longer.

THE TYNE AND THE TWEED

Designed by Robert Stephenson, the High Level Bridge across the Tyne at Newcastle was opened by Queen Victoria in 1849, its 1,337ft span also carrying a road on a lower level. Less than a year later John Dobson's fine Central station was also opened

Thompson Class 'B1' 4-6-0 No. 61191 passes through Morpeth with a train of empty coal wagons in the early 1960s. All ECML trains are still severely speed restricted through the station due to a 90-degree curve immediately to the south.

Ex-LNER Class 'J39/2' 0-6-0 No. 64897 draws through Alnmouth station, to shunt on to other wagons before leaving with a southbound freight. Seen here on 29 May 1962, Alnmouth was also the start of the branch line to Alnwick, which remained steam-hauled until 1966, before closing in 1968.

by the queen, but, until the opening of the King Edward VII bridge in 1906, all trains were forced to reverse here before resuming their journeys to the north or south. The missing link at Berwick, Robert Stephenson's iconic Royal Border Bridge over the Tweed, was also opened by Queen Victoria in 1850 and, for the first time, through trains could run between King's Cross and Edinburgh – north of Berwick the railway to Edinburgh had already been opened by the North British Railway in 1846.

FEW BRANCH LINES

Apart from the network of coal-carrying railway lines already converging on the Newcastle area, the Newcastle & Berwick Railway (and its successors) north of Morpeth spawned very few branch line offshoots. This is hardly surprising in this sparsely populated farming region but there were a few exceptions: the first was a 5¾-mile branch line from Chevington to the port of Amble, opening in 1849. Designed primarily as a freight line, passengers were carried between 1879 and 1930, although the line continued in use for freight until 1969. A second branch line, from Alnmouth to a grand overall-roofed terminus at Alnwick, opened in 1850. Steam-hauled until 1966, the line finally closed in 1968, although there are currently plans by the Aln Valley Railway Society (see page 205) to reopen it. The terminus building at Alnwick has been preserved and now houses a large second-hand bookshop.

One of the strangest railways in Britain was the 4-mile North Sunderland Light Railway, which opened between Chathill and the coastal harbour village of Seahouses in 1898. Remaining totally independent until its closure, the railway hired a motley collection of locomotives from both the North Eastern Railway, the LNER and later British Railways. Passengers were carried in vintage Highland Railway, North Eastern Railway and Great Eastern Railway carriages until closure of the line in 1951.

To the north, a branch from Tweedmouth and across the border to Kelso was opened in 1851, making an end-on connection with the North British Railway's line from St Boswells. During the severe flooding of 1948, when the East Coast Main Line north of Berwick was closed, this cross-country route saw extraordinary scenes when trains such as the 'Flying Scotsman' were diverted along it, continuing their journey to St Boswells and up the Waverley Route to Edinburgh. Passenger services were withdrawn in 1964 and the line closed completely in 1965, with Tweedmouth shed closing on 19 June 1966.

Under the North Eastern Railway, a 35½-mile branch line was opened between Alnwick and Coldstream (on the Tweedmouth to Kelso branch) in 1887. Despite the line serving only a sparsely populated agricultural region, the company built rather grandiose station buildings along its route line, which closed to passengers as early as 1930. Freight services carried on until the line was severed by floods in 1949 when it effectively became two separate branches: Alnwick to Ilderton

With the North Sea in the background, Peppercorn Class 'A1' 4-6-2 No. 60129 'Guy Mannering' restarts the 2.25pm Edinburgh to Newcastle stopping train from Beal on 31 May 1962. Built at Doncaster in 1949, this loco had had only 16 years of service when it was withdrawn in 1965.

Shortly before the end of steam north of Newcastle, ex-LNER Class 'V2' 2-6-2 No. 60836 looks in fine fettle at Tweedmouth shed in March 1966. Tweedmouth shed closed only three months later.

BR Standard Class 2 2-6-0 No. 78049 crosses the Royal Border Bridge over the River Tweed with the 4pm train from St Boswells to Berwick on 25 May 1962. This train travelled via the former North British line to Kelso and then over the former North Eastern line to Coldstream and Tweedmouth (where it reversed). By this date, there were only two return trains each weekday over this rambling Borders line, which closed to passengers on 15 June 1964.

and Coldstream to Wooler. The former closed in 1953 while the latter remained open until 1965.

ELECTRIFICATION

The York, Newcastle & Berwick Railway had become part of the North Eastern Railway in 1854 and soon Anglo-Scottish expresses made up of East Coast Joint Stock, the forerunner of the 'Flying Scotsman', were a daily feature on the main line between Newcastle and Berwick. During the 20th century, under LNER and later BR management, Gresley's 'A3' and 'A4' Pacifics and the later Thompson 'A2' and Peppercorn 'A1' Pacifics held sway on these trains until the introduction of 'Deltic' diesels in the early 1960s. These were in turn replaced by HST sets until electrification in 1990.

Although electrification of the East Coast Main Line was not completed until 1990, the North Eastern Railway became one of first railways in the world to introduce electric suburban trains. Using a 600V DC third-rail system, the North Tyneside circular line from Newcastle Central to Tynemouth, Whitley Bay, Monkseaton, Benton and South Gosforth was opened in 1904. It was an immediate success, taking custom from the recently opened electric street tram network and remaining in use until 1967 when the electric trains were replaced by diesel multiple units. They, in turn, were replaced by the overhead-electric 1500V DC Tyne & Wear Metro, which opened in the early 1980s.

▲ **A busy scene at Berwick-upon-Tweed station as Peppercorn Class 'A2' 4-6-2 No. 60537 'Bachelor's Button' arrives with the 6.50am stopping train from Edinburgh on 2 June 1962. Judging by the activity on the platforms, the contents of a couple of pigeon trains are in the process of being released. The loco was withdrawn only six months later.**

▼ **Leaking steam, Peppercorn Class 'A1' 4-6-2 No. 60137 'Red Gauntlet' leaves Berwick-on-Tweed station with the previous day's 11.50pm King's Cross to Edinburgh Waverley train on 31 May 1962. The loco had just over four months left before withdrawal.**

THE LINE TODAY

Passenger services between Newcastle and Berwick-upon-Tweed are operated by East Coast and CrossCountry. Local services between Newcastle, Morpeth, Alnmouth and Chathill are operated by Northern Rail.

HERITAGE RAILWAYS

HEATHERSLAW LIGHT RAILWAY

Ford Forge, Heatherslaw, Cornhill-on-Tweed, Northumberland TD12 4TJ

Website: www.heatherslawlightrailway.co.uk

Tel: 01890 820317

Route: Heatherslaw to Etal village

Length: 2 miles

Nearest main-line station: none in area

Situated on the Heatherslaw Estate, with its restored watermill and blacksmith's forge, this 15in-gauge miniature railway was built from scratch in 1989 and follows the picturesque River Till with trains operated by 0-4-2 steam locomotive 'Lady Augusta', built in 1989, and recently introduced 'Bunty'. Passengers are carried in a variety of disc-braked coaches, all built in the railway's workshops.

NORTH TYNESIDE STEAM RAILWAY AND STEPHENSON RAILWAY MUSEUM

Middle Engine Lane, West Chirton, North Shields, Tyne & Wear NE29 8DX

Website: www.ntsra.org.uk

Tel: 0191 200 7146

Route: Percy Main to Middle Engine Lane

Length: 1¾ miles

Nearest station: Percy Main (Tyne & Wear Metro)

Both the museum and the railway share the same buildings, originally used as the Tyne & Wear Metro Test Centre. The museum displays the progress of railways with a collection of vintage and more modem steam, diesel and electric locomotives. Exhibits include Killingworth Colliery 0-4-0 'Billy' dating back to the early 19th century and Bo-Bo electric locomotive No. E4 built by Siemens in 1909. The 1¾-mile standard gauge steam railway connects the Tyne & Wear Metro station at Percy Main with the site on summer Sundays and Bank Holiday Mondays.

MUSEUMS

NORHAM STATION MUSEUM

Station House, Norham, Northumberland TD15 2LW

Website: n/a

Tel: 01289 382217 (weekdays only)

Nearest main-line station: Berwick-upon-Tweed (7 miles)

This privately owned museum on the former North Eastern Railway branch from Tweedmouth to Kelso features the original signalbox, booking office and porter's room. The station, opened in 1849 and closed in 1964, now houses a museum, cared for by the wife of the last man to work at the station.

ALN VALLEY RAILWAY SOCIETY

Longhoughton Goods Yard

Website: www.alnvalleyrailway.co.uk

Nearest main-line station: Alnmouth

Presently based at Longhoughton Goods Yard north of Alnmouth and also at Wooler, the Aln Valley railway Society was first formed in 1995 and is dedicated to reopening the branch line from Alnmouth to Alnwick. Northumberland County Council have recently approved the scheme, although it will be some years before steam is seen again in Alnwick.

▼ Built at the Ravenglass & Eskdale Railway's workshops, 0-4-2 'Lady Augusta' waits at Etal station on the Heatherslaw Light Railway.

SCOTTISH REGION

Preserved Stanier 'Black Five' No. 45487 heads 'The Jacobite' train from Fort William to Mallaig across Loch nan Uamh Viaduct between Polnish and Arisaig on 16 October 2010.

THE ROAD TO SKYE

Inverness to Kyle of Lochalsh

As the first railway route to the north-west west coast of Scotland, the Dingwall & Skye Railway suffered several setbacks in its formative years. The line escaped closure on several occasions in the late 20th century and is now considered to be one of the most scenic rail journeys in the UK.

Amid great rejoicing in the town, Inverness had been reached by the Inverness & Nairn Railway in 1855. Within two years the line was being worked by the Inverness & Aberdeen Junction Railway, which itself merged with the Inverness & Perth Junction Railway in 1865 to form the Highland Railway.

The Inverness & Ross-Shire Railway had been born in 1860 to build the circuitous 31-mile line from Inverness to Invergordon. The heavily engineered line, which included bridges over the Caledonian Canal, the River Conon and the River Beauly, was opened for the 18½ miles to Dingwall in 1862 and farther north to Invergordon a year later.

SPEED, BONNIE TRAIN

At this time the only way to reach Scotland's west coast and the Hebridean islands was by boat from Glasgow – a long-winded journey that left seasick passengers at the mercy of gales and rough seas. Dingwall was an obvious springboard for a railway to the west coast and so the Dingwall & Skye Railway was authorised in 1865 to build a 63-mile line from Dingwall westwards across sparsely populated country to Kyle of Lochalsh on the west coast, where boats would then convey passengers on the short sea journey to the Isle of Skye.

All did not go well for the Dingwall & Skye as its original route would have taken it through the spa village of Strathpeffer, where a few misguided local gentry objected to the railway being built through their land. Consequently, the railway was forced to divert 2 miles north of the village, the new route involving a steep climb to the summit at Raven Rock. The villagers of Strathpeffer did eventually get their own branch line from Dingwall in 1885, but by that time it was too late and the village has suffered ever since – the branch was closed to passengers as early as 1951.

▼ 'Blood-and-custard' days at Inverness – complete with single-line token-exchange apparatus on the cabside, Stanier 'Black Five' 4-6-0 No. 45192 stands at Inverness station before departing with the 7.10pm train to Kyle of Lochalsh in July 1955.

▶ Serving a small and isolated community, Achnasheen station is an important midpoint passing loop between Dingwall and Kyle of Lochalsh. Seen here c.1955, Stanier 'Black Five' 4-6-0 No. 45361 pauses at the station en route for Inverness with a loaded fish van and a train of blood-and-custard stock. Sadly, the Station Hotel has since burned down.

▲ Compared to today's scene at Kyle of Lochalsh, fish traffic was still important in this September 1957 view. Here, with the mountains of the Isle of Skye in the background, Stanier 'Black Five' 4-6-0 No. 44722, fitted with a small snowplough, waits to leave the station with an evening train for Inverness.

▲ Built in 1863, the semi-roundhouse at Inverness shed was approached through a grand stone archway surmounted by a large water tank. Viewed from the turntable in front of the shed, Stanier 'Black Five' 4-6-0 No. 45117, complete with snowplough, awaits its next turn of duty shortly before the end of steam in June 1961.

ONWARDS TO LOCHALSH

The next sorry chapter in the life of the Dingwall & Skye came in 1868 when it abandoned plans to build the line as far as Kyle of Lochalsh, instead opting for a terminus alongside Loch Carron at Stromeferry. This decision was taken because of the high cost of engineering work needed to reach Kyle along the rugged south shore of Loch Carron – on a cost per mile basis it was the most expensive railway ever built at the time. Ten and a half miles short of its goal, the Dingwall & Skye Railway opened for business in 1870 with trains connecting with steamers at Stromeferry for the crossing to the Isle of Skye and the Isle of Lewis. The Dingwall & Skye was worked from the outset by the Highland Railway and was absorbed by that company in 1880.

To coincide with the opening of the railway to Stromeferry, the Dingwall & Skye Railway had purchased two steamers to operate the daily service to Portree and a weekly service to Stornoway. These continued until 1880 when MacBrayne took over the services.

▶ Sporting a 63A (Perth) shedplate, Stanier 'Black Five' 4-6-0 pauses at Plockton station with the Inverness to Kyle leg of the RCTS/SLS 'Scottish Rail Tour' on 14 June 1962. By this date steam had been ousted from the Kyle line and Kyle of Lochalsh shed was due to close completely only four days later.

Main image The scenic delights of the Kyle line in June 1958. A Stanier 'Black Five' heads the 5.45pm train from Kyle of Lochalsh to Inverness away from Plockton along the shore of Loch Carron towards Strome Ferry.

On a wet and windy 16 August 1960, ex-Caledonian Railway 0-4-4T No. 55227 of 1915 vintage shunts a train of fish wagons in the yard at Kyle of Lochalsh. Five of these sturdy and versatile locos were then allocated to Kyle of Lochalsh's mother shed, Inverness (60A).

The ferry operations from Strome Ferry were not a resounding success due to the strong currents encountered and, spurred on by the building of the West Highland Line to Fort William with a possible extension to Mallaig, the Highland Railway went back to the original Dingwall & Skye plan to continue westwards to Kyle of Lochalsh. The remaining 10½ miles of this route were blasted out of rock and the extension opened to a new pier at Kyle of Lochalsh in 1897. Ferry operations from Strome Ferry were then abandoned in favour of Kyle.

THE KYLE LINE

Services on the single-track Kyle line were never heavy and three return passenger trains each day have sufficed until recent improvements have seen this increase to four each day. With very little local traffic generated along the line, these trains once connected with steamers to and from Portree and Stornoway. Although mail, livestock and fish traffic was initially important, the Kyle line lost much of its freight to the Mallaig Extension of the West Highland Railway when it opened in 1901. Even after the Highland Railway became part of the LMS in the 1923 Grouping, the Kyle line was synonymous with the Jones 'L' Class 4-4-0s, more commonly known as 'Skye Bogies' that were built at the HR's Lochgorm Works between 1882 and 1901. These powerful mixed-traffic locos did much sterling service on the line until they were withdrawn around 1930. Under the LMS and later British Railways, motive power was provided by ex-Highland Railway 'Clan Goods' and later by Stanier 'Black Five' 4-6-0s from Inverness shed until dieselisation by BR on 10 June 1961. In an attempt to generate more tourist traffic, an observation car previously used on the Southern Railway's 'Devon Belle' was attached to the rear of an Inverness to Kyle return train on weekdays during summer months from 1961 until 1967. Prior to that an ex-LNER 'Coronation Beaver Tail' observation car had also been used with some success.

The Kyle line, along with the Far North Line to Wick and Thurso, was listed for closure in Dr Beeching's report of 1963, but was saved from oblivion by both public and political pressure and, in particular, by Frank Spaven, the first head of planning for the Highlands & Islands Development Board. The transfer of MacBrayne's Stornoway ferries from Kyle to Ullapool in 1972 brought further closure threats to the line but these were all seen off with the promise of increased freight traffic to a new offshore oil platform construction site at Strome Ferry. Unfortunately, this had closed by 1977 and, despite a short-lived experiment with container loads of supermarket produce, the opening of the road bridge to Skye in 1995, along with road improvements from Inverness, has brought further doubts about the line's viability.

◀ **In the days before the road economy, everything that was meaningful was transported by rail as illustrated by this scene at Kyle of Lochalsh around the time of nationalisation in 1948. In the sidings wagons, from the LMS, GWR and SR stand along with stacks of fish boxes, testament to a thriving Scottish fishing industry. At the platform stands a passenger train, complete with flat wagon behind the engine. The train is hauled by ex-Highland Railway Superheated Goods 4-6-0, still numbered with LMS No.17955.**

THE LINE TODAY

That the scenic Kyle line still exists today against all odds is not only a miracle but is also due to the many people and local organisations who have fought for over 40 years to save it from numerous threats of closure. Train services between Inverness and Kyle of Lochalsh are currently operated by First ScotRail who operate four return journeys each weekday throughout the year. There is a reduced Sunday service. The line's scenic nature, particularly along the south shore of Loch Carron, has made it a hit with tourists from all over the world with passenger numbers nearly doubling in the past five years.

MUSEUM

FRIENDS OF THE KYLE LINE

Kyle Railway Station, Kyle of Lochalsh IV40 8AQ

Website: www.kylerailway.co.uk

Tel: 01599 534824

With Charles Kennedy as its President, the 'Friends of the Kyle Line' operate a museum and shop at Kyle of Lochalsh station. The museum contains railway memorabilia related to the Kyle line and a collection of photographs depicting day-to-day scenes from the Lochalsh and Skye areas. 'The Friends' are also hoping to restore the Kyle of Lochalsh signalbox to its former glory. Kyle station occasionally sees the arrival of charted steam trains while the nearby pier is also visited by the *Waverley* paddle steamer during summer months.

▲ **The Kyle of Lochalsh is occasionally visited by steam charter trains. Here, preserved Stanier 'Black Five' 4-6-0 No. 45407 arrives at Kyle of Lochalsh with the 'North Briton' charter train in 2008.**

THE WEST HIGHLAND LINE

Glasgow to Fort William and Mallaig

Now billed as the most scenic railway journey in the world, the West Highland Line opened in 1894; along with the 1901 Mallaig Extension, it transformed the fortunes of this long-neglected and isolated region of Scotland.

Railways came to the West Highlands and the west coast of Scotland late in the day – Oban was reached by the Callander & Oban Railway in 1880, Kyle of Lochalsh by the Highland Railway in 1897. Meanwhile, Inverness had been reached from the south by the Inverness & Perth Junction Railway (via Pitlochry, Aviemore and Forres) in 1863 – two years later this railway amalgamated with the Perth & Dunkeld Railway to become the Highland Railway. Although this provided a through route from Glasgow it was anything but direct.

Despite the spreading network of railways around the rest of Britain, the West Highlands were still virtually inaccessible by the late 19th century – there were no roads to speak of and the sea journey from Glasgow was slow and tedious at best and dangerous at worst. Following years of the despicable 'clearances', what was left of the indigenous population were impoverished, with the majority barely scratching a living from the land or sea. The coming of the railway to Oban in 1880 soon showed the benefits for the local population, opening up the region to Victorian tourists for the first time and enabling cattle and fish to be transported quickly to distant markets. Thus, with one eye on social need and another on the profit to be made by tapping into the hidden beauty of the West Highlands, the proposed Glasgow & North Western Railway (G&NWR) was born.

▼ The 10.15am Glasgow Queen Street to Mallaig train is seen tackling the formidable 1 in 41 Cowlairs Bank on 12 August 1960 headed by Stanier 'Black Five' 4-6-0s Nos 44975 and 44973 plus a banking engine at the rear. Diesel locos put an end to this sight.

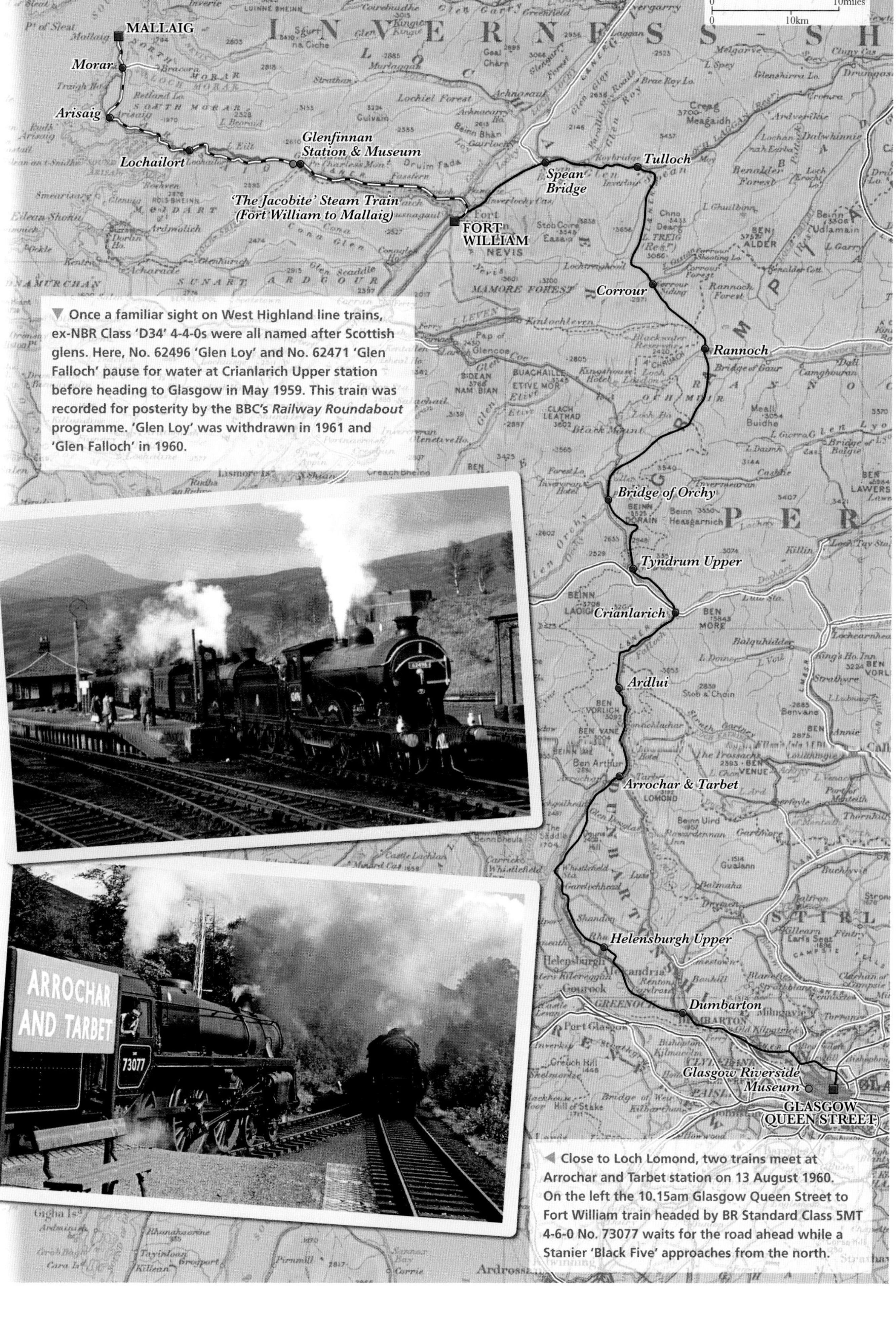

▼ Once a familiar sight on West Highland line trains, ex-NBR Class 'D34' 4-4-0s were all named after Scottish glens. Here, No. 62496 'Glen Loy' and No. 62471 'Glen Falloch' pause for water at Crianlarich Upper station before heading to Glasgow in May 1959. This train was recorded for posterity by the BBC's *Railway Roundabout* programme. 'Glen Loy' was withdrawn in 1961 and 'Glen Falloch' in 1960.

◀ Close to Loch Lomond, two trains meet at Arrochar and Tarbet station on 13 August 1960. On the left the 10.15am Glasgow Queen Street to Fort William train headed by BR Standard Class 5MT 4-6-0 No. 73077 waits for the road ahead while a Stanier 'Black Five' approaches from the north.

HIGHLAND PROPOSAL

The grandiose but apparently realistic G&NWR scheme, initially backed by the North British Railway and money from the City of London, planned for a direct railway to link Glasgow with Inverness via Loch Lomond, Rannoch Moor, Glen Coe, Fort William and Loch Ness. The G&NWR bill went to Parliament in 1882 but was strongly opposed by the Caledonian Railway, the Highland Railway and west coast ferry operators such as MacBrayne, all of whom saw the new railway encroaching into their territory. Following seven months of legal wrangling in Parliamentary committees, the bill was eventually thrown out in May 1883 and the Glasgow & North Western bit the dust.

After this bit of bad news, the inhabitants of Fort William and the Lochaber region struggled on for 11 more years, their only link with the outside world via a 6½-hour stage-coach journey to the Highland Railway's main line station at Kingussie. Eventually the North British Railway eventually came to their rescue by backing the proposed West Highland Railway, which, despite opposition from the usual suspects (Caledonian Railway and Highland Railway), was incorporated on 12 August 1889 to build a line from Craigendoran, west of Glasgow, to Fort William via Long Long, Loch Lomond, Crianlarich and Rannoch Moor.

Glorious Highland scenery on the Mallaig Extension – viewed from the rear of the 5.45am Glasgow Queen Street to Mallaig train, Class 'K1' 2-6-0 No. 62052 is working hard as it climbs away from Glenfinnan station on 26 May 1961.

Double-headed by Class 'K1' 2-6-0 No. 62034 and Class 'B1' 4-6-0 No. 61342, the 1pm Mallaig to Glasgow Queen Street train approaches Fort William station on 20 May 1961.

▶ Class 'K1' 2-6-0 No. 62052 again, this time near Lochailort with a Mallaig-bound train on 21 June 1960. Opened in 1901, the Mallaig Extension was built through difficult terrain by an army of 3,500 navvies blasting a route through solid rock.

At Craigendoran the new railway would follow the route of the existing North British suburban Clydeside line into Glasgow Queen Street station.

A PRECARIOUS LINE

With Formans & McCall as engineers, construction of the line started in October 1889 and soon temporary 'wild west' camps housing thousands of Irish navvies had sprung up at remote locations all along the route. Conditions for the navvies were harsh and progress was slow across difficult terrain, which involved the building of 19 viaducts (including the famous Horse Shoe Curve) and more than 100 bridges. Wherever possible, the railway clung precariously to mountainsides and despite serious labour disputes it was completed in 1892, apart from the small problem of crossing Rannoch Moor. This missing 20-mile link was ingeniously constructed by 'floating' a raft made up of layers of turf, brushwood and ash across the bleak bog. By 1894 the entire single-track route from Craigendoran to Fort William had been completed. The line unofficially opened for passengers on 7 August with a special ceremonial train running eight days later – the people of Lochaber were beside themselves with joy. However, operating the line across Rannoch Moor in the winter soon proved a major problem and a series of snow fences and a snow shed were soon installed to prevent the line being blocked by snowdrifts.

While a 2½-mile branch line west of Fort William to a pier on Loch Linnhe at Banavie had opened in 1895, a proposal to build a rack railway to the summit of Ben Nevis never materialised. The opening of the West Highland Railway brought much needed tourist traffic to the West Highlands during the summer months and Fort William became a frontier boom town.

THE LINE TO MALLAIG

While Banavie was at the west end of the line, this situation soon changed with the authorisation of the Mallaig Extension in 1894. However, the high cost of building this line to the small fishing port of Mallaig was totally dependent on a government grant, and the Guarantee Bill for this had a rough ride through Parliament, first being rejected in 1895 before finally being approved a year later.

The Mallaig Extension was built by Robert McAlpine (known as 'Concrete Bob') & Sons along with a team of 3,500 hardy navvies housed in various makeshift camps along the 38¼-mile

With a scorched firebox door, Eastfield-based Thompson Class 'B1' 4-6-0 No. 61342 heads away from Mallaig alongside the Sound of Sleat with a train for Fort William on 21 June 1960. Steam was ousted from the West Highland line on 18 June 1962 when the Fort William and Mallaig sheds closed.

61342

route between Banavie and Mallaig. Heavily engineered with numerous cuttings blasted out of solid rock, the line is a showcase for Robert McAlpine's use of concrete, never before employed on such a massive scale. The most famous example of concrete engineering is the curving 21-arch Glenfinnan Viaduct, but there are other structures such as the viaduct over Loch nan Uamh and the bridge at Borrodale. At the time of building, the 40-metre span of the latter was the longest single-span concrete bridge in the world.

The new railway to Mallaig opened for business on April Fool's Day, 1901. By then a new harbour had been built and a new steamer service to Portree and Stornoway was introduced to coincide with train arrivals and departures. As with the West Highland Line, the Mallaig Extension was worked by the North British Railway from the outset, with a through carriage being conveyed during weekdays to and from King's Cross via the GNR and NER. Until 1909, trains out of Glasgow (Queen Street) were hauled up the 1 in 42 Cowlairs Incline by a steel hawser – after that time trains were banked in the rear by powerful tank locomotives built at Cowlairs Works.

▲ Observation cars were once attached to certain trains between Fort William and Mallaig during the summer months. Here, a former LNER Coronation 'Beavertail' car has just been turned on Mallaig's turntable before being attached to the rear of the 1pm train to Glasgow Queen Street on 26 May 1961.

Not only did the opening of the Mallaig line greatly improve transport links between the Hebridean islands and the mainland but it also opened the door for freshly caught fish to be carried overnight to distant markets such as Billingsgate in London. These were boom times for Scottish fishermen.

THE GLENS AND THE CHIEFS

The West Highland Railway and the Mallaig Extension were taken over by the North British Railway at the end of 1908, which, in turn, became part of the London & North Eastern Railway in 1923. Under the NBR, motive power on this long and highly demanding route first came in the form of Holmes's Class N 4-4-0s (known as 'West Highland Bogies') and were followed by Reid's famous 'Glen' Class 4-4-0s, which were the mainstay of loco power on the line until the late 1930s. Under LNER management and with heavier trains to haul, 13 of Gresley's Class K2 2-6-0s, all named after Scottish lochs, were introduced in 1924–25 and, along with the 'Glens', provided the majority of motive power between Glasgow (Queen Street) and Mallaig until the introduction of six, more powerful, purpose-built Class K4 2-6-0s in 1937–39. Apart from the first loco, which was named 'Loch Long', the rest were named after clan chiefs.

Following nationalisation in 1948, other locomotive types also appeared on the West Highland line including ex-LNER Class 'B1', ex-LMS Stanier 'Black Five' and BR Standard Class 5 4-6-0s. By the early 1960s the 'Glens' and 'K4s' had all been withdrawn and steam workings ceased on 18 June 1962 when Fort William and Mallaig engine sheds were closed. Steam was replaced by Type 2 diesels, all of which have long since disappeared to the great diesel knacker's yard in the sky and replaced by multiple units and the daily Class 67 diesel-hauled sleeper train. Fortunately, both the West Highland and Mallaig Extension escaped Dr Beeching's closures and in 1975 the original terminus at Fort William was demolished to make way for a new road with the new station being re-sited half a mile to the north.

◀ The grimy state of locomotives during the last years of steam on the Mallaig Extension is fairly obvious here as Fort William-based Class 'K1' 2-6-0 No. 62011 prepares to leave Mallaig terminus with a late-afternoon train for Fort William on 13 August 1960. Behind the loco are two fish vans carrying the catch of the day to distant markets.

THE LINE TODAY

Described as the most scenic railway journey in the world, the West Highland Line and the Mallaig Extension are still open for business today. Passenger services from Glasgow are operated by First ScotRail. The Highland Caledonian Sleeper operates daily (except Saturday nights) between London Euston and Fort William. 'The Jacobite' steam-hauled tourist train operates during summer months between Fort William and Mallaig (see below). The West Highland Line still carries freight traffic to and from the aluminium smelter at Fort William and a new sawmill at Corpach.

▲ Winter in the Highlands – preserved Stanier 'Black Five' 4-6-0 No. 45305 heads across the iconic Glenfinnan Viaduct with a train for Mallaig in 1987.

▲ The small Glenfinnan Station Museum houses a collection of railway memorabilia from the Mallaig Extension line

HERITAGE TRAIN

'THE JACOBITE'

West Coast Railways, Jesson Way, Crag Bank, Carnforth, Lancashire LA5 9UR

Website: www.westcoastrailways.co.uk/jacobite/jacobite_details.html

Tel: 0845 1284681

Route: Fort William to Mallaig

Length: 42 miles

Nearest main-line station: Fort William

'The Jacobite' is a steam operated tourist train that runs from Fort William to Mallaig and back between mid-May and the end of October each year. It was originally introduced by British Rail in 1984 when it was called the 'West Highlander' and later named 'The Lochaber'. Since privatisation of British Rail in 1994 the train, now with its present name, has been operated by West Coast Railways. Motive power usually consists of preserved LNER Class 'K4' 2-6-0 No. 61994 'the Great Marquess', LNER Peppercorn Class 2-6-0 No. 62005 'Lord of the Isles' or a LMS Stanier 'Black Five' 4-6-0, of which 18 have been preserved around the UK.

Recently described as one of the great railway journeys in the world, 'The Jacobite' passes through magical Highland scenery taking in Glenfinnan Viaduct (made famous in the Harry Potter films – some of the carriages used in 'The Jacobite' were also used for the 'Hogwarts Express'), the village of Arisaig, the silver sands of Morar (made famous in the film *Local Hero*) and the fishing port of Mallaig.

MUSEUMS

GLENFINNAN STATION MUSEUM

Station Cottage, Glenfinnan, Inverness-shire PH37 4LT

Website: www.glenfinnanstationmuseum.co.uk

Tel. 01397 722295

Nearest main-line station: Glenfinnan

The Glenfinnan Station Museum was set up in 1991 to save the redundant station buildings on the down platform of Glenfinnan station from being demolished. The restored booking office contains exhibits that illustrate the history of the Mallaig Extension Railway, which opened in 1901. A dining car set in a BR Mk 1 coach offers homemade cakes and meals during the daytime and evening (check for reservations Tel: 01397 722300) and a self-catering sleeping car that sleeps up to 10 people is available for hire. Cycle hire is also available but do check before visiting.

RIVERSIDE MUSEUM

100 Pointhouse Place, Glasgow G3 8RS

Website: www.glasgowmuseums.com/riverside

Tel: 0141 287 2729

Nearest station: Partick and Kelvingrove subway stations

Located on the River Clyde and opened in summer 2011, Riverside Museum is a new visitor attraction and, among other exhibitions, houses the collection from the closed Glasgow Transport Museum that was situated in Kelvin Hall. Railway exhibits include Caledonian Railway 4-2-2 No. 123, Highland Railway 'Jones Goods' 4-6-0 No. 103 and Great North of Scotland Railway 4-4-0 No. 49 'Gordon Highlander' as well as examples of Glasgow trams and the Glasgow 'Subway' system. The museum also features a recreated street from the first decade of the 20th century and 3,000 artefacts from the collections.

OVER THE BRIDGES

Edinburgh to Aberdeen

For 42 years rail travellers between Edinburgh and Dundee endured the misery of ferry journeys across the Firth of Forth and Firth of Tay. This important railway route came into its own only following the opening of the second Tay Bridge in 1887 and the Forth Bridge in 1890.

Railway travellers between Edinburgh and Dundee had to wait until the last decade of the 19th century before they could make the entire journey by train – and for that they could thank the disgraced engineer Thomas Bouch.

Long before the building of the Tay and Forth bridges, the county of Fife possessed its own network of railways, many of them serving the coalfields in the south of the county and later the small fishing villages along the east coast. The main north–south railway linking the Firths of Tay and Forth was the Edinburgh, Perth & Dundee Railway formed by an amalgamation of the Edinburgh, Leith & Granton and the Edinburgh & Northern railways in 1847. The latter which linked the Firth of Forth at Burntisland and the Firth of Tay at Tayport opened in 1848. Passengers were carried across the two firths by company-owned ferries – 5 miles across the Forth between Granton and Burntisland and 2 miles across the Tay from Tayport to Broughty Ferry. From here the Dundee & Arbroath Railway (worked by the Caledonian Railway until 1880) took over for the last few miles into Dundee. Goods were carried separately in what was probably one of the world's first railway wagon ferries, which started operation in 1849.

The Edinburgh, Perth & Dundee (EP&DR) was taken over by the North British Railway (NBR) in 1862, but passengers between Edinburgh and Dundee still continued to endure two

▼ A regular sight on trains from Edinburgh to Dundee and beyond were Gresley's Class 'V2' 2-6-2s. Here, No. 60931 casts a pall of smoke over Princes Street Gardens as it leaves Edinburgh Waverley with a train for Dundee on 12 June 1964.

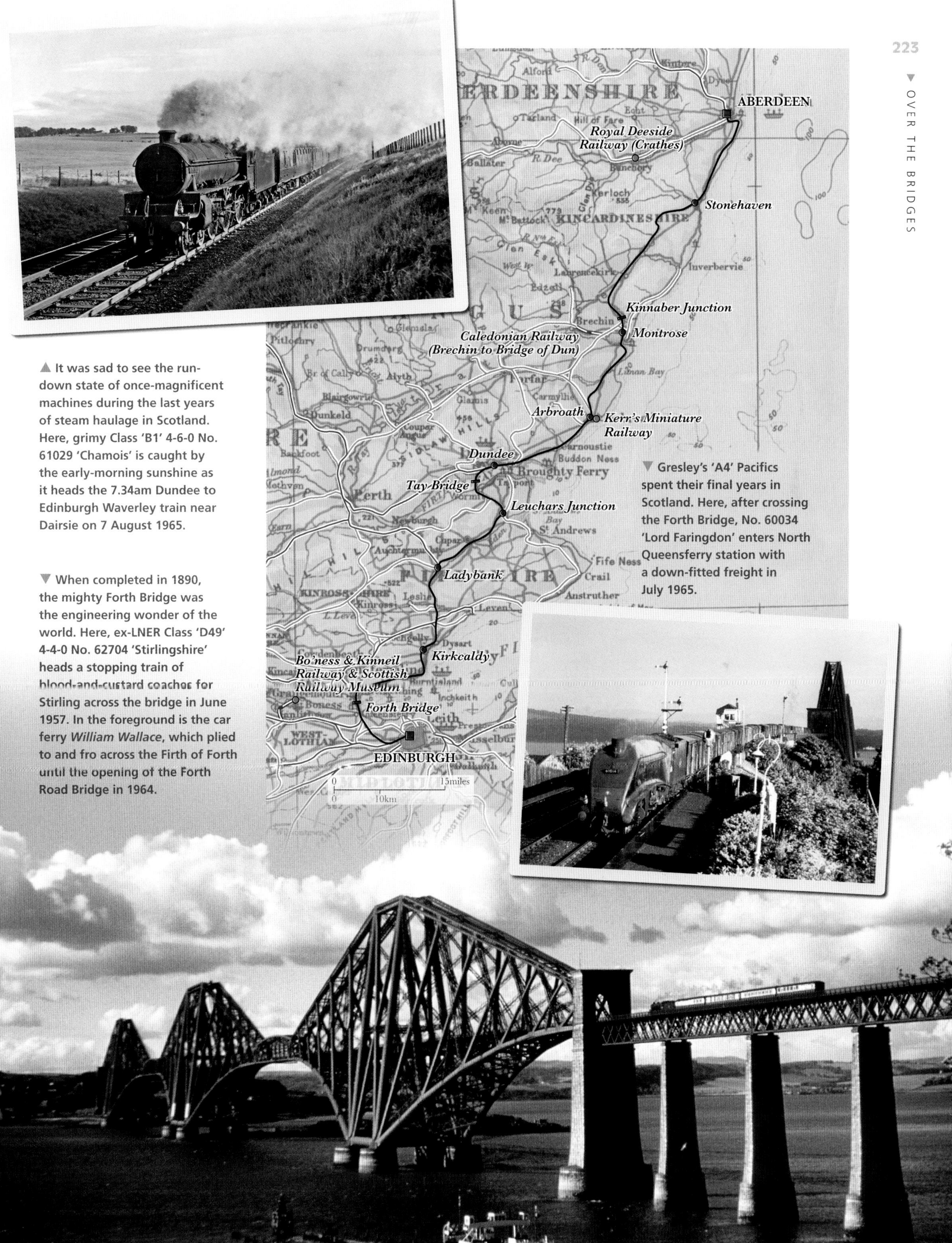

▲ It was sad to see the run-down state of once-magnificent machines during the last years of steam haulage in Scotland. Here, grimy Class 'B1' 4-6-0 No. 61029 'Chamois' is caught by the early-morning sunshine as it heads the 7.34am Dundee to Edinburgh Waverley train near Dairsie on 7 August 1965.

▼ Gresley's 'A4' Pacifics spent their final years in Scotland. Here, after crossing the Forth Bridge, No. 60034 'Lord Faringdon' enters North Queensferry station with a down-fitted freight in July 1965.

▼ When completed in 1890, the mighty Forth Bridge was the engineering wonder of the world. Here, ex-LNER Class 'D49' 4-4-0 No. 62704 'Stirlingshire' heads a stopping train of blood-and-custard coaches for Stirling across the bridge in June 1957. In the foreground is the car ferry *William Wallace*, which plied to and fro across the Firth of Forth until the opening of the Forth Road Bridge in 1964.

uncomfortable ferry crossings or had to take the Caledonian Railway's long way round via Stirling. Although matters improved slightly in 1867, when the NBR introduced a much shorter crossing of the Firth of Forth between North and South Queensferry, these convoluted working arrangements were unsatisfactory.

BOUCH AND THE HIGH GIRDERS

Formerly manager of the EP&DR, Thomas Bouch had gone on to become a railway engineer, putting forward schemes to build bridges across the two firths as early as 1854. None of these saw the light of day, not only because of the high cost but also because of the seemingly insoluble engineering problems that would be encountered in building such immense structures. Despite this, Bouch's scheme for a bridge across the Firth of Tay was given Royal Assent in 1870. Plagued from the outset by problems with contractors and design faults, the single-track 85-span cast-iron bridge took nine years to complete and was officially opened by Queen Victoria on 1 June 1878 (although the first engine crossed in September 1877). The NBR were now able to run through trains from North Queensferry right through to Aberdeen and had soon totally eclipsed the Caledonian Railway in passenger numbers and freight tonnage along this route. On paper, the bridge – the longest at that time in the world – was a total success but something was seriously amiss.

On 28 December 1879, gale-force winds from the North Sea caused the collapse of the centre section of the High Girders portion of the bridge just as a train from North Queensferry to Dundee was passing over. All of the 75 passengers, along with the train crew and guard, perished in the icy waters of the Tay. The blame for the disaster fell on the bridge's designer and engineer, Thomas Bouch, who had only recently been knighted; he died a broken man a year later. Bouch had also designed a suspension bridge to cross the Firth of Forth but, following the Tay Bridge collapse, his design was scrapped and replaced by a cantilever bridge designed by John Fowler and Benjamin Baker. The main contractor was William Arrol, who simultaneously built the replacement double-track Tay Bridge and Tower Bridge in London. When completed in 1890, the Forth Bridge at 1½ miles was the largest cantilever bridge in the world and the first major structure to be built of steel (65,000 tons of it) in Britain. It has stood the test of time and weather, still performing its task today after more than 120 years of continuous use.

THE DIRECT ROUTE

Meanwhile the new 2¼-mile Tay Bridge had already opened in 1887 and, with the opening of the Forth Bridge, the NBR finally had its direct route between Edinburgh and Aberdeen. North of Dundee, North British Railway trains ran over the Dundee

◀ Once a star performer on the ECML out of King's Cross, by 1965 'A4' 4-6-2 No. 60027 'Merlin' had been relegated to more mundane duties in Scotland. Seen here passing Lunan Bay south of Montrose with a southbound block cement train on 5 August, this loco was withdrawn less than a month later.

▶ Ferryhill's Peppercorn Class 'A2' 4-6-2 No. 60532 'Blue Peter' passes Kinnaber Junction with the 1.30pm Aberdeen to Glasgow express on 30 July 1966. The loco was withdrawn at the end of the year. Following a campaign by the BBC children's TV programme of the same name, it was saved for restoration and can now be seen at Barrow Hill Engine Shed in Derbyshire.

Soon after leaving Wormit (Goods), 'B1' Class 4-6-0 No. 61404 starts its journey across the 2¼-mile Tay Bridge to Dundee on 6 August 1965. Designed by disgraced engineer Thomas Bouch, the original bridge was destroyed in a gale in 1879 and a new bridge was built alongside, opening in 1887. Steam haulage survived in Fifeshire until spring 1967 when Thornton Junction, Dunfermline and, across the water, Dundee Tay Bridge sheds all closed.

& Arbroath Joint Railway to Arbroath – this quirky railway had originally been opened in 1838 and laid to a 5ft 6in gauge. It was converted to standard gauge in 1847 and in 1880 became a joint undertaking worked by the Caledonian Railway and the North British Railway. North of Arbroath, the North British opened its direct line through Montrose to Kinnaber Junction in 1881. From here NBR trains ran over Caledonian Railway metals to Aberdeen.

In 1890, the important East Coast route from Edinburgh to Aberdeen was in place and through trains were introduced between London (King's Cross) and Aberdeen, first from London to Doncaster over the Great Northern Railway, to Newcastle and Berwick over the North Eastern Railway and then over the North British Railway to Edinburgh and Aberdeen. As early as 1860 through trains were being run from King's Cross to Edinburgh. The three companies involved had developed special rolling stock for this service known as East Coast Joint Stock. Although the journey originally took 10½ hours (with a stop for lunch in York), the journey was down to 8½ hours by the end of the century.

▼ Ousted from the ECML by 'Deltic' diesels, Gresley's 'A4' 4-6-2s spent their last years hauling the 3-hour Glasgow to Aberdeen expresses. Here, the 5.30pm from Glasgow Buchanan Street, the 'St Mungo', is seen south of Stonehaven in July 1964 behind No. 60009 'Union of South Africa'.

RACE TO THE NORTH

Kinnaber Junction, a few miles north of Montrose, was, for a short time, the finishing post for the famous 'Railway Race to the North'. In 1895 there was great competition between the two rival railway routes for the fastest journey times for overnight trains between London and Scotland. The West Coast Main Line consisted of the London & North Western Railway's route from Euston to Carlisle and the Caledonian Railway's route from Carlisle to Aberdeen. The East Coast Main Line from King's Cross met the West Coast Main Line at Kinnaber Junction and both routes strove to beat the other to this point – whoever got there first had won because the route north of Kinnaber had to be used by both trains. The East Coast Main Line achieved a milestone on 20 August when the 523-mile journey from King's Cross to Aberdeen was covered in 8 hours 40 minutes at an average speed of just over 60mph. While this was a great publicity coup for the railways involved, passengers were no better off as they arrived at Aberdeen at an unearthly hour in the morning. The competition between the two routes continued until 1896 when a high-speed derailment at Preston put an end to the racing. Strict speed limits were imposed on both routes and remained in force until the early 1930s when the race was renewed with the streamliners.

With the opening of the Forth Bridge north of Edinburgh, the new direct route saw a massive increase in traffic, both freight

and passenger, for the North British Railway. In addition to the through expresses from Aberdeen to the south, the route became an important artery for Fifeshire coal, cattle, agricultural produce and fish – all now able to reach important markets in the south overnight. The NBR's locomotive, carriage and wagon works at Cowlairs near Glasgow turned out prodigious numbers of successful steam locomotives and rolling stock during the reigns of chief mechanical engineers Matthew Holmes and William Reid. So successful were some of the freight locos – notably Holmes's Class J36 of 1888 and Reids' Class J37 of 1914 – that they remained in service into the British Railways era and the end of steam in Scotland.

PEPPERCORN STARS

Meanwhile, the North British Railway had become a major constituent company of the newly formed London & North Eastern Railway in 1923 and with Nigel Gresley in charge as Chief Mechanical Engineer the route north of Edinburgh soon saw his famous locomotive designs taking over the duties of former NBR locos. Notable among these were his highly successful mixed-traffic three-cylinder Class V2 2-6-2s, which were introduced in 1936 and gave sterling service on the route hauling fast fitted freight and fish trains until their final demise in 1966. Introduced in 1942, Thompson's Class B1 4-6-0s also became regular performers on passenger and freight workings over the two bridges. But without a doubt the star performers north of Edinburgh were the later Peppercorn Class A2 4-6-2s, with Dundee Tay Bridge shed retaining several famous examples of this class until 1966. The northerly section from Kinnaber Junction to Aberdeen also witnessed the swan song of Gresley's famous A4 Pacifics hauling the three-hour Aberdeen to Glasgow expresses until they were withdrawn in 1966.

The end of steam came in the spring of 1967 with the closure of the last steam sheds at Aberdeen Ferryhill, Thornton Junction, Dunfermline, Dundee Tay Bridge and Edinburgh St Margaret's. Despite this, the occasional steam special across the magnificent Forth Bridge can still rekindle the fading memories of those halcyon days.

▼ Our final glimpse of an 'A4' is close to the North Sea above Nigg Bay. This time it is No. 60010 'Dominion of Canada' climbing away from Aberdeen with the 6pm train to Glasgow Buchanan Street on Sunday, 5 July 1964. Carrying what appears to be two milk tank wagons at the rear, the train travelled via Arbroath and Dundee, arriving in Glasgow at 10.15pm.

THE LINE TODAY

The non-electrified Edinburgh to Aberdeen line via the Forth and Tay bridges is still open for business, with local trains operated by First ScotRail and long-distance trains from King's Cross operated by the recently nationalised East Coast. A few long-distance services from Penzance and Plymouth are operated by Arriva CrossCountry.

▼ Originally one of six locos built specifically to work on the West Highland line, preserved ex-LNER Class 'K4' 2-6-0 'The Great Marquess' hauls a train alongside the Firth of Forth on the Bo'ness & Kinneil Railway.

HERITAGE RAILWAYS

BO'NESS & KINNEIL RAILWAY

Bo'ness Station, Union Street, Bo'ness, West Lothian EH51 9AQ

Tel: 01506 822298

Website: www.srps.org.uk

Route: Bo'ness to Manuel

Length: 5 miles

Nearest main-line station: none in area

This former colliery line along the foreshore of the Firth of Forth was originally built in 1851 as the Slamannan Railway, being later absorbed by the North British Railway, and finally closed to all traffic by BR in 1979. The Scottish Railway Preservation Society

had already set up a base on the line and reopened it in stages, from Bo'ness to Kinneil in 1984, to Birkhill in 1989 and to Manuel in 2010. The SRPS collection of locomotives and rolling stock, formerly based at Falkirk, were moved to Bo'ness in 1988. Visitors to the railway can also visit the clay mine near Birkhill station. A large collection of finely restored steam and diesel locomotives are based at Bo'ness, including such historic items as LNER Class D49 4-4-0 No. 246 'Morayshire', built in 1928 and North British Railway Class J36 0-6-0 'Maude', built in 1891.

KERR'S MINIATURE RAILWAY

West Links Park, Arbroath, Angus

Website: www.kerrsminiaturerailway.co.uk

Route: Adjacent to the Aberdeen to Edinburgh railway line at Arbroath

Length: 400yd

Nearest main-line station: Arbroath

This family-run miniature railway began operations in 1935 as a 7¼in-gauge line, and was converted to 10¼in during 1938. Since opening it has carried two million passengers and in 2010 celebrated its 75th birthday. The entire route is alongside the main Edinburgh to Aberdeen main line, from the main terminus at West Links, which has three platforms, a booking office, footbridge, signalbox, turntable and three-road engine shed. En route the line passes through a 40ft-long tunnel before reaching a run-round loop at Hospitalfield Halt. Six locomotives operate on the line including a steam 4-6-2, steam 0-6-0, two internal combustion Bo-Bo diesel outlines and two internal combustion steam outlines

▲ A line-up of locomotives at Kerr's Miniature Railway in Arbroath.

CALEDONIAN RAILWAY

The Station, Park Road, Brechin, Angus DD9 7AF

Website: www.caledonianrailway.com

Tel: 01356 622992

Route: Brechin to Bridge of Dun

Length: 4 miles

Nearest main-line station: none in area

The former Caledonian Railway line from Montrose to Brechin via Bridge of Dun opened in 1848 and was built as a branch line with its terminus at Brechin. From here another line left for Edzell and the Brechin to Forfar railway. Passenger services on the Brechin to Bridge of Dun section lasted until 1952, when many of the other lines in the county of Angus also lost their services. However, the main line through Bridge of Dun continued with a passenger service until 1967, when all Aberdeen to Glasgow trains were rerouted via Dundee. A single line from Kinnaber Junction was retained for local freight and in 1979 the Brechin Railway Preservation Society took over the shed at Brechin. BR finally closed the freight-only line in 1981. The trackbed to Bridge of Dun was purchased with the assistance of Angus District Council, Tayside Region and the Scottish Tourist Board. First trains ran to Bridge of Dun in 1992 and stock from the closed Lochty Railway also augmented the line's potential. Locomotive stock consists of ex-BR diesels (including examples of Classes 20, 26 and 27) owned by the Caledonian Railway Diesel Group and industrial steam and diesel locomotives.

ROYAL DEESIDE RAILWAY

Milton of Crathes, Banchory, Kincardineshire AB31 5QH

Website: www.deeside-railway.co.uk

Tel: n/a

Route: Milton of Crathes towards Banchory

Length: 2 miles

Nearest main-line station: none in area

The 43¼-mile branch line from Aberdeen to Ballater opened in stages between 1853 and 1866, although an extension to Braemar was never finished following pressure from Queen Victoria. Famous for its royal trains, the line closed in 1966. Since then much of the trackbed has become a footpath and cycleway known as the Deeside Way. However, the Royal Deeside Railway Preservation Society has relaid track for 2 miles from their headquarters at Milton of Crathes towards Banchory. Trains, at present normally diesel-hauled, run on most weekends between April and September and during December.

MUSEUM

SCOTTISH RAILWAY EXHIBITION

Bo'ness Station, Union Street, Bo'ness, West Lothian EH51 9AQ

Website: www.srps.org.uk

Tel: 01506 822298

Opened in 1995, this large railway museum is situated adjacent to the Bo'ness & Kinneil Railway station (see left). By using the Scottish Railway Preservation Society's large collection of rolling stock, the exhibition traces both the practical and social aspects of the development of railways in Scotland. Star of the museum is ex-NBR Class D34 4-4-0 No. 256 'Glen Douglas'.

THE CLYDE VALLEY

Glasgow to Carlisle

Opened by the Caledonian Railway in 1848, the gruelling Carlisle to Glasgow line is a fitting memorial not only to the great railway engineer Joseph Locke, but also to the legendary locomotive designs of John McIntosh, William Stanier and Robert Riddles.

▲ **Resplendent in its maroon livery, Crewe North's 'Coronation' Class 8P 4-6-2 No. 46246 'City of Manchester' prepares to leave Glasgow Central with the up 'Royal Scot' on 21 July 1959. Time was running out for these fine machines.**

The success of what became the first through railway route linking London with Scotland is due, in no small way, to the meticulous planning of the railway engineer Joseph Locke. Locke's early career was marked by his close association with George Stephenson during the building of the Liverpool & Manchester Railway, the world's first inter-city railway, before going on to become chief engineer of the Grand Junction Railway (Warrington to Birmingham) and then the Lancaster & Carlisle Railway, which opened in 1846 (famous for its demanding route through the Lune Gorge and over Shap).

Locke's faith in the ability of powerful steam locomotives to haul heavy trains over this demanding route paid off and, together with Robert Stephenson's London & Birmingham Railway in the south, the trunk route from London to Glasgow was nearing completion. Before long the entire route between Euston and Carlisle had become part of the mighty London & North Western Railway.

The final section of what came to be known as the West Coast Main Line was also surveyed by Joseph Locke in 1836 but the eventual route up Annandale, over Beattock and down the Clyde Valley to Glasgow nearly didn't see the light of day. Locke's faith in the power of steam locomotives to overcome the line's steep gradients wavered and he recommended a less demanding,

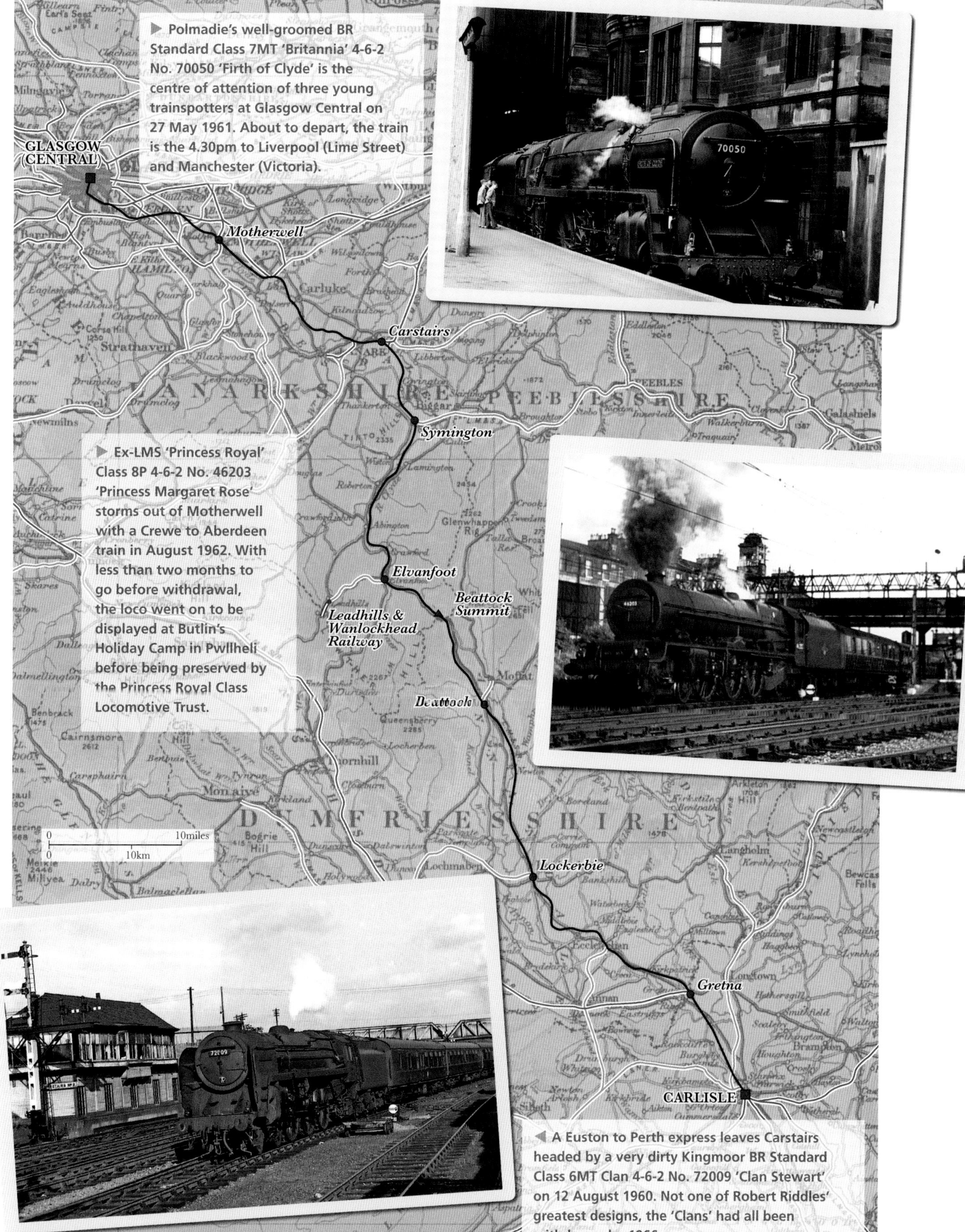

▶ Polmadie's well-groomed BR Standard Class 7MT 'Britannia' 4-6-2 No. 70050 'Firth of Clyde' is the centre of attention of three young trainspotters at Glasgow Central on 27 May 1961. About to depart, the train is the 4.30pm to Liverpool (Lime Street) and Manchester (Victoria).

▶ Ex-LMS 'Princess Royal' Class 8P 4-6-2 No. 46203 'Princess Margaret Rose' storms out of Motherwell with a Crewe to Aberdeen train in August 1962. With less than two months to go before withdrawal, the loco went on to be displayed at Butlin's Holiday Camp in Pwllheli before being preserved by the Princess Royal Class Locomotive Trust.

◀ A Euston to Perth express leaves Carstairs headed by a very dirty Kingmoor BR Standard Class 6MT Clan 4-6-2 No. 72009 'Clan Stewart' on 12 August 1960. Not one of Robert Riddles' greatest designs, the 'Clans' had all been withdrawn by 1966.

longer route to the west. At its northern end this would have connected with the planned Glasgow, Paisley, Kilmarnock & Ayr Railway, but this was not to be.

That the final route up Annandale saw the light of day is down to one man – the 7th Earl of Annandale and Member of Parliament for Dumfriesshire, John Hope-Johnstone, who had wanted the railway to pass through his vast estate. He persuaded Locke to reappraise the original route and a new survey confirmed its feasibility.

▼ The hard slog over Beattock – BR Standard 9F 2-10-0 No. 92012 climbs Beattock bank near Greskine with a northbound oil tank train, banked in the rear by Fairburn 2-6-4T No. 42273 on 12th August 1965.

What was to become one of Scotland's most powerful railway companies, the Caledonian Railway (CR), was authorised by Act of Parliament in 1845 to build a main line along Joseph Locke's surveyed route between Glasgow and Carlisle together with a junction at Carstairs for a branch to Edinburgh. With the takeover of the Glasgow, Garnkirk & Coatbridge Railway in 1846, the new company would open up the industrial belt and coalfields of Central Scotland to new markets in England.

NEW MARKETS, HEAVIER LOADS

The new railway opened from Carlisle to Beattock on 9 September 1847 and from Beattock to Edinburgh and Glasgow on 15 February 1848. A connection with the Scottish Central Railway at Castlecary was opened on 7 August 1848 and a new terminus at Buchanan Street in Glasgow in 1849. The Caledonian Railway lost no time in making full use of its rail connection with England and had soon usurped the East Coast Main Line (which still required a change of trains at Newcastle and Berwick) for the carrying of mail and passengers, becoming the first railway to convey through carriages between Scotland and London. Soon, vast numbers of Scottish cattle were heading for lucrative markets down south. The Caledonian Railway expanded its empire with the acquisition of the Scottish Central Railway (1865) and the Scottish North Eastern Railway (1866). Buchanan Street station in Glasgow was proving unable to cope with the increased traffic so the company opened Central station north of the Clyde in 1879; it was enlarged to its present grandeur between 1901 and 1905.

Having a close working relationship with the LNWR south of the border, meant the Caley route between Carlisle and Glasgow saw the introduction of the famous 'Royal Scot'

▼ Green-liveried 'Coronation' Class 8P 4-6-2 No. 46252 'City of Leicester' looks a fine sight matched with the eight maroon coaches of a Euston to Perth express as it leaves Beattock station on 20 May 1961. Beattock shed, home to the Fairburn 2-6-4T banking engines, can be seen on the right.

It's November 1964 and BR Standard Class 6MT 'Clan' 4-6-2 No. 72008 'Clan Macleod' heads a stopping train for Glasgow over the River Eden north of Carlisle. In 1966 this loco was the penultimate member of its class to be withdrawn. None of the ten locomotives was preserved, but a new locomotive, No. 72010 'Hengist', is currently being built in Lancashire.

express between Euston and Glasgow as early as 1862. By the end of the 19th century this 10am departure from Euston was being hauled north of Carlisle behind McIntosh's legendary 'Dunalastair' 4-4-0s (a product of the Caledonian Ralway's St Rollox locomotive works), which were putting in electrifying performances over Beattock. Following the 'Big Four Grouping' of 1923, the Caley became part of the newly formed London, Midland and Scottish Railway and the introduction of Fowler's 'Royal Scot' Class 4-6-0s in 1927 led to greatly improved timings with heavier loads. These, in turn, were replaced by Stanier's 'Princess Royal' Pacifics in 1933 and his streamlined 'Coronation' Class Pacifics in 1937 – the latter hauled the newly introduced non-stop 'Coronation Scot' express, which ran until the outbreak of the Second World War.

DEATH BY DIESEL

Following the end of the war and nationalisation in 1948, motive power on the Anglo-Scottish route continued to be dominated by Stanier's Pacifics operating out of Polmadie shed until the introduction of English Electric Type 4 diesels in the early 1960s. In addition to the 'Royal Scot', other named expresses to use this route during BR steam days were 'The Caledonian', 'The Mid-Day Scot' and 'The Royal Highlander' sleeping car train. By 1964 the writing was on the wall for steam but the Carlisle to Glasgow line provided the swan song for BR Standard 'Britannia' Class Pacifics that had been sent en masse to the London Midland Region following the diesel invasion in the Eastern and Western Regions.

The 10 miles of northbound 1-in-75 climb from Beattock to Beattock Summit was always a gruelling test for steam

locomotives and the vast majority of freight and passenger trains had to be banked in the rear by banking locomotives from Beattock shed. This practice continued until the end of steam on 1 May 1967. Steam was followed by the short interregnum of Class 50 diesels, until they were replaced by electrification in 1974. Today 'Pendolino' tilting trains hurtle up Beattock without even a second thought.

▼ On the right, BR Standard Class 6MT 'Clan' 4-6-2 No. 72006 'Clan Mackenzie' of Kingmoor shed prepares to leave Carlisle with the 1.05pm (Sundays only) Manchester Victoria to Glasgow Central train on 30 June 1963. In the centre road 'Coronation' Class 8P 4-6-2 No. 46249 'City of Sheffield' waits to relieve the engine working the down 'Royal Scot' from Euston.

THE LINE TODAY

While most intermediate stations, apart from Motherwell, Carstairs and Lockerbie, have been closed, passenger services between Glasgow and Carlisle are currently operated by TransPennine North West, Virgin Trains and CrossCountry. The route is also heavily used by intermodal freight trains between England and Scotland.

HERITAGE LINE

LEADHILLS & WANLOCKHEAD RAILWAY

Station Road, Leadhills ML12 6XP

Tel 01555 820778

Website: www.leadhillsrailway.co.uk

Route: Leadhills to Glengonnar Halt

Length: 1½ miles

Nearest main-line station: none in area

The former Caledonian Railway branch from Elvanfoot, on the Glasgow to Carlisle main line, to Wanlockhead was built in 1902 as a light railway to serve the local lead-mining industry. Gradients as steep as l-in-35 were encountered and as a light railway the trains were restricted to a maximum speed of 20mph. At 1,405ft above sea level, Wanlockhead was one of the highest standard gauge railway stations in Britain and the summit of the line, at 1,498ft, was the highest in Britain. In the 1930s a Sunday service operated using a Sentinel steam railcar but trains were usually operated by a CR 0-4-4 tank engine kept at Leadhills shed. Following closure of the lead mines, the railway was eventually closed in 1938. Rispin Cleuch Viaduct, built by 'Concrete Bob' McAlpine, was demolished in 1991. A preservation group was formed in 1983 to reopen part of the route as a narrow gauge railway and work commenced in 1986. A limited diesel service operated 1988–89 and in 1990 the railway borrowed a steam engine. Passengers are carried in fully air-braked coaches with sprung axles. At present the line stops less than a mile short of the former terminus at Wanlockhead but it is hoped it will be extended for about 1 mile to the east of Leadhills in the near future.

▼ 0-4-0 diesel 'Clyde' with a short train from Glengonnar Halt on the Leadhills & Wanlockhead Railway.

THE ROAD TO NORTHERN IRELAND

Ayr to Stranraer

Built by three separate railway companies, the long and winding line from Ayr to Stranraer took 21 years to complete. While its early years were marked by financial difficulties and temporary closure, its later years brought a reprieve from the 'Beeching Axe'.

The important harbour town of Stranraer (then only a small village) was first reached by the Portpatrick Railway in 1861, itself dependent on traffic across the wilds of Galloway from the Castle Douglas & Dumfries Railway, which had already opened in 1859 (later absorbed by the Glasgow & South Western Railway 'GSWR' in 1865). Portpatrick, then the harbour for the short sea crossing to Northern Ireland, was reached in 1862. However, the harbour at Portpatrick and its approaches along the steeply graded line soon proved totally unsatisfactory and a new ferry terminus was opened at Stranraer Harbour in 1874.

NORTH AND SOUTH OF STRANRAER

In 1877, the Wigtownshire Railway opened for business from Newton Stewart, on the Portpatrick Railway, to the Isle of Whithorn but, within a few years, this company and its neighbour were both struggling to survive. Despite passing through very sparsely populated country, the Portpatrick Railway was an important link for Northern Ireland traffic from some of the bigger railway companies – the Glasgow & South Western, the Caledonian, the London & North Western and the Midland railways all had a vested interest in its survival. In 1885, these four companies took control over both the Portpatrick and Wigtownshire railways, forming the Portpatrick & Wigtownshire Joint Railway with day-to-day operations under the control of the GSWR and the CR.

To the north of Stranraer, the harbour town of Ayr had already been reached by the Glasgow, Paisley, Kilmarnock & Ayr Railway as early as 1839 and in 1850 this company amalgamated with the Glasgow, Dumfries & Carlisle Railway to become the Glasgow & South Western Railway. Building the railway southwards from Ayr proceeded in fits and starts, first with the Ayr & Maybole Junction Railway, which opened in 1856, followed by the Maybole & Girvan Railway, which opened

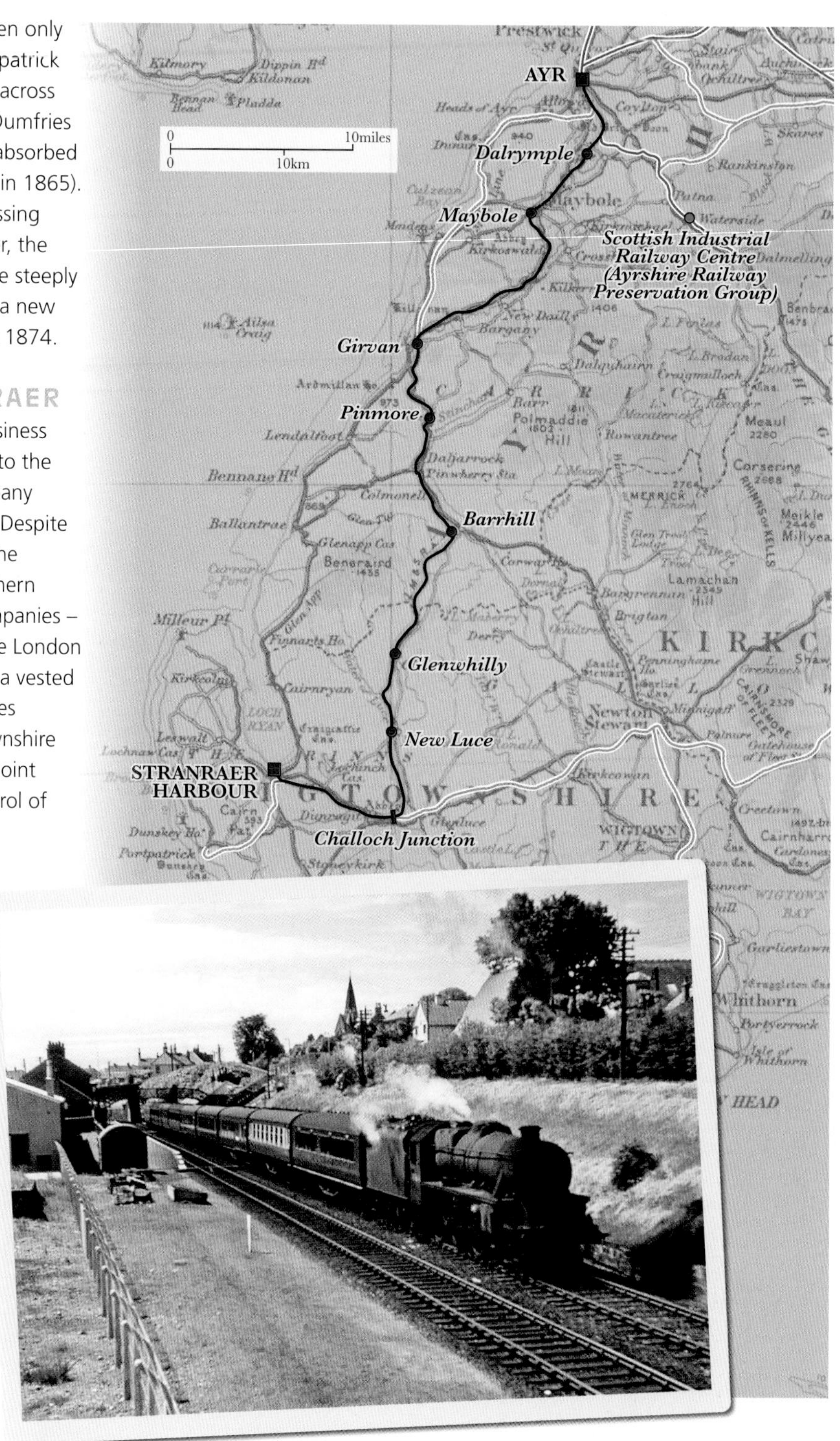

▶ **A Stranraer Harbour to Glasgow train leaves Maybole station behind Stanier 'Black Five' 4-6-0 No. 44778 in 1958. The line was singled in 1973 when the up platform and awning were removed.**

in 1860. Worked by the GSWR, both of these railways took a meandering inland course through rich agricultural land – the coastal route via Turnberry only being opened by the short-lived Maidens & Dunure Light Railway as late as 1906.

Girvan remained the southern terminus for the next 10 years, the wild country to the south proving a major barrier to any further development. Eventually, the Girvan & Portpatrick Junction Railway was authorised in 1865 to build the 32-mile missing link between Girvan and Challoch Junction on the Portpatrick & Wigtownshire Joint Railway. Trains from Girvan would run the last 8 miles from Challoch Junction to Stranraer Harbour over P&WJR metals.

THE LOSS-MAKING LINE

The building of the railway south of Girvan was fraught with problems including the collapse of a viaduct, lack of funds and poor management. That the railway opened at all in 1877 was a miracle, but the years following brought further

▲ **Following closure of the Dumfries to Challoch Junction line on 14 June 1965, trains for Newcastle or Euston from Stranraer were routed via Girvan and Mauchline. Here, double-headed by Stanier 'Black Five' 4-6-0s Nos 45486 and 45120, the 1.55pm Stranraer Harbour to Newcastle relief train passes Pinmore station on 31 July. The station, having already lost its passing loop, closed just over a month later on 6 September.**

Between Ayr and Girvan the line makes a long inland loop away from the coast. Here, south of Maybole, Stanier 'Black Five' 4-6-0 No. 45365 leaves Kilkerran with the 10.28am Paisley to Girvan relief train of non-corridor suburban coaches on 31 July 1965.

The 11.02 Glasgow St Enoch to Stranraer Harbour boat train storms up Glendoune Bank on the approach to Pinmore Tunnel behind Corkerhill's BR Standard Class 5MT 4-6-0s Nos 73120 and 73079 on 31 July 1965.

misery. For 2½ years, between 1882 and 1884, trains from the north were not allowed to run over the P&WJR from Challoch Junction to Stranraer due to unpaid tolls. Then in 1886 the G&SWR, which had been operating the loss-making line, pulled out and the line closed for three months. It survived only after it was taken over by the newly formed Ayrshire & Wigtownshire Railway in 1887, which itself became part of the G&SWR in 1892.

With very little local traffic, train services over the Ayr to Stranraer line never amounted to more than around 4 to 5 return journeys each day, with most of them originating at Glasgow St Enoch and connecting with ferries for Larne, Northern Ireland, at Stranraer Harbour. Even as late as 1964, when DMUs had replaced steam, two of these trains were grandly named in the timetable – the 'Stranraer Larne Boat Train' and 'The Irishman'. Despite the dieselisation of regular passenger services as early as 1959, steam in the shape of Stanier 'Black Five' and BR Standard Class 5 4-6-0s continued to haul freight and special boat trains until closure of Stranraer shed in October 1966.

▲ Not all trains ran to Stranraer Harbour. Here, at Stranraer Town station, Stanier Black Five' 4-6-0 No. 44723 prepares to leave with a train to Dumfries via Castle Douglas on 20 April 1965. Less than two months later, on 14 June, the line from Challoch Junction to Dumfries was closed. On the right is a DMU bound for Glasgow St Enoch while on the far left can be seen Stranraer shed (68C).

▼ The winter of 1962/63 was particularly harsh and caused severe delays for months on the rail network. Here, Stanier 'Black Five' 4-6-0 No. 45126 makes full use of its snowplough at Barrhill while hauling a Glasgow St Enoch to Stranraer Harbour train in January 1963.

Both routes to Stranraer were listed for closure in the Beeching Report of 1963, but although the line across Galloway from Dumfries to Challoch Junction succumbed on 14 June 1965, the line from Ayr was reprieved. From that date the 'Northern Irishman' sleeping car train from Euston to Stranraer was diverted to run via Mauchline, Ayr and Girvan for a short time and all intermediate stations between Stranraer and Girvan were closed with the exception of Barrhill. Freight continued to use the route until 1991 when the BR Railfreight Distribution depot at Stranraer Town closed. Now there are only three passing loops on the 38 miles of single track south of Girvan, although the train frequency (6–7 per day) is a vast improvement compared to earlier years.

▶ Repeated at engine sheds all over the country, this scene at Stanraer shed on 27 June 1964 tells its own sad story. With only one engine in steam, the rest of the locos, including Stanier 'Black Five' 4-6-0 No. 44957, are stored out of use awaiting their last trip to the scrapyard. Once providing significant business for the railways, the cattle pens on the right stand empty.

Stanier 'Black Five' 4-6-0 No. 44935 leaves Stanraer Harbour station alongside Loch Ryan with the 1.40pm train for Dumfries on 12 July 1963. The long train of flat wagons indicates the amount of container freight traffic to and from Northern Ireland that was once handled by the railway here. Now it all goes by road.

THE LINE TODAY

Passenger trains between Stranraer Harbour and Ayr are operated by First ScotRail. Most trains continue on to Kilmarnock or Glasgow Central. There are plans to relocate Stranraer station about 500yds farther east when the Stena Line terminal at Cairnryan is opened in 2011. Rail-ferry traffic will then be via a bus link from Girvan station, while the newly-sited Stranraer station will form part of a new interchange serving southwest Galloway.

▲ Seen at Minnivey Colliery before its move to Dunaskin, the Scottish Industrial Railway Centre's former NCB Andrew Barclay 0-4-0ST No. 2244 is seen in action on the overgrown line on an early Open Day.

RAILWAY CENTRE

AYRSHIRE RAILWAY PRESERVATION GROUP

Dunaskin Heritage Centre, Waterside, Ayr KA6 7JF

Website: www.arpg.org.uk

Tel: 01292 313579 (evenings only)

Route: within site

Nearest main-line station: none in area

Operated by the Ayrshire Railway Preservation Group, the Scottish Industrial Railway Centre was originally on the site of the former Minnivey Colliery, which was once part of the industrial railway system of the Dalmellington Iron Company. This commenced operations in 1845 at Dunaskin (Waterside), and as the ironworks grew so did the railway system. The period after the First World War brought a slump in demand for iron and coal, and the ironworks closed in 1922, although coal continued to be mined and the colliery was nationalised in 1947. Production at Minnivey continued until 1976, with the last mine closing at Pennyvenie in 1978. The railway line from Dunaskin to Minnivey was lifted in 1980 but it remained *in situ* up to Pennyvenie. In 1988 Chalmerston opencast mine was opened and the railway from Dunaskin was relaid by British Coal. The Ayrshire Railway Preservation Society took the lease of the derelict site at Minnivey in 1980 until 2002, when the centre was closed and all stock moved farther down the line to Dunaskin, where the group now runs occasional steam days. Planned future developments may include use of the former NCB locomotive shed at Dunaskin to display various items from the group's large collection of steam and diesel industrial locomotives.

THE WAVERLEY ROUTE

Edinburgh to Carlisle

Once a major Anglo-Scottish trunk railway, the Waverley Route's fortunes and those of the Border towns it served hit rock bottom when the line closed in 1969. Now the townsfolk of Galashiels await its northern renaissance with baited breath.

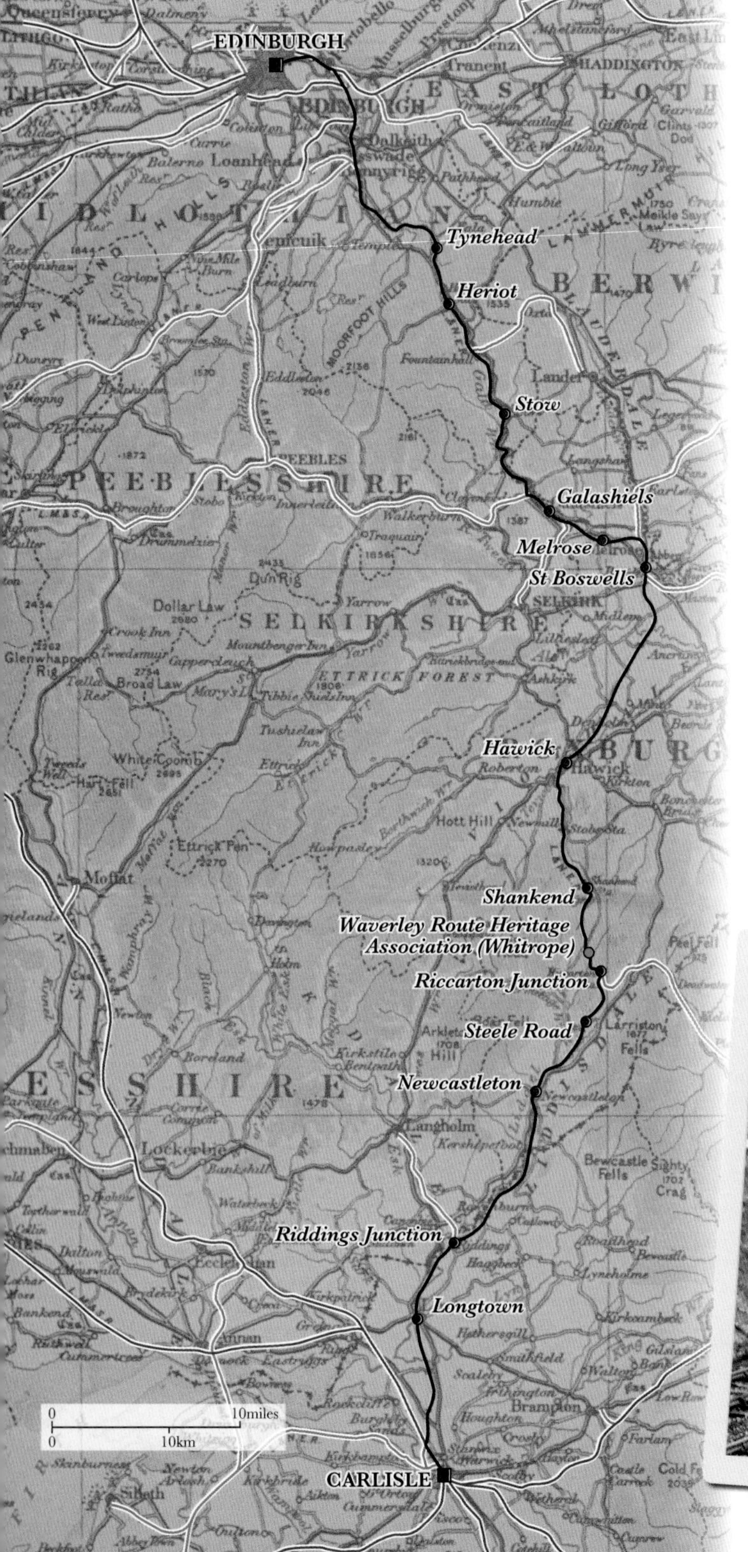

The closure of the 98¼-mile Waverley Route in 1969 must go down in history as one of the most short-sighted political acts ever carried out on Britain's railways, leaving vast swathes of the Border regions without rail connections to the outside world. However, the Waverley Route had humble beginnings in the Edinburgh & Dalkeith Railway. It was one of Scotland's first railways and consisted of a horsedrawn 4ft 6in-gauge tramway that opened in 1835 to carry coal from mines south of Edinburgh to the docks at Leith. It was later bought by the fledgling North British Railway (NBR) in 1845, regauged and reopened with steam power in 1847.

Meanwhile, the nominally independent Edinburgh & Hawick Railway had already been authorised in 1845 – in reality it was then owned by the North British, who had set their sights on building an Anglo-Scottish route across the Borders to Carlisle. The line, initially taking in the route of the old Edinburgh & Dalkeith railway, headed off in a southeasterly direction down the valley of Gala Water to Galashiels and Melrose before striking south across hill country to the important mill town of Hawick. Despite the building of numerous bridges along the Gala Valley, the double-track line was opened in 1849.

▼ As well as being a useful diversionary route when the ECML was closed, the Waverley Route was also an important Anglo-Scottish freight route. Edinburgh St Margaret's ex-LNER Class 'V2' 2-6-2 No. 60813 was a regular performer on the route and is seen here near Stow with a fitted freight c.1960. The line from Edinburgh to Galashiels and Tweedbank may reopen in 2014.

St Boswells was once the junction for two former NBR meandering cross-country lines, one to Duns and Reston and the other to Jedburgh, Kelso and then via the NER route to Tweedmouth. Here a southbound diverted ECML express leaves the station behind Haymarket's ex-LNER Class 'A4' 4-6-2 No. 60009 'Union of South Africa' in 1954. The train would have travelled via Kelso, Coldstream and Tweedmouth, where it would have rejoined the ECML.

Pounding its way through remote Border country, ex-LNER Class 'V2' 2-6-2 No. 60840 heads a northbound freight at Whitrope Summit on 8 July 1961. Today this trackbed can be walked or cycled as far as Riccarton Junction and Steele Road.

◀ On a cold, wintry day in January 1950, ex-LNER Class 'A3' 4-6-2 No. 60095 'Flamingo' leaves Galashiels and passes Kilknowe Junction with a stopping train to Edinburgh Waverley. The track on the right is the Peebles Loop Line, which closed on 5 February 1962.

◀ A busy scene at Hawick in April 1954 with Carlisle Canal's ex-LNER Class 'D49/1' 4-4-0 No. 62734 'Cumberland' entering the curving station with a southbound freight, while locally based (64G) Class 'J36' 0-6-0 No. 65317 stands to the right.

THE C&SBR

The North British Railway's dream of reaching the London & North Western and Caledonian railways stronghold of Carlisle took another 13 years to come to fruition but in the meantime a much smaller operation, the 13-mile Carlisle & Silloth Bay Railway & Dock Company, unwittingly held the key to Carlisle's back door. The line had opened in 1856, but traffic proved disappointing – the company owned no steam engine, occasionally borrowing one from a neighbouring company, and passenger services were horsedrawn. The little line struggled on for six more years until an unusual saviour came knocking.

Back at North British headquarters in Edinburgh, the directors had been planning their next move to reach northwest England and in 1859 the Border Union (North British) Railway was authorised to extend the NBR's Edinburgh & Hawick Railway to Carlisle. Despite strong protests and blocking tactics at Carlisle from both the LNWR and the CR, the new railway was opened throughout across the sparsely populated Borders region in 1862 – the key to the NBR's success in reaching Carlisle was to lease the Carlisle & Silloth Bay Railway & Dock Company at the same time. Serving nothing more than a few villages along its route and lonely

The midday stopping train from Edinburgh Waverley to Carlisle arrives at Newcastleton behind St Margaret's grimy ex-LNER Class 'A3' No. 60057 'Ormonde' on 8 July 1961. The station was the site of a famous 'sit in' on the night of 5/6 January 1969 when protestors temporarily blocked the final train.

Riccarton Junction, the double-track railway was a feat of engineering with the long Whitrope tunnel and Shankend Viaduct today standing as a lasting memorial to their optimistic Victorian engineers.

▲ **Once a familiar sight on Waverley Route trains, ex-LNER Class 'D49' No. 62712 'Morayshire' receives the undivided attention of a young duffel-coated trainspotter at Carlisle Citadel station on 30 July 1960. With only one year to go before withdrawal, this loco was lucky to be saved from the scrapyard and is now preserved.**

THE WAVERLEY ROUTE EMERGES

Featuring a route running through countryside immortalised by Sir Walter Scott in his Waverley Novels, the new line was romantically advertised as the 'Waverley Route' by the NBR. Although initially slow to develop as a major trunk route, once the Midland Railway had reached Carlisle in 1876 via the Settle & Carlisle line (see pages 154–161) it came into its own. Soon through trains were running from London St Pancras to Edinburgh via the Settle & Carlisle and the Waverley Route. Despite its scenic attractions, however, this Anglo-Scottish route could never compete with the faster timings achieved on the rival East and West Coast main lines. Introduced by the LMS in 1927, the 'Thames-Forth Express' became the principal train each day between St Pancras and Edinburgh along with an overnight sleeping car train. The former was renamed 'The Waverley' after

Kingmoor's Stanier 'Black Five' 4-6-0 No. 44792 slows for the stop at Kershopefoot with a Carlisle to Edinburgh stopping train on 25 February 1967. Steam was soon to end on the Waverley Route with Edinburgh St Margaret's shed closing on 1 May.

the Second World War and ceased to run in September 1968. The sleeping car train continued until closure of the line on 6 January 1969. Even so, the Waverley Route's success lay in the amount of through freight traffic that it carried, with heavy trains labouring up to Whitrope Summit with banking assistance in the rear.

Following the 'Big Four Grouping' of 1923, the Waverley Route came under the management of the newly formed LNER and soon locomotives of that company along with tried and tested NBR locos were in service on the line. From the early 1930s Class D49 4-4-0s became a familiar sight on passenger trains, while after nationalisation in 1948 these were increasingly in the charge of Gresley 'A3' Pacifics and 'Thompson' 'B1' 4-6-0s from Carlisle Canal and Edinburgh St Margaret's sheds. 'A1', 'A2' and the occasional 'A4' Pacifics were also drafted in to work this demanding route. From the 1930s, heavy freight was often handled by Gresley's 'K3' 2-6-0s and his versatile 'V2' Class 2-6-2s, their familiar three-cylinder beat stirring the heart of any railwayman while struggling with a northbound heavy freight through lonely Riccarton Junction in the dead of the night.

PROTESTING TO THE END

The year of 1963 not only saw increasing dieselisation of the Waverley Route with 'Peak' Class diesels taking over the long-distance expresses, but also the publication of Dr Beeching's infamous report. Arguing that its route was already duplicated by the East and West Coast main lines, Beeching listed the entire line for closure. Admittedly it was expensive to maintain and operate, while the line south of Hawick served nowhere in particular, but its closure in the early hours of 6 January 1969 was the end of a long and bitter struggle by local authorities, politicians, unions and passenger user groups. Closure had originally been scheduled for 2 January 1967 but a reprieve was given pending a review, all to no avail. Closure was finally scheduled for 5 January 1969 and the last train to travel over it was the Edinburgh to St Pancras sleeper train – among its passengers, David Steel, MP for Roxburgh, Selkirk and Peebles.

Feelings were high among local protestors by the time the train arrived at Newcastleton, where they had blocked the line by locking the level crossing gates shut. Tempers were also high and a few arrests were made before the train was able to continue, though it didn't complete its journey on the Waverley Route until the 6th. Tracklifting operations began in almost indecent haste, but this was suspended for some months while fruitless negotiations were held with the Border Union Railway, who wanted to keep the line open. Not surprisingly, this all came to nothing and by June 1972 the Waverley Route had been totally ripped up.

THE WAVERLEY
60099
64B
A-3

Carrying 'The Waverley' headboard, ex-LNER Gresley 'A3' Class 4-6-2 No. 60099, 'Call Boy', at that time an Edinburgh Haymarket (64B) engine, waits to depart from Carlisle to Edinburgh on 12 September 1957. Originating at St Pancras, the express was originally called 'The Thames-Forth Express' but lost its name at the outbreak of the Second World War, only to be resurrected under its new name in June 1957. Plagued by delays caused largely by mining subsidence along its diagrammed route, 'The Waverley' became a summer-only working after 1964 and continued in that vein until September 1968 when it was withdrawn.

THE LINE TODAY

Much of the infrastructure of the Waverley Route exists today including the impressive 23-arch Lothianbridge Viaduct at Newtongrange, the 15-arch Shankend Viaduct south of Hawick and the ¾-mile long Whitrope Tunnel, although the latter is now fenced off since a roof collapse in 2002. At the site of Whitrope Siding, the fledgling Waverley Route Heritage Association has opened a heritage centre and hopes one day to reopen the line to Riccarton Junction. Meanwhile, the route south from Whitrope to Riccarton Junction and on to Steele Road can be followed for 5 miles on foot or by bike along what is now a forestry track. The island platform at ghostly Riccarton Junction has been cleared, a short length of track laid and a new station nameboard erected.

While Galashiels, Melrose and Hawick have been the most isolated towns in Britain for more than 40 years, the new Borders Railway is due to reopen along the Waverley Route from Edinburgh to Tweedbank in 2014. Enshrined in the Scottish Parliament's Waverley Railway (Scotland) Bill of 2006, the project is now at the tendering stage for the construction contract. If all goes well the northern part of the Waverley Route will soon be open for business again.

RAILWAY CENTRE

WAVERLEY ROUTE HERITAGE ASSOCIATION

Whitrope Sidings, TD9 9TY

Website: www.wrha.org.uk

Nearest main-line station: none in area

This fledgling group has recently opened a new heritage centre at the site of Whitrope Sidings, 11 miles south of Hawick. Its long-term aims are to open a heritage railway from the centre southwards to Riccarton Junction. In the meantime the group are busy reconstructing Whitrope signalbox, building a new platform, erecting signs, benches and tourist information along the 5 miles of trackbed as far as Steele Road and surveying Whitrope Tunnel (currently out of bounds to walkers because of a roof collapse).

▲ A sign of things to come? The Waverley Route Heritage Association has laid track at Whitrope Sidings towards the southern portal of Whitrope Tunnel.

INDEX

D

E

F

H

I

J, K

L

M

S

T

U,V

W

Acknowledgements

The author and AA Publishing would like to thank the following photographers and organisations for their assistance in the preparation of this book.
r = right; l = left; t= top; b = bottom; m = middle

John Ashman: 55mr; 57mr
Hugh Ballantyne: 4ml; 11tl; 22/23b; 24ml; 65ml; 68/69b; 80t; 98b; 103br; 104tl; 109mr; 111tr; 136/137b; 234/235b
I S Carr: 200t
H C Casserley: 84mr; 162mr; 166t; 186t; 188ml; 192tr
Richard Casserley: 194ml; 198bl
Colour-Rail: 5bl; 10; 16b; 18; 20mr; 20b; 24bl; 26tl; 30ml; 30bl; 31br; 34/35; 34tl; 37; 39b; 41b; 42ml; 42b; 44b; 46mr; 47b; 49t; 53tr; 54mr; 57t; 58tl; 59tr; 59mr; 60t; 61ml; 62/63; 64mr; 65t; 66ml; 66b; 67t; 69tr; 70b; 72ml; 73t; 86mr; 93tr; 95tr; 97br; 98mr; 102tr; 104b; 105tl; 105b; 106tl; 109t; 109b; 110ml; 112bl; 115tr; 115bl; 118tr; 118b; 123tr; 129b; 132tr; 132b; 138br; 139tr; 141tr; 142mr; 144tl; 149bl; 151b; 155bl; 159b; 160b; 164/165b; 165tr; 177tl; 178tl; 179tr; 180tl; 182mr; 184/185b; 192b; 195t; 201t; 203tr; 208b; 209tr; 209bl; 209br; 210/211; 211tr; 212t; 215ml; 218t; 218/219; 222b; 223mr; 223b; 231mr; 235br; 236br; 239b; 240/241t; 242br; 244t; 246tl; 248/249
Mike Esau: 19b; 61t; 73b; 75b; 82bl; 83br; 85b; 206/207
John Goss: 7; 25t; 38; 66tl; 75tr; 82t; 84b; 88b; 92ml; 99tr; 149; 150; 156t; 156/157b; 157t; 159tr; 160tr; 221mr; 223tl; 224/225b; 225tl; 225mr; 232ml; 237tr; 237b; 238; 239tr
Kenneth Gray: 198ml
Tom Heavyside: 74; 94mr; 113br; 145ml; 147ml; 148bl; 161mr; 173tr; 173bl; 205b; 241tr
G F Heiron: 58/59b
R W Hinton: 138bl
Colin Hogg: 8/9
Julian Holland: 25br; 31t; 93mr; 249br
Alan Jarvis: 27t; 28/28; 28tl; 45; 46b; 87b; 90bl; 95mr
T Lakin: 23tr
Michael Mensing: 3; 11br; 12mr; 12b; 13t; 13b; 14/15; 15br; 32tr; 33mr; 36b; 43t; 50tr; 50ml; 50b; 51t; 51mr; 52b; 90/91b; 95b; 96/97; 100/101; 103tl; 108bl; 117tr; 124ml; 124b; 127b; 133bl; 134br; 136tl; 137tr; 137mr; 183tl; 183; 184t; 201br; 202b; 203b; 204tr; 204b; 216/217; 216b; 220tr; 226b; 227b; 231tr; 240/241b
Brian Morrison: 116/117b
Gavin Morrison: 33tl; 36mr; 75tl; 77b; 78bl; 80/81b; 83t; 87tr; 89tr; 107tr; 119; 120b; 129tl; 142/143t; 143b; 148t; 152tl; 153b; 154b; 155tr; 158/159; 161tr; 168tl; 169tr; 169br; 170/171; 171tl; 172t; 176/177b; 178ml; 178/179b; 180br; 189; 190t; 190/191b; 191tr; 193br; 196/197; 214b; 215bl; 220bl; 221tr; 229tr; 230t; 231bl; 232b; 244b; 245b; 246/247b
Milepost 92½: 19t; 39tr; 48tr; 52t; 54tl; 64t; 76tl; 77t; 102b; 110/111b; 114; 116ml; 122t; 125; 126t; 126b; 127tr; 130/131; 134t; 135; 140t; 141b; 146t; 155mr; 163tr; 163b; 166b; 174/175; 185tr; 212b; 243; 245t
Ivo Peters Collection: 89b; 92bl
Peter J Robinson: 233
Brian Sharpe: 4tr; 17; 40t; 71b; 79t; 79br; 106br; 113tl; 121tr; 128t; 145t; 167b; 181tr; 187b; 198br; 199t; 213br; 228b
J R Smith: 1; 56
T E Williams: 21